Life's a Gamble

Mike Sexton

First published in 2016 by D&B Publishing
Copyright © 2016 Mike Sexton

British Library Cataloguing-in-Publication Data
A catalogue record for this book is available from the British Library.
ISBN: 978 1 909457 56 0

Cover and book design by Horacio Monteverde.

Photo of American Poker Awards Lifetime
Achievement Award courtesy of Revolutionpix

Photo of Mike, Lynn Gilmartin & Vince Van Patten on the
WPT set courtesy of Joe Giron/PokerPhotoArchive.com

Endorsement photos by PokerPhotoArchive.com

Printed and bound by Versa Press in the US.

All sales enquiries should be directed to D&B Publishing:
info@dandbpoker.com

In loving memory of the two most special people in my life:

my father
Ray Sexton Jr. (1919-2008)

my brother
Tom Sexton (1946-2013)

and

in honor of my son,
who fills my life
with love, laughter,
and pride.

Ty Michael Sexton

(born August 21, 2008)

Contents

Foreword

by *Vince Van Patten*

I've had the privilege of co-hosting the World Poker Tour (WPT) with Mike Sexton since day one. We're now heading into Season 15. You couldn't find a better partner to work with. The energy, excitement, and enthusiasm you see from Mike on television is real. He has a passion for poker like no one I've ever seen.

Like Mike, I grew up playing poker. We really are poker guys who became poker commentators – not commentators who became poker guys. And Mike is as professional as they come. In 14 seasons, he's contributed greatly to the success of the WPT, both on camera and behind the scenes, and he hasn't missed one televised final table in the history of the WPT.

Life's a Gamble tells the story of Mike's life and how "action" has been a part of his life all his life. It also lets you in on the key roles he played in the development of online poker with partypoker, which he helped grow to the number-one site in the world, and televised poker, with the WPT. But to me, the highlights of the book are the countless gambling adventures that he shares with the readers. These stories, involving some of the most legendary figures in poker history, are fun to read and extremely entertaining.

Once you start the book, it's hard to put down. You'll keep reading, wondering, and asking for more. And when you think his stories can't get more fantastic, they do. He tops every story with a better one.

Mike is a visionary who saw the future of poker years ahead of everyone else. He is a writer, lecturer, philanthropist, and amazing poker player, and has been one of poker's premiere ambassadors for over 20 years. And when it comes to ideas to help grow the game we love, he's not a talker, he's a "doer". He has a sign in his office that reads, "Those who achieve success are those who take a dream and make it come true." That's Mike.

He was integral to the creation and success of two mega events in the poker world, the Tournament of Champions of Poker and the partypoker Million. He was also a key player in the growth of Party-Gaming, a company whose success was mind-blowing. In less than four years after the launch of partypoker, that company went public on the London Stock Exchange for $8.5 billion, the largest float in five years!

Mike was a star gymnast at Ohio State and following college, he joined the Army to become a paratrooper. His patriotism shines when he pays tribute to those who served, as well as with the work he does for the Paralyzed Veterans of America, the Wounded Warriors, the Special Olympics, as well as other charities.

Throughout his life, as you will learn in *Life's a Gamble*, Mike has been an action man. Danny Robison, his buddy growing up, steered him into a "bet on everything" lifestyle, and he's lived it. He is accustomed to a life of winning and losing a lot of money on the turn of a card, the roll of a golf ball, a bet on a football game, or a prop bet involving untold sums.

I'm an action man myself. Mike and I have made side bets on nearly every outcome of WPT final tables, including the "over and under" of what time the table will finish. Hey, we're action guys.

What can I say?

Few writers can tap into our vicarious lust. Mike Sexton gives us permission to enjoy it and keep it our little secret. In the book, you'll get an insight into the high-stakes poker players' insatiable need for action. His tales about high rollers, celebrities, and the rich and famous run rampant throughout the book.

I'm confident that you will enjoy his humble and humorous style of story-telling. His way of telling golf stories will make you feel like you're on the course and right in the middle of the high-stakes action. You'll actually feel the "thrill of victory and agony of defeat".

Mike divulges the ups and downs of gambling. He also talks about his success and mistakes along the way. He knows he's not the only man in this layered mirror of life. Many a man has left the table with pockets full of money and chips. Others, not so lucky, leave penniless, homeless, and drug-addicted. A number have died lonely deaths after reaching heights we can only dream of.

High-stakes gambling is like walking the high wire or traversing a minefield. Danger lurks with every step along the way. Life's a gamble, but this book isn't.

Enjoy!

Vince Van Patten,
WPT Commentator
Writer, Director, Producer

Preface

Full definition of GAMBLE

Intransitive verb

1: to play a game for money or property

2: to bet on an uncertain outcome

3: to stake something on a contingency: take a chance

Transitive verb

1: to risk by **gambling**: wager

2: **venture, hazard**

Let's face it – life's a gamble. And I'm not just talking about when you roll the bones on the dice table, bet on a football game, or play bingo, I mean L-I-F-E. Nearly everything we do is a gamble. We take a chance when we ask someone out, play sports, choose a college, select employment, get married, move to another state, buy a house, borrow money, invest in the stock market, drive a car, fly on a plane, hire a new baby-sitter, etc., etc., etc.

I have bet on an uncertain outcome and wagered far more than most in my lifetime. Gambling has been a big part of my life for nearly all my life. Most of the time that hasn't been a good thing, but it is a fact – and it's how and why this book was written.

I have chronicled my life story as a Poker Hall of Famer who played a key role in the recent growth and popularity of poker, sometimes referred to as the "poker explosion". This explosion occurred just after the turn of the century, and it changed the poker world forever!

These accounts are honest and real and recount amazing, blow-by-blow stories involving some of the most unique characters and risk takers in poker history. If this kind or any kind of 'action' interests you, then you're going to love *Life's A Gamble*.

Enjoy!

Mike Sexton

Introduction

Many of you know me as the commentator and co-host (with my partner, Vince Van Patten) of the televised WPT. In my 50-plus years of playing poker, I've done well as a cash game player and have had my share of success on the tournament circuit.

I learned the game at the age of 13 and became a full-time professional poker player in 1977. What is not generally known, however, is the story of how my early passion for cards and gambling eventually led to my induction into the Poker Hall of Fame, to my involvement with one of the world's most lucrative and innovative internet gaming companies of all time, PartyGaming, and my role in helping bring the WPT to fruition.

Now that my parents have passed away and I have become the father of a young son (Ty Michael Sexton), I feel that the time is right to tell what happened in between: how my early life shaped me to become who I am today and about the cast of characters I had the good and, sometimes, ill fortune to know, and to recount the incredible but true stories of the remarkable ventures in which I was involved or witnessed.

These true stories come from the poker table, the golf course, and gamblers who, in their quest for action, create bets on everything – even weight gain or loss. The trip I took down memory lane while writing this book was a bumpy one. I was hooked on "action" at 13. In reflecting, I remembered things that made me smile and a few things that made me sad. But most of all, I was able to recall things that have helped me understand how gambling came to define me. Life's a gamble and this is how it all began...

1 Hooked on Action

There's one thing in the whole world that has the ability to change our whole life in an instant... it's ACTION!
Old School Gambler

Danny Robison, a neighbor who lived a few doors down, was the gambling influence in our neighborhood. He flipped coins for money and bet on any kind of card games, especially gin rummy and poker. He also bet on bowling, ping-pong, wiffle ball, golf, shooting baskets, and everything else. Therefore, so did I. Who knew that my good friend, Danny Robison, was a genuine card genius who would grow up to become a poker legend? (Sadly, Danny passed away in 2014.) All I knew back then was that he kept me broke most of the time.

It was Danny who taught me how to play poker when I was 13

years old. He was 15 and those two years gave him a big edge at almost everything in those days. He was better than me at every game and nearly every sport – which is not good if you bet on everything!

In a brilliant scheme that let me think he was doing me a big favor, Danny sold me his *Dayton Journal Herald* paper route. This meant that I, not Danny, would get up every morning at 4 am to deliver papers. Looking back, I'm sure his plan was to let me do all the work and then beat me out of the money I earned when we played cards. And it was a good one – for him.

It was another Friday night. I was 14, had just collected money from my newspaper route, and I can still see him now – the kid down the street, Danny Robison, shuffling cards, perched like a vulture on the stoop of our little house in Kettering, OH – waiting to beat me out of my money for what seemed like the hundredth time.

When I lost, which was nearly every time, I would go into the house with my chin down and my mother would look at me, shake her head, and say, "Don't play cards with Danny, he's too good for you." Week after week, she'd say the same thing. Most parents would have screamed at their kid or chased the other kid away, but my mother didn't operate that way. Like everyone, she liked Danny and I guess she was hoping I'd see the light and quit playing with him on my own.

One day, after another losing session, I came in with that sad, puppy dog face, and she said, "You know, if you're so goddamn stupid to get up at four o'clock in the morning, work all week long, and then go lose all your money to Danny, you don't deserve to have any money!"

I remember thinking, *maybe she is right*. Maybe Danny was just too good for me. But win or lose, by that time, I was hooked on action… and I have been from that time to this.

2 A Forked Family Tree

*When a man with money meets a man with experi-
ence, the man with experience leaves with the money
and the man with money leaves with experience.*

Unknown

My mom, Gloria, and dad, Ray, met while teaching ballroom dancing
at the Arthur Murray Dance Studio in Indianapolis, IN. Talk about taking a gamble: they were married within two weeks of meeting each
other. They had two sons, my brother, Tom, and a year later, me. We
lived in Shelbyville, a town of about 11,000 people located 30 miles
south of Indianapolis.

My dad was a terrific athlete. He was the city champion at tennis, bowling, and pool. Dad also liked to gamble on card games, was

an excellent gin rummy player, and ran a popular dice game at the bowling alley his father owned. He also liked to bet on sports (like father, like son).

The ups and downs of being the wife of a gambler became a problem for my mom. She couldn't take the financial swings, and with the responsibilities of 4- and 5-year-old boys, she needed more stability. After six years of marriage, she divorced my dad.

Mom decided to make a fresh start in Dayton, OH, about a hundred miles east. This was a bold move for a single parent with two young children. With no money and uncertainty about the future in a new location, it was a very rare and gutsy move for a woman back in those days. Our mother was an unusual woman in many regards and, for the most part, I say that with admiration.

Within a couple of years, both my parents remarried. My mom had a daughter, Loni, with her new husband, Elmer, an electrical engineer who worked at Wright-Patterson Air Force Base. Not surprisingly, my dad met another dance teacher (Beverly) at Arthur Murray's. Dad and Beverly ended up having four children: Jeffrey, Rodney, Stephanie, and Lance.

Even though we have a forked family tree, I was always close to all five of my brothers and sisters. Tom and I, who were as close as brothers could be, lived with our mom, but we always looked forward to summer vacations and Christmas, when we visited our dad and his new family in Indianapolis.

From the first grade on, I lived in Kettering, a middle-class suburb of Dayton, OH. My school years bring back so many wonderful memories. Like our father, Tom and I were totally involved in sports, which was a good thing because, back in those days, if one was into sports (which nearly all of my friends and I were), smoking, drinking and drugs didn't exist – not in my world, anyway. I had never seen or known about drugs or drug use and I didn't have my first beer until I was in college. But, because of my closeness to Danny, I did like to bet on uncertain outcomes.

To me, my small town and middle-class upbringing in the 1950s and '60s were the perfect place and time to grow up. There were no R-rated movies, hardly anyone was fooling around sexually, and except for the few hoods, nobody was drinking or smoking.

School spirit was *huge* at our school. There were pep rallies all the time and nearly everyone went to all the football and basketball games. We decorated our cars (which we borrowed from our parents on Friday nights) and would caravan to away games. When I was in high school, earning a varsity letter and wearing a letter jacket was as good as it could get. I loved those days.

We were raised by a mother who was ahead of her time, especially when it came to women's lib. But, even with her uniqueness, we were just like all the other kids and were involved in everything a kid could be. All in all, we really were good kids. No, we didn't smoke or drink or get into too much trouble, but we did gamble when we had a little money (and sometimes, even when we didn't).

Gambling without money reminds me of one of my favorite lines of all time. It was when golfer Lee Trevino was leading the US Open going into the final round. A reporter asked, "Lee, how will you handle the pressure today?" Trevino smiled and said, "Pressure? What pressure? I'll get a good check wherever I finish today. That's not pressure. Pressure is playing a $10 Nassau when you don't have a dime in your pocket." (And Trevino won.)

One of the best lessons I ever learned from my mother was when I was 11 years old. She sat my brother and me down on the couch and said, "I want to talk to you about smoking. It's a filthy habit."

She continued, "I smoke, so I can't tell you not to, but I can tell you that you're dumbasses if you ever start. It costs money, gives you bad breath, stains your teeth, burns holes in the furniture, makes your clothes stink, to say nothing of emphysema, cancer, and who knows what else it causes." And then she said again, "But because I do it, I can't tell you not to do it. All I can tell you is that you're complete idiots if you ever start."

I thought about what she'd said and wondered why anyone

would ever smoke. To this day, I've never had a cigarette in my life and I believe it's because of that one conversation my mother had with us. Had she shaken her finger at us like all of the other parents were doing and said "Don't you dare smoke", we'd probably have run around the corner and smoked like some other kids did. Her approach, I believe, was brilliant. It sure worked for us.

My friends in high school didn't smoke, but when I got to college, it seemed like just about everybody was lighting up. And later, as I entered the poker world, almost all the players smoked. Still, in college and all those poker games, being around all those smokers, I've never had a cigarette. I give my mom a lot of credit for that.

Our mother believed we should be independent and she wanted us to be leaders, not followers. When we wanted to do something because the other kids were doing it, she would say, "I don't give a shit what those other kids are doing, you're not doing it." She also believed that if you wanted a school ring, varsity jacket, or whatever, you needed to go out and earn the money for it. And we did.

She also told us, "If you ever get kidnapped, you better try to escape because I'll never pay a penny in ransom money to get you back – not only because I don't have it, but because if I paid it, I think they'd kill you anyway. Why would kidnappers want to keep anyone alive who could identify them?" She believed that if nobody ever paid a ransom, there would be no kidnappings or hijacked planes.

She said if we ever knocked up a neighborhood girl, she'd kill us, but if we were curious and wanted to learn about sex, she'd get a hooker for us. (And no, we didn't take her up on that one.) My mom was quite unusual in her ways but far from perfect.

Sadly, she was a heavy drinker and became a volatile alcoholic. At times, mostly during a drinking binge, my mom was unnecessarily gruff. She was a bad drunk and the friction her drinking caused eventually culminated in her second divorce, just after Tom and I started high school. She would remarry a third time while my brother and I were in college. Because of her drinking, she died of kidney disease when she was just 50 years old.

3 The Sporting Life

The mark of a top player is not how much he wins when he is winning, but how he handles his losses.

Bobby Baldwin

In my young years, it seemed that Danny Robison was as much of an influence on me as were my brother and my parents. Not only was Danny a fast talker and a gambler extraordinaire, he was a great athlete. He was the number-one man as a sophomore on the Fairmont High School golf team that won the Ohio High School State Championship, and upon graduation received a golf scholarship to Ohio University.

His dad Rex, a very good golfer himself, wanted Danny and his brother Jimmy to be pro golfers and paid them a salary to hit golf balls. He also put a cement basketball court in their backyard. It was a half court that took up the whole backyard and was a popular hangout for wagering.

In addition to being a golf standout, Danny was also the starting point guard on a basketball team that went to the regional finals of the state championship. There, they lost to Dayton Belmont, which was one of the best (if not *the* best) high school teams in Ohio history. Belmont averaged 83 points a game (with no three-point shot) and conceded only 55 points per game to their opponents. They beat the number two team in the state (Canton McKinley) 80–56 and won the state championship game against Cleveland East 89–60.

On that Belmont team were two guys who became college All-Americans – Don May and Bill Hosket. It was the first time in Ohio history that two players from the same team were first team all-Ohio. May went to the University of Dayton and Hosket went to Ohio State. Incredibly, both led their teams to the National Collegiate Athletic Association (NCAA) Final Four. Dayton went in 1967 (finishing runner-up) and Ohio State in 1968. Dayton also won the National Invitation Tournament in '68 with May winning the Most Valuable Player award.

In the NCAA Final Four, both lost to John Wooden's UCLA (University of California, Los Angeles) Bruins, led by the great Lew Alcindor, who later became Kareem Abdul-Jabbar, the number-one scorer in National Basketball Association history. The high scorer in that high school regional championship game, however, was not the future collegiate All-Americans, it was Fairmont's Danny Robison.

Danny was good at everything: golf, basketball, bowling, ping-pong, baseball, gin rummy, poker, you name it. And, of course, he was gambling on everything possible and was kind enough to allow those of us in the neighborhood to gamble with him. Under Danny's indoctrination, I too liked to bet on anything and everything.

Junior High Entrepreneurs

My mom might have appreciated that the experience I got playing against Danny was priceless. (Going broke is educational.) Early in life, I learned to equate gambling with business, as you will see in this story.

When Tom and I went to Van Buren Junior High School in Kettering, OH, we needed to hustle up some extra money. So, while in the ninth grade, we ran a mini-casino in the boys' restroom a couple days a week before class. We brought in a roulette wheel from a game called Tripoli and set up another area for cards and dice. We also pitched coins to the wall.

Our little enterprise was doing pretty well until our assistant principal, Mr. Bridgeman, who was in charge of discipline, made an announcement over the morning public address system: "There has been a report of a gambling ring going on in the boys' restroom. Do you know how bad this looks for Van Buren Junior High School?" With his voice rising, he continued, "This will immediately cease or there will be serious consequences! Those responsible better listen up."

Well, we continued running our little gambling parlor but took extra precautions. We paid one kid a dollar every morning to be our lookout. If we were raided and the lookout gave the signal, we had a plan in place. All the players were assigned specific positions to take care of, and they quickly picked up any gaming equipment and money, and then raced for the urinals or stalls to look innocent.

One morning the janitor snuck up on us, burst through the door, and caught us. (The genius lookout said he was looking for teachers.) He herded all of us down to Mr. Bridgeman's office and, boy, was he hot! His neck bulged and his face turned beet red as he read us the riot act. He screamed, "Do you know how bad this makes our school look?" He continued to rant and rave and seemed ready to beat us all with his legendary paddle. (In case you're thinking paddling = "lawsuit", forget about it. Our mother told us, "If you get a paddling at school, don't tell me about it. If you do, you'll get another one when you get home.")

Standing between Tom and me was the biggest hood in the school. He was listening to Mr. Bridgeman's tirade, and all of a sudden, burst out laughing. Mr. Bridgeman glared at him, stepped toward him, and yelled, "You think this is funny?" And the hood snarled back and said, "Well, maybe I do."

With that, Mr. Bridgeman clenched his fists and in a karate-type move punched both fists into the kid's chest. The poor kid literally flew back past us and hit the wall with a thud. After that, Mr. Bridgeman said, "All right, all of you out of here... now!" So Tom and I scurried out with everyone else, even though we were the ringleaders. The hood that mouthed off saved us. This ended our little casino adventure in the junior high boys' room, but it sure was good while it lasted.

Tumbling into College

After my sophomore year, the population of Kettering had grown so much that two high schools were needed. Our high school, Fairmont High School, was separated into two schools – Fairmont East and Fairmont West. I lived in the section designated for Fairmont East, the new school. But because the administration didn't want to take the seniors out of their old school environment, the new school (Fairmont East) would only have juniors and sophomores in it that first year. The would-be seniors would stay where they were (Fairmont West).

So, as a junior, it was like being in the senior class. I essentially had two senior years, which was actually a very cool thing. But without a senior class, our school lacked the experience they needed to excel at the major sports.

Our football team was average, our basketball team really struggled, but we did have a pretty good track team. I played on the golf team (which anyone reading this book who has played with me will find hard to believe) and we weren't very good. But, we did have an entertaining quality about us – we could all juggle! Luckily, because of my brother Tom and me (we were in the same grade because my mother had held Tom back in eighth grade), we had a phenomenal high school gymnastics team.

We would have won the Ohio High School State Championship our junior year, but sadly Tom broke his ankle dismounting from the high bar during practice two weeks before the state meet. But in our senior year, we were undefeated and won the state championship. To win a state championship before you even had a graduating class at your high school was considered pretty big stuff. The Monday after the state meet, they had a special assembly in the school auditorium with the entire student body and all the local politicians there to honor our team. That was special.

Our school had tremendous school spirit. Students supported all sports, and that included our gymnastics team. Because our team was so good and so many students wanted to go to the state championship meet in Columbus, held at Ohio State, Fairmont East chartered four buses so students could go to watch the meet. I'm very confident that this has never been done before or since by any school in Ohio – certainly not for gymnastics.

Tumbling Our Life Away

So, how did Tom and I get into gymnastics? Well, when we were 8 and 9 years old, a friend of ours belonged to the Dayton YMCA, and he took us there as his guest one day. We absolutely loved it and wanted to join the "Y". Luckily, our mom recognized our passion for the "Y" and signed us up.

Every Saturday morning they had relay races, swimming, and sports of all kinds. It was like paradise to us. Much of our youth was spent there.

We never missed going on Saturday mornings, and soon discovered that on Tuesday and Thursday nights they had a tumbling class. Tom and I joined it. Before long, we were pretty good tumblers. They put us on the "Y"'s tumbling team and we would do exhibitions all

over town. We tumbled first, then started bouncing on the trampo-
line, and then graduated to gymnastic apparatus. Fortunately for us,
when we later got to high school, our high school had a gymnastics
program.

To illustrate just how the "Y"'s programs influenced our lives, my
brother Tom liked to tell this story:

> *Back in the early 1960s, Mike and I used to do a lot
> of tumbling shows for the Dayton YMCA. But sometimes,
> just for fun, we would walk down stairs on our hands in
> unique locations, such as stores in downtown Dayton, or
> kick up to a handstand riding the escalator, while one of us
> would hang a hat on the other's foot to watch the reaction
> of people going the other way on the opposite escalator.*
>
> *We might kick up to a handstand in front of an el-
> evator and say "excuse me" as we walked into it on our
> hands, to the surprise of customers who were getting off.
> We might do a tumbling show on the courthouse lawn
> downtown, or do front and back flips off the huge cannon
> in front of the courthouse as buses went by.*
>
> *One Saturday afternoon we were returning a tram-
> polette [a smaller, portable version of a trampoline] we
> had borrowed from the "Y". We were riding on the city bus
> with a few other kids when one of them offered Mike a
> challenge. He said, "Sexton, I'll bet you a dollar you don't
> have the nerve to go to the main floor of Rike's Depart-
> ment Store [the largest store in Dayton] and do a front flip
> off the trampolette." Mike immediately laughed and said,
> "You've got a bet." [Life's a gamble, but this was a sure
> thing.]*
>
> *Our whole group followed Mike into the department
> store as he set up the trampolette. He cleared everyone
> back, then took off running to do a high, front somersault
> off the trampolette. There was a huge crowd shopping that*

day and they broke into applause. So, Mike did it again. Then we all joined in and started doing our tricks with Mike.

A bigger crowd gathered and the applause got louder. All of a sudden a store employee showed up and said, "What the hell do you kids think you're doing?" Mike, who has always had a quick mind as well as a quick wit, immediately spoke up: "We were hired to do a show today for the sporting goods department. They asked us to do two shows today because they have a sale going on this weekend. I'm surprised you haven't heard about it." The employee replied, "Oh, I'm sorry, I didn't know that. Well, you're all doing a great job... carry on." With that, we did a few more tricks for the delighted audience, scooped up our trampolette, and went on our way. It was another fun time, back in the day!

We were always doing somersaults somewhere. One way Tom and I earned money was when we were in a restaurant with Danny and he would give us 50 cents each to do a back flip off the table. He loved watching us do that and we loved getting his money!

Flipping Our Way Through College

Our high school gymnastic team won every meet (by a wide margin) our senior year. In our high school's state championship meet, my brother Tom won three event gold medals plus the Best All-Around Award. Every college in the country with a gymnastics team was trying to recruit him. Most wanted me as a throw-in. We took numerous recruiting trips, and every school offered Tom a full scholarship and me a half scholarship – with the exception of Ohio State, which, I'm sure in order to lure Tom, offered both of us a full ride.

Tom didn't want to go to Ohio State, though, as they weren't too good in gymnastics at that time. (They have since become one of the top programs in the country.) He wanted to go to a school that was in the hunt annually to win the NCAA title. He decided to go to Oklahoma (a new program at the time). I went to Ohio State because that's the only school that offered me a full scholarship (four-year tuition, room and board, books, laundry money, the works).

I remember calling the Ohio State coach, Joe Hewlett. I said, "Coach, I'm sorry that Tom decided to go to Oklahoma, but you offered me a full scholarship, too. Do I still get it?" And he said, "Yes. I offered you one and you get it if you want it." Yes! I got a full scholarship to Ohio State because of my brother – and he didn't even go there. As close as Tom and I have always been, I went to a separate college (Ohio State) since it was the only way I could get a full scholarship as well.

Tom had a great career at Oklahoma. He became the first All-American gymnast ever at Oklahoma. I won the high score award every year at Ohio State and the Most Valuable Gymnast award in my senior year. College worked out well for both of us. One thing is for sure – I will always love the Buckeyes!

As for college experiences, one of the greatest lessons ever for me came the first day I walked on to the Ohio State campus. After unloading my stuff in my dorm room at Park Hall, I went downstairs to the rec room. As I was walking around and looking at the ping-pong tables, a guy came up to me and said, "Do you play ping-pong?"

I said, "Yes, I play ping-pong" and he continued, "There's a guy who's supposed to be real good and he's looking for a game tonight at 7 pm. Would you play him?" I said, "Sure." (FYI, I thought I was a *great* ping-pong player. I never lost at the "Y" and was my high school's intra-mural ping-pong champion.)

I went down to the rec room just before 7 pm and, to my surprise, the place was packed. The guy I met earlier in the day then blurted out, "There's the guy who's gonna play him." All eyes turned to me.

A guy in shorts carrying a gym bag walked over to me and said "Hi". I said "Hello" and he unzipped his gym bag and in it I saw about 20 ping-pong paddles. I thought, *Hmmm. I could be in trouble here.*

He pulled one out where the face of the paddle was smaller than the handle. (Take your thumb and forefinger and form a circle with them and then open it about a half an inch. That's how big the face of his paddle was!) I walked over to the wall and got my paddle off the rack.

Perhaps sensing my embarrassment, he said, "You don't mind if I warm up with this paddle, do you?" I said, "No, I don't mind." Within 20 seconds of volleying, I could see I was in big trouble. The crowd knew it, too, as I heard their murmuring.

He didn't change paddles after warm-ups and beat me 21–4 and 21–6 – with a miniature paddle that you could hardly see the face on! I was so embarrassed. The funny thing is, I thought I was so good at ping-pong. And just like that, 'bam', I got a real wake-up call. Like Dorothy in *The Wizard of Oz*, I discovered, "You're not in Kansas any more."

I think I learned more in that rec room on my first day on campus than in my next four years at college. It's a lesson I've never forgotten – when you think you're good at something, there's always someone else who's better – and in this case, a lot better. It turns out this kid was the third ranked table tennis player in the US and was on a tennis scholarship to Ohio State. He played the world champion from China at halftime of one of the basketball games – and almost beat him!

4

Pack up and Get Out

You can't leave your children on the street.

Doyle Brunson

My mom had her pluses and minuses. She was certainly unique and, for sure, she was ahead of her time. She was married and divorced twice before I was a junior in high school. She owned her own business, Gloria's Dance Studio, and, like my dad, was a superb dancer and excellent ballroom dance teacher.

One of the things I remember proudly about my mother was her kindness, especially for those who were under-privileged or handi-capped. She had a soft spot for orphans and she taught free dance classes to those children (I started dancing in those kid classes). The real topper: she taught a free class for the blind and another for the deaf – and as you can imagine, neither of those is easy to do. Unfortunately, even though she did so many good things for people, as I mentioned earlier, she was an alcoholic.

My mom did things other parents probably would never understand. And as a parent, put me on that list. For example, I don't think she ever came to one of my Little League games. I remember making the All-Star game one year and I hit a single and a triple in that game. I was thrilled, but at the same time I was sad because nobody from my family was there to see it. (Tom, a year older, was playing on another team at the time.)

No doubt, my mom was different. As good as Tom and I were in gymnastics, she came to only one or two of our meets in high school, and none in college. If we ever needed to get somewhere, she wouldn't take us. She would tell us to hitchhike or take the bus. (We hitchhiked everywhere back then, something that is not done at all today.) If we needed money to buy something, she insisted that we get a job and pay for it ourselves. Tom and I sold everything door to door from donuts to encyclopedias, but mostly we caddied when we needed money growing up. My first job with a paycheck was working as a busboy at Imperial House South in Centerville, OH.

Our mom forced us to be independent. The week after we got out of high school, she said we had to pay her $15 a week rent to stay in the house. When we questioned her about that, she said, "If you can find anywhere to live cheaper than $15 a week, I suggest you go there." We both got jobs (I taught ballroom dancing at Arthur Murray's in Dayton and Tom got a construction job) and we paid her the $15 a week rent.

During our freshman year at college, she married for a third time. He was a very nice guy, Adam Geisel, a factory worker at Delco. He was good for her in that he looked out for her while letting her do her own thing (drinking), and he was nice to us. Tom and I went home for the summer after our freshman year and lived with them. Tom got another construction job and I was a forklift driver at a factory. So we were doing well, making money, and – again – paying rent at home.

One night, my mom came in drunk at 2 am. She'd obviously closed down the bar... again. She turned on the lights in our room and started yelling, "Get up! Get your asses out of bed!" I was hoping this was a bad dream, but sadly, it wasn't. I said, "Come on, Mom. We're tired. Let's talk about whatever you want to talk about tomorrow." She passionately continued, "Goddammit, I said get out of bed *now*!"

We were mumbling and started moving, but apparently not fast enough for her. She went over to our trophy case and swept her arm across it, knocking all our trophies to the floor. Well, when you're a kid, trophies are more valuable than hundred-dollar bills. We immediately jumped up and said, "What are you doing? Are you crazy?"

She looked at us and said, "You two don't know shit about the world. You've got no idea how tough it is to make it in the world. You don't know what a quart of milk costs. You go to college and they pamper you because you're athletes. You swing around a bar like monkeys – big goddamn deal."

Shockingly, she then said, "You've got 30 minutes to pack up your stuff and get out of the house. Go out and see what it's like in the real world." This was the middle of the night and she was throwing us out of the house.

So, we gathered up our stuff, went down to the YMCA, and got a room there. My brother was engaged and he and his girlfriend were going to be married at the end of the summer before he went back to college for his sophomore year. Her parents could not believe that our mother had thrown us out in the middle of the night for no reason. And neither could we!

We just didn't get it. We were both on full scholarships to college, had good jobs in the summer, and were paying rent, and still we were tossed out of the house. It was an eye-opening experience, to say the least. Tom moved in with his fiancée's parents to save money and I stayed at the "Y". About a month after she threw us out, my mom called me and said, "I think by this time you know a little bit about the world and you're welcome to come home now." I told her I'd rather just stay down at the "Y" for the rest of the summer. And I did.

As harsh and painful as that experience was, I must say, I really did grow up that summer.

5 College and the Army

*Beating the games was the easy part. Getting out
of town with the money was the tough part.*

Johnny Moss

Once I got to Ohio State, I discovered that I was much more talented than the other guys in the dorm at playing cards, whether it was gin rummy, hearts, euchre, or poker. As a kid I had paid my dues with Danny, but I discovered that I was now in a clover patch in college. These guys were not nearly as good as I was at any card game. It was time to get some "Danny money" back.

I won at whatever card game we were playing most of the time. Whenever someone on the floor asked how the game came out, the answer was usually, "Sexton smoked 'em again." Because of that, the guys in the dorm started calling me "Smoker". I never told anyone about that nickname after I left college. I didn't like that nickname because I thought it would make everyone think I smoked – which I didn't. Maybe I should have kept it. Nicknames go a long way in getting publicity in the poker world.

I also learned how to play bridge in college (ironically, from Danny's older brother, Jimmy). And I played a lot. Jimmy was three years older than Danny and had gone into the Air Force after high school, so I didn't really know him well when we were kids. But after he got out of the Air Force, he went to Ohio State and we became good friends and bridge partners.

We started playing bridge together nearly every day – at the student union in the afternoon and at the dental fraternity or local bridge club at night. You might say we became obsessed with bridge – and we started getting pretty good at it. (Jimmy later became a world-class bridge player, an American Contract Bridge Grand Master, and I later taught bridge classes in North Carolina.)

Between bridge and poker, I played cards just about every day during my college years. You could safely say that I majored in cards in college. And it worked out well for me.

Bridge Ace at Bragg

Having done somersaults all my life, it was only natural that I wanted to jump out of planes. So, after college, I joined the Army. I wanted to be a paratrooper. (Hey, life's a gamble!) It was during the Vietnam era and my draft number was high enough that I wouldn't have been drafted, but I always believed (and still believe) that everyone should serve a couple of years in the Armed Forces. (Speaking of side bets and gambling, on our dorm floor, we put up a pool of $5 each, that whoever's birthday was called first on the day of the draft lottery would win the money.)

I can remember how crazy everyone thought I was for volunteering to go in the Army. They thought for sure that I would go to

Vietnam. They also said I'd make a lot of money playing cards. Well, that turned out to be rubbish. I didn't find a poker game over a 25 cent limit until I got to jump school.

After basic and advanced individual training at Fort Knox, KY, I went to jump school at Fort Benning, GA (August 1970). After just a few days there, I got an opportunity to play in my first poker game in the Army.

During my first week of Airborne training, a guy was going around asking, "Does anybody play poker? Anybody play poker?" I said, "Yes. I like to play." And he said, "Great. If you want to play, we're going to have a $5 limit, Seven Card Stud game tomorrow night on the latrine floor after lights out. Cash only. It'll be a $1 ante and $5 limit." I said, "OK. I'll see you tomorrow night." That may seem like a small game, but when you're only making $138 a month with an additional $55 for jump pay, it was pretty big.

I showed up in the latrine the next night (we played there because that was the only place the lights were on) and six of us sat on the tile floor and started playing. After about an hour and a half, the officer of the day came in and just glared at us. He then bellowed out, "You guys haven't got enough to do around here, huh? Well, we'll see if we can change that."

He put us on Kitchen Police (KP) for three days. From 4 am until about 11 pm, we were assigned to the mess hall. My assignment was to scrub pots and pans. It was brutal. (When they got rid of the draft and went to an all-volunteer Army they did away with KP duties for soldiers. They had to if they wanted anybody to join.) I'll never forget that poker night though, not just because we got busted, but because I beat the game for $43.

After jump school, I was assigned to the 82nd Airborne Division at Fort Bragg, NC. This division had just returned from its second tour of duty in Vietnam, which turned out to be a blessing for me, as I didn't have to go to Vietnam. In fact, I never left Fort Bragg while in the Army.

I was assigned to Headquarters & Headquarters Company and

worked for the 82nd Airborne Division Schools Detachment, which ran the Jumpmaster School and the Recondo School, and sent guys to the Non-commissioned Officer Academy and other schools. I had a great job working in an office. I was allowed to live off post and miss reveille and morning formation every day. I just had to show up for work and everything was Jake. Airborne!

It was a great setup for me because I loved to make parachute jumps. I could go out to the drop zone with the Jumpmaster School, jump out of helicopters a few times with the students, and drive back in, all in an hour or two. When the rest of the division made a jump, they had to go to the Green Ramp at Pope Air Force Base about 5 am, sit there for a few hours, fly around all day, and then jump once late in the afternoon. I did that once and it was a very long day. Give me those chopper jumps!

It's amazing what you can do in the Army if you try. Here's a fond memory. I played a fair amount of bridge back then and wanted to go to the American Contract Bridge League Nationals, which were being held in Atlanta – and I came up with an idea. The Army sent guys to sporting events temporary duty, so I thought, *How about the Army sending me to the National Bridge Championships?*

The guy I worked for at the Schools Detachment thought this was a great idea and felt challenged to do it. He looked in all the Army Regulations but couldn't find anything about sending someone to a bridge tournament. He then said, "Let's forget about the Army sending you. Let's see if the 82nd Airborne Division will send you."

He put together a letter with a list of my qualifications, wrote that I was an outstanding soldier, that I would wear my uniform when I played, that I'd represent the 82nd Airborne Division in an outstanding manner, and that I'd report back daily on how I was doing. He sent the letter to the commanding general of the 82nd Airborne Division for approval.

The truth is that my qualifications were a joke to any serious bridge player – I was an advanced senior master – which is below Life Master (and Life Masters were a dime a dozen). I won the Ohio collegiate championships (a designated tourney at the Ohio Union one Sunday where five or six other teams from colleges around Ohio came and played that day), etc, etc, – but I knew my "qualifications" would look impressive to someone who didn't play bridge.

I was, however, a good soldier – clean, smart, did what I was told, always maxed the physical training tests, and would represent the 82nd well. Sure enough, the 82nd Airborne Division approved it. They sent me temporary duty to Atlanta for two weeks to play bridge!

I was happy to get to go, but was now worried about getting results as I had to report in daily. Luckily, I somehow won a one-session event (all the major events were two- or four-session) called the Georgia Pairs, but still that was a good result. I called the guy who sent me and told him about my win. He was feeling good knowing the brass would eat this up.

When I got back to Fort Bragg a reporter came to see me. I thought he was with the *Paraglide* (the 82nd's newspaper) but it turned out he was with the *Army Times* (a paper that goes all over the world). I did the interview and the next week nothing appeared in the *Paraglide*.

Two weeks later, on the top of page 2 of the *Army Times*, in bold print, the headline read, "Bridge Ace at Bragg!" It was an article on me that took up over half the page. I had brought good publicity to the 82nd Airborne Division and my man was right, the brass was happy about it. In today's terms, it went viral. It's amazing what can be done if one just tries.

I loved the Army. I came very close to making it my career. Then, I realized I might have to leave Fort Bragg some day. With that in mind, when my enlistment was up, I left the service.

6 Back to the Ballroom

I look at a man from the ankles down. I don't care if he's rich or good looking, if he can't dance, I'm not wasting my time on him.

Suzie Matthews

While at Fort Bragg, I had a cushy office job, which meant I didn't have to go out into the field. That allowed me time to work at night if I wanted to and that worked out well for me. I went to the local YMCA with plans to teach gymnastics.

While I was there applying for the job, I saw a guy teaching a ballroom dance class. I watched for a while and then said hello to him after his class. His name was Roland Bersch. I told him I taught one summer at the Arthur Murray Dance Studio in Dayton, OH. He lit up

Life's a Gamble

like a Christmas tree. It turned out he had worked at the Oshkosh, WI, Arthur Murray Studio, now had a studio of his own in Fayetteville called Roland's Dance Studio, and needed a male teacher.

He showed me a step list, asked me if I recognized it, and when I told him I did, he said, "You'll make twice as much teaching for me part time as you will teaching gymnastics here at the 'Y'." I said, "Great! You've got a new teacher."

I taught ballroom dancing part time at Roland's Dance Studio at night and continued doing that long after I got out of the Army. While working at the studio, I met a couple who took lessons and the husband was a successful businessman. He told me he was starting a new business, a military sales company called All-American Sales. (I thought that was a clever name as the 82nd Airborne Division is called the All-American Division.)

The company would sell products to the PX's (Post Exchanges) and commissaries in North and South Carolina. I'd never been in sales, other than my youth days selling stuff door to door, but looking at his success (he was a millionaire), I figured it was worth a shot. Hey, life's a gamble, right?

I worked as a sales rep for several years. I learned a lot on that job about marketing and selling (mostly how important "the buyers" thought they were and how you had to grease them to get your products in). From a business and life perspective, that job was a very educational and an enlightening experience for me.

Father and Son: a Bond

My dad was a ballroom dance teacher, but not your ordinary dance teacher. He started out like all dance teachers – teaching at a studio – but later did something that to my knowledge has never been done before or since.

Not long after my dad remarried, he and his new wife, Beverly, had their first child, Jeffrey. He then left the Arthur Dance Murray studio in Indianapolis and went to California to manage the Arthur

Murray Studio in Santa Monica. Because of him, it became one of the top studios in the country.

When it came to teaching dancing, my dad had a dream he wanted to pursue: he wanted to teach *couples* to dance. He knew the happiness that dancing brought to people, the difference it made in their lives, and he wanted to provide that joy.

My dad thought dance studios were too expensive and too sales oriented, which they were. One needed deep pockets to take lessons at Arthur Murray's. Most of the students there were widows who had plenty of free time and money. It was good for them, don't misunderstand me, but young couples with kids or people who had average jobs could never afford lessons at an Arthur Murray Studio.

My dad felt that young couples should have the opportunity to dance together and do so at an affordable price. He wanted to provide them with something that they could and would enjoy all their lives as a couple. (When you think about it, there really are very few things you do and enjoy as a couple. Dancing can be one of those.)

So, he returned to Indiana to do what he believed could be done, to teach one couples-only class each night (8–10 pm) in small towns. He felt his dance class would be the "social thing" for people to do in those towns. For $40 a couple, he would sign them up for a 10-week course. (And, incidentally, he did this for more than 20 years before he ever raised his rates.) The catch was that they had to pay for the course months in advance. Amazingly, they did it!

He started knocking on doors and got one class going, then another, then another. His only advertising was word of mouth. He knew that getting couples to pay in advance, as well as rotating dance partners around, were the two things that *must* be done for him to be successful over the long haul. With his great teaching ability and smooth selling style, his classes filled up fast.

My dad taught dance classes in small towns in Indiana for more than 30 years – strictly group classes, not private lessons. He'd knock on doors during the day to sell classes that would not take place for several months and then teach one at night that he sold months ago. It might not sound that impressive to you, but I promise, to my knowledge, it's something that's never been done anywhere in the country before or since.

He taught at the Elks and Moose Lodges in little towns in Indiana including Columbus, Bloomington, Andersonville, Seymour, Martinsville, and Muncie. My dad, who died at age 88 in 2008, is still a legend back in those towns. It really was "the social thing to do" to take Ray Sexton's dance classes. The people loved it. In some of those towns today, even though he left Indiana in 1990, they still have a Sexton Dance Club.

In the winter of 1989, my dad slipped and fell on the ice and had to have a metal plate inserted in his head. I was living in Las Vegas and told him, "Look, you can't spend another winter in Indiana. Your doctor said another fall could kill you. I want you to move out here."

At his third wife's (Sandra's) insistence, they moved to Vegas a few months later. I was thrilled to have him with me in Las Vegas and for him to witness my rise to the top. He (and my brother Tom) played a key role in my career by giving me confidence in my abilities and advising me on decisions regarding my Card Player columns, the Tournament of Champions (TOC), partypoker, and the WPT.

Change of Plans

My dad had been teaching dance classes for years, but right before I got out of the Army in 1972, he called me up and said he was in big trouble. He had gotten a second DUI (penalty for drinking under the influence). They were taking his driver's license away from him for six months. It was bad. He needed someone to drive him around so that he could continue to make a living.

He knew it wasn't fair to ask me to do it – as he knew I'd gotten a good job offer as a sales rep after I was discharged from the Army – but he was desperate. He and Beverly had four kids, all in high school or below. He didn't know where else to turn.

I went to my prospective employer, explained the situation, and asked if I could delay starting the sales job for six months. He understood and said OK. So I took a six-month hiatus before I started with All-American Sales. It turned out to be one of the best things I ever did. And my dad learned his lesson. He never had another drink.

During those six months, I lived with my dad and his family in Indianapolis. I drove him around, knocked on doors with him, went into every living room, saw how people adored him, witnessed his selling expertise, and went to the classes with him. Watching him sell the lessons was like watching Muhammad Ali in his prime, and seeing him teach dancing could be compared to watching Picasso paint. He was that good at both.

Once in a while, he would get in a gin rummy game. I got to sweat those – as well as baseball and football games we had vested interests in. We became very close during those six months. It amazed me how much alike we were even though I didn't grow up with him. I appreciated what he was doing because I, too, had been in the dance business and knew that his concept was unique, to put it mildly.

I saw the joy and happiness he brought to all those people's lives. He was special. Had I not gone into poker, I could and probably would have done just what my dad did. I'd have taught dance classes for a living in small towns, and I know I would have been very content doing it.

There's one thing that I'll always believe – *those who dance enjoy life more than those who don't*. Nobody will ever get me to change my mind about that. I've seen it and I've lived it. It doesn't matter if you're rich, it doesn't matter if you're poor. People who dance have more fun in life than those who don't. Period.

7

Turning Pro

*The only difference between a
winner and a loser is character.*

"Nick the Greek" Dandolas

After the Army and the six-month stint with my dad, I moved back to
Fayetteville, NC, worked as a military sales rep, and got married to a
local girl, Pam Sharpe. I taught ballroom dancing part time, but I also
managed to find some home poker games.

I loved playing in those games — and did well in them. After
three and a half years of marriage (and no kids), my wife and I got a
divorce. We were young. I was gone pretty much all the time and was
certainly not giving her the time and attention she needed – probably
playing too much poker. Live and learn.

When I worked as a sales rep, it would kill me to quit my poker game at 1 am, which is what I had to do so I could drive to Camp Lejeune or another base the next day (where I might or might not sell something and make some money). I knew I could make money in that poker game.

After becoming single again, I thought, *I love to play poker and I'm single. Screw it. Life's a gamble. I'm just going to quit my job and play poker in these home games. If I get broke, I can always get another job.* So, that's what I did.

In 1977, I officially became a professional poker player. I played nearly every day, and for the next 23 years, I never had a paycheck. I played in North Carolina home games for nearly eight years. Then, in January 1985, I moved out to Las Vegas and have been there ever since.

I always tell anyone who is thinking about becoming a professional poker player that even if you have the talent to do it and are a winning player, if you don't love to play poker – not like to play, but *love* to play – don't do it, because you'll be miserable. I was fortunate because I always loved playing poker. I never got tired of it. When one game was over, I couldn't wait for the next day to go to the next game.

Sexton's suggestion: The one attribute you must have if you want to live a successful, happy life as a poker player is a love of the game. If you don't *love* to play, forget about doing it for a living.

A Life-changing Experience

We all have certain moments and experiences that change our lives forever, many that are the epitome of *taking a chance*. I had one in 1984, the first time I played in the World Series of Poker (WSOP).

Even though I'd been a pro player for seven years and had been to Las Vegas numerous times, I'd never played in the WSOP. I met my second wife-to-be in 1978. We were married in 1980. She had a son (Michael) who was playing Little League baseball (10–12 year olds) when I met her. I became fascinated with it.

After my wife's son aged out, I wanted a team of my own. I was ecstatic when I got one. I coached the Honeycutt Pirates in Fayetteville for six years. My number-one passion in life in those days was coaching Little League baseball. I can honestly say that nothing I've ever done in my life has given me more joy.

To give you an idea of my passion for Little League, here's one of my favorite stories. We had a beautiful time-sharing place in the Outer Banks the second week of June every year. One year, the Pirates were tied for first place and scheduled to play our rivals, the Astro's, the following Friday night. Naturally, I would much rather have been at the game than the beach, but this was a sensitive issue to bring up with the wife as she looked forward to our beach trip every year.

I had an idea – to charter a plane back for the game. I was looking in the yellow pages for private jets when my wife inquired what I was doing. I said, "I'm seeing what it costs to get a private jet back and forth from the Outer Banks so I can go to our game on Friday."

She couldn't believe what she was hearing. She stared blankly and said, "Now I know that you've lost your mind. Do you think any Little League coach in the world would leave a luxury beach resort for one Little League game – and charter a jet to do it?" I said, "I don't know, but I want to."

We ended up with a compromise, and it didn't take a private jet. She invited a girlfriend to the beach for the weekend and they would ride back together at the week's end. I drove home that Friday morning. I was so happy to get to go to the game. And we won!

In those days, the WSOP took place in April and May, which is exactly when Little League season was. We started practicing in April and the season started in May. At that time in my life, my devotion to Little League outweighed my desire to play in the WSOP.

Finally, I decided that, since I was a professional poker player, I needed to take a week off Little League practice to go to the WSOP. In those days, the WSOP was not like it is today. In 1984, you could play only one event every other day. They played down to the final table on Day 1 of a tournament and then played the final table on Day 2 (with no other event going on). That meant if you went to Vegas for a week, you could play in only three events. And that's what I did.

Out of three events, I made two final tables – one in Seven Card Stud 8 or Better and the other in Pot Limit Omaha (PLO). It was the first time in WSOP history they had a PLO tournament and, as the tournament got under way, I really felt I played as well as anyone. I sincerely believed that I had as good a chance as anyone to win it, especially after I made it to the final table.

Sadly, I took a bad beat with five players left, one I will never forget. Nobody likes to hear bad beat stories, and I don't tell many, but I'll tell you this one. Skip the next few paragraphs if you don't like bad beat stories, but it's my book so I'm telling it.

I had average chips with five players left. Included in those remaining players were the reigning world champion of poker, Tom McEvoy, famed author David Sklansky, and a high-stakes cash game player named Bill Bennett (who won the tournament).

I'd never met or played with McEvoy, and although he had won the WSOP main event the year before, I wasn't impressed with his overly aggressive style playing PLO. (I'm guessing he wasn't impressed with my tight play, either.) Anyway, McEvoy was raising nearly every pot, and after another of his raises, I looked down at A-K-Q-8 double suited (A-Q of diamonds and K-8 of clubs). I called (and don't scream at me for not re-raising – I said I played tight) and the flop comes Q-8-3 with two hearts.

McEvoy said, "I'll bet the pot." Well, I know this is it as I'm going with this hand. McEvoy, who was staring at me, read me well. He sensed that I was going to play and said, "If you raise, I'm going to set you all-in." In those days, you could say what you wanted at the table with no penalties. I said, "Well, I guess you're setting me in, then, because I raise the pot."

True to his word, McEvoy then set me all-in and I called. We tabled our cards. I turned up my A-K-Q-8 for top two pair, and he turned up 3-4-5-8, bottom two pair with no flush draw! *Yes!* I was way out front and my heart was pounding. I was on the verge of nearing the chip lead with just a few players left. I was envisioning becoming rich and that championship bracelet going back to North Carolina with me!

Then it happened: a 7 came on the turn and a 6 on the river. *Boom!* He back-doored a straight and, just like that, I was out in fifth place. You could hear the thud of my heart hitting the floor. Bye-bye, Mike. Bye-bye, bracelet.

It was so painful. I couldn't imagine an icepick in your eye feeling much worse. I still remember the agony of that loss. I wanted to win so badly. We all take bad beats, but because it was my first WSOP and I had a real shot to win, that's one I've never forgotten.

As for McEvoy, I learned to respect him as a person – not only because he was one of the good guys in poker but because he and Casey Kastle were the first to campaign and petition for getting smoking out of poker tournaments – something many thought would never happen.

It's hard to imagine nowadays how prevalent smoking was back then. To get this done was like climbing Pike's Peak. Tom and Casey knew they had to get the high-stakes players on board to be successful with this venture. So, they went to the biggest cash game and asked those players if they would sign their no smoking petition. Chip Reese quickly said, "Yes! Where do I sign?" Doyle Brunson followed with, "Yes. Give it here. I'll sign it, too."

Jack Binion, Bob Stupak, and other casino owners used to say, "Drinking, smoking, and gambling all go together and I'm not telling a big pit player that he can't smoke when he plays poker." In my opinion, all of us who play poker today owe Tom and Casey a debt of gratitude for leading the charge.

You can't really appreciate what they accomplished unless you were a nonsmoker who played during the time they allowed smoking in tournaments. Today, you can hardly find a smoking tournament anywhere in the world. Thank you Tom and Casey.

After that beat in the WSOP, I went home to regroup. I thought to myself, *if I'm going to be a professional poker player, maybe it's time that I moved out to Las Vegas.* I knew for sure that I never wanted to miss another WSOP. I was hooked and set my dreams on winning a bracelet. In January 1985, I moved to Vegas, and in '89, I fulfilled my dream of winning a bracelet. To this day, I've never missed a WSOP.

I often wonder, had I not had a good World Series showing, had I not made those two final tables out of three tournaments, would I have ever moved to Las Vegas? What would have happened to me if I'd stayed in North Carolina?

It just shows you how weird life is – one pivotal experience or twist of fate often determines whom you marry, what your job is, where you're going to live. I moved to Las Vegas because of the success I had at my first WSOP. Fortunately, that gamble in life worked out well for me.

8 Off to Vegas

Part of it went on gambling. Part of it went on women. The rest I spent foolishly.

George Raft

After college, Danny went back to Dayton and played gin rummy and poker around town, where he met and became friends with David "Chip" Reese. Chip was an Ohio boy wonder: one of the smartest in his class at Centerville High School, a debate champion, player on the football team, and a superb poker player. He went to Dartmouth, where he majored in economics and, upon graduating at the top of his class, was accepted to Stanford Law School.

Chip never made it to Stanford. In the unforgettable summer of 1974 following Chip's graduation from Dartmouth, Danny and Chip decided to become gambling partners on a trip to Las Vegas. They went there with a $1,000 bankroll and started out by playing the same money in 12-hour shifts around the clock ($15/30 and $30/60 Seven Card Stud, mostly at the Sahara). They did well.

After a successful month or so at the Sahara, Chip, after watching the big game (which was held at the Flamingo at that time), convinced Danny he could beat it, took a shot, and they never looked back.

After several months, they turned their bankroll into a million dollars! And, as they say, "the rest is history." Because of their youth and phenomenal success, Danny and Chip were known as "the Gold Dust Twins" and became Las Vegas icons and poker legends within a short period of time.

Fueled by their success, Danny and Chip decided to make Las Vegas their home. Like most gamblers, they lived high and weren't afraid to spend money. To most, at least to those aspiring to get to the top of the poker world, they were living the dream – and I was their biggest fan.

I'll never forget my first trip to Vegas. I thought I'd died and gone to heaven. Danny was always inviting me to visit him but I was married, had a job, and just didn't have the time to go. Finally, after getting a divorce in 1977, I took Danny up on his invitation. I went to Vegas and stayed at Chip and Danny's house.

I was wowed. I thought it was the greatest bachelor pad in the world. That house had all you could dream of: two master bedrooms, a swimming pool (complete with naked girls lying around), a 10-foot home theater (nobody had one back then), a collection of 500 movies, a pool table, a fabulous bar, and a couple of great dogs (who ate as well as Chip and Danny – on steaks delivered by taxi from the best restaurants in town). To me, their life was paradise.

This was the first time I'd met Chip. Although he was from the Dayton area (Centerville) like I was, he was five years younger. I was off to college and the Army before he got into poker. I was flabbergasted that two guys from my hometown could do so well in Las Vegas.

I remember how excited I was to finally be in Vegas. That first night, I asked Danny, "What's on the schedule for tomorrow?" He chuckled and said, "I'm playing golf with a guy who weighs 400 pounds." I said, "You're playing golf with a guy who weighs 400 pounds? What are you spotting him?" And he said, "A half a shot a side." *WTF?* How was that possible?

Danny was a phenomenal golfer growing up. He was a star golfer at Fairmont High School (that won the Ohio State High School Championship), got a golf scholarship to Ohio University, and he won the City of Dayton Championship when I caddied for him a few years later (a week-long match play tourney that is one of the biggest amateur tournaments in Ohio). The guy could play. I know it was 10–12 years later since he was a star golfer, but I still couldn't believe what I was hearing – that Danny only had to give a half shot a side to play a guy who was that big.

I said, "There's nobody in the world who weighs 400 pounds who can beat you only getting a half shot a side." He laughed and said, "It'll be a tough match. We're playing a $20,000 Nassau [three-way bet: front nine, back nine, and total] with one automatic press (a second bet that begins during the round and runs concurrently with the original bet) a side [a two-down press]. You can have a piece of it if you like." It was one round of golf with a potential win/loss of $100k. This was the big time.

My total net worth of $2,500 was in my pocket. Nevertheless, I said, "I'd love to have a piece. I'll bet a $500 Nassau on you." That meant I could win or lose five bets – so my whole bankroll would be on the line. He said, "OK. You're in action."

I was so excited that I couldn't sleep that night. I truly thought I would be stealing. Here I was in Vegas, staying with Danny and Chip in this dream house, and I was going to double my bankroll the first morning I was in town by having the nuts in this golf match. How could life get any better?

We went to the Las Vegas Country Club the next day and, over on the putting green, I see Danny's opponent – none other than Doyle Brunson, the reigning world champion of poker. We went over and Danny introduced me to Doyle (who really was close to 400 pounds at that time). Just looking at Doyle, I couldn't imagine he would have a chance against Danny playing golf. How could a guy this big beat Danny at golf?

They finished warming up and we all headed to the first tee. Danny teed off first and drove it perfectly down the middle. *How sweet it is*, I thought. Doyle then stepped up and hit a low line drive down the middle. As we drove over the hill, I could see that one ball was about 40–50 yards in front of the other. I thought to myself, *If that's Doyle's ball out front, I could really be screwed.* Sure enough, it was Doyle's ball out front. (The fairways are like the greens at Las Vegas Country Club and low line drives, like Doyle hits, tend to roll forever.)

Doyle shot even par (72) from the back tees that day. Danny lost four bets and I lost $2k, nearly my entire bankroll. I hated Doyle that day for breaking me but I couldn't help but admire him at the same time. I couldn't believe anyone his size could play that well. It was a good lesson for me – you've never got the nuts when you're gambling, especially in Vegas.

On my next visit to Danny and Chip's, something happened that I'll never forget – and to say it was an eye-opener is putting it mildly. I walked into the rec room and it looked to me like somebody had spilled a pile of sugar on the bar. I asked Danny, "What's this?" He chuckled at my naivety and said, "That's cocaine."

Stunned, I said, "Cocaine? What are you doing with cocaine?" I'll never forget the words he said to me for as long as I live: "Sexton, coke is a rich man's habit and I'm a rich man."

To this day, I think about that experience and Danny's words. It shocked me that a guy I grew up with, who never smoked, drank, or used drugs in high school, ended up addicted to cocaine. What began as a recreational, rich man's train ride, sadly turned into a pile of wreckage.

Las Vegas is a 24-hour town, and if you have any vices, Vegas will find them. In my opinion, it's a town where you either have to work for a living or gamble for a living. It's *very* tough to do both. You might be able to survive in Vegas with one vice, but if you have more than one, it's difficult, in fact, nearly impossible, to stay afloat. Unfortunately for Danny, he found one – and it was the worst one. He became addicted to cocaine.

Cocaine has ruined the lives of successful people in all fields, including poker. In addition to Danny, former world champions Sailor Roberts, Jack Straus, and Stu Ungar all got hooked on cocaine and all paid the price. Joey Hawthorne (who wrote the lowball chapter of Doyle Brunson's book *Super System*) was another. It was so sad to see all these poker legends and so many others destroy their lives by getting hooked on drugs.

It's hard for most who don't use drugs to really understand the depth of addiction and to recognize that it really is a sickness. (I understand the addiction part as I had my own "drug" – betting on sports.) But, I grew up with Danny and knew he never did drugs, so I asked him, "Seriously, Danny, why in the hell are you doing cocaine?" And he said to me, "Mike, you'll never understand why people do cocaine unless you get on the train." Fortunately, I never boarded that train.

9 Amazing Gambling Stories

*The safest way to double your money is
to fold it over once and put it in your pocket.*

Kin Hubbard

I was good friends for a long time with a number of the characters in this book: Puggy Pearson, Amarillo Slim, Chip Reese, Danny Robison, Jack Straus, and Stu Ungar. Doyle Brunson remains a good friend today. These were men who could have me roaring with laughter and mesmerized by their abilities. They were high-stakes gamblers beyond most people's comprehension – or, as I like to call them, gamblers extraordinaire. Two things are for sure: they were smart and they had balls. You have to be and have both if you gamble high and are successful.

The 10 of Diamonds

I'm often asked, "Who do you think is the greatest poker player of all time?" Chip Reese is the greatest all-round poker player I've ever seen, but I believe Stu Ungar is the greatest No Limit Hold 'Em player of all time. (Without a doubt, he's the best gin rummy player ever to walk the planet.) This story may help you understand why.

Stuey called me one day and wanted me to go to Bob Stupak's Vegas World with him. (It's where the Stratosphere now sits.) He wanted to see Stupak to talk to him about playing blackjack there as Stuey had been barred from playing nearly everywhere in Vegas. I was happy to go with him, so he picked me up and we headed to Vegas World.

Bob Stupak was an original. He was a casino owner, promoter, and huckster extraordinaire, and loved playing poker. He primarily played high-stakes No Limit 2–7 draw and won a WSOP bracelet in that event in 1989. In business, public relations (PR) was his specialty.

Stupak did many things to get publicity for himself and Vegas World. For example, he publicly proclaimed he was betting $1,000,000 on Super Bowl XXIII – Bengals/49ers. He called the press, and with great fanfare, carried $1m in cash into Little Caesars, a sports book owned by Gene Mayday, and made the bet with entourage in tow. (He took the Bengals +7, which he won.) What the public didn't know was that he bet back $900k on the other side – just in case.

When Stupak remodeled Vegas World and wanted to promote the place, he paid a stuntman $1m to jump off the roof (on to a big air mattress in front of Las Vegas Blvd). It made the wire services and TV news programs across the country. The PR was great. What the public didn't know was that Stupak paid him $1m to jump off the building but, in the guy's contract, Stupak charged him $990k to land on his property!

Once, while flying back to the US on the Concorde, Stupak invited Alaskan Perry Green, also on the flight, to play him a little heads-up poker. I was sitting right across from them and watched them play. Two days later, the papers proclaimed Stupak recently played in "the *highest* poker game of all time".

Another time, he paid $100,000 to play basketball with the Harlem Globetrotters in Madison Square Garden. You have to say one thing about Bob Stupak – he knew how to generate publicity.

Anyway, when Stuey and I got to Vegas World, Stupak met us and took us to the coffee shop for lunch. He was well aware that Stuey was barred from playing blackjack about everywhere in Vegas, so he asked Stuey how allowing him to play blackjack in his joint would benefit him. Stuey told him he would only make bets in one or two units ($5k or $10k) to discount any edge he might have, but Stupak wasn't buying it.

As the blackjack discussion stalled, Stupak proposed a proposition bet to Stuey. He said he would get a deck of cards, turn them over one at a time in 1–2 second intervals, and bet $10k that Stuey couldn't name the bottom card on the deck. Stuey thought for a few seconds and said, "You've got a bet."

A deck was brought in, Stupak shuffled the cards, and he started turning them over one at a time. Stuey watched closely. When Stupak reached the last card, Stuey said, "It's the 10 of diamonds." Sure enough, it was the 10 of diamonds! Stupak proclaimed, "That's it! You'll never play a hand of blackjack in here as long as you live."

Stupak paid him and we left. I was mesmerized by it all. I said, "Stuey, that was amazing! How did you do that?" He replied, "Mike, it was really pretty easy. I gave all 52 cards a unique number from 1 to 52. For example, the ace of clubs = 1, ace of diamonds = 2, ace of hearts = 3, ace of spades = 4, deuce of clubs = 5, etc. That 52-card total equals 1,378. I then just added up the points as he turned over each card and subtracted that number from 1,378. Whatever number is left is the card on the bottom of the deck. In this case it was 38, the 10 of diamonds. If it was 52, it would have been the king of spades." It pays to have a genius IQ and a photographic memory.

Hollywood Legend

Years ago, I was playing in a $30/60 game of Seven Card Stud 8 or Better at the Dunes Hotel (where Bellagio now sits). It was midnight on a Saturday night and a buzz started around the room because Hollywood star Telly Savalas had stopped by the poker room and was over talking to the floorman.

At that time, Savalas was about as big a movie star as you could find. He had done a number of movies (a couple I really liked were *The Dirty Dozen* and *Kelly's Heroes*) but he was most famous for being the star of *Kojak*, the number-one-rated TV show for several years. (He won an Emmy and two Golden Globe Awards for Best Actor in a TV drama for that role.)

After speaking with Telly, the floorman started walking toward our table. He said, "Mike, can I speak to you for a moment?" I stepped away from the table and he continued, "Telly Savalas loves to play poker and Hi/Lo split is his favorite game. He wants to know if he could watch someone play so he could learn the game better. I think you'd be the perfect guy for him to sweat. Would that be OK with you?" Obviously flattered, I said, "Sure!"

The appreciative floorman headed back to the podium and spoke with Telly, who turned and said good night to his entourage. Then, with all eyes in the room on them, they started heading to our table. The floorman introduced Telly to me, explained to the table that Telly was going to sweat the game for a while, and pulled a chair up for him. Everyone was excited to have this Hollywood legend watching our game (and immediately about 10 new names went on the waiting list).

Telly watched the game intensely and didn't get out of his chair until 6:30 am. He loved sweating the game. And let me add, not one person in the game quit while he was there. I would play a hand and then whisper to him what my thought process was and why I had played it like I had. He would nod. It was a great night, not only because I met and became friends with Telly Savalas, but because I beat the game for $2,600.

A couple of years later, in 1985, Telly went on a cruise vacation with a group of high-stakes players including Doyle Brunson, Chip Reese, Puggy Pearson, Amarillo Slim, and Bob Stupak. Eric Drache, the tournament director at the WSOP, put the trip together. I won the $12,500 trip by winning a $300 satellite they held at the Horseshoe during the WSOP (by outdrawing Oklahoma Johnny Hale playing heads-up with the A/7 of clubs vs. his A/J, all-in pre-flop).

It was the vacation of a lifetime – a week's cruise from New York to England on the *QEII*, staying at a lavish hotel in London for a week with side trips to Wimbledon, and then flying back on the Concorde. We played poker every day on the ship, and Telly obliged every person (hundreds over the course of a week) who came up to the table and asked for an autograph or a picture (including when he was big loser).

He was the best – he didn't turn down anybody! And if it were a woman who wanted a picture, he'd have her sit on his knee and say, "Who loves ya, baby?" I've never seen a celebrity as kind and courteous to the public as Telly Savalas. The guy was amazing.

In 1987, Telly made the final table at the WSOP in Seven Card Stud 8 or Better (finishing fifth). Just after that tournament, he came up to me and said, "Mike, I would have never made that final table had I not watched you that night at the Dunes. Thank you again for that." In 1992, Telly finished 21st in the main event at the WSOP. He loved poker and the poker world loved him.

If Money Can Solve It

I've had the good fortune to play in a number of private games in Beverly Hills with big-time Hollywood celebrities such as Ben Affleck, Toby Maguire, James Woods, Leonardo DiCaprio, and others. These guys love to play poker, and not just for the challenge of the game and as an escape from their real-life jobs, but because at the poker table they're treated like regular people. At the poker table, no one cares that they're Hollywood celebs, they just want their money.

But trust me, some of them, particularly Affleck and Maguire, play well enough to be pros.

A number of years ago, I was a regular in a weekly No Limit Hold 'Em game ($25/50 blinds with a $5k buy-in) held on Mondays in a private club in Beverly Hills. On the day after Ben Affleck won the 2004 California State Championship, a $10k buy-in event at the Commerce Casino, we had our weekly game. (I told you he could play.)

We were all thrilled that Ben had won the title. He came to the game that night grinning from ear to ear, with his trophy and a bag of cash ($356,000 – his first place prize money). He put the trophy and the cash (he didn't take a check) on the table and proudly said, "Boys, you're looking at the California State Poker Champion." Everyone laughed and said, "Ben, that's nice, but those were tournament players. We play for cash here. Now sit down and let's play some poker."

Every time Ben lost a pot that night, the needling would start: "Ben, you better stick to those tournament players," or, "Ben, if you were the best player in that tournament, I'll be playing that tournament next year," and on and on. It was one of those nights you put in a frame and hang on the wall – truly one of the most fun nights of poker I've ever had.

Another night we were playing in the same private club and it was closing time. (The game always stopped at 1 am.) Ben, who had a chartered jet waiting to fly him back east after the game, still wanted to play more. He said he'd put the jet on hold, and suggested that whoever wanted to could stay and play a $5k freeze-out tourney. Five other guys, as well as myself, said they would stay and play.

Then, the manager came in and said we had a problem – that the valet guy had to leave. Ben told the manager to send him up. When the valet guy came in, Ben handed him $500 and said, "Can you stay for another hour or so?" The guy looked at the money and happily said, "I'll be glad to." As the guy left, Ben said, "If money can solve it, it's not a problem." Incidentally, with his private jet on hold,

Ben won the freeze-out. I'm sure he had a very enjoyable flight back east – a flight that we paid for!

It Pays to Have a Gift of Gab

Once, when I was in the Army stationed at Fort Knox, KY, I decided to hitchhike back to Dayton for the weekend. (Back in those days, when you hitchhiked in uniform, it usually didn't take 10 minutes to get a ride.) I got back on Friday evening and called Danny to see what was going on. He said he had a date that night but was playing poker at Briar's (the perfect name for this guy) on Saturday night and that if I wanted to go, he would pick me up and take me. I told him I'd love to go.

Danny picked me up at 7:30 pm the next night and we went to Briar's game, whose place was on the north side of Dayton. They played $15/30 Seven Card Stud and the game was in a house solely used to play poker. The living room had an old couch and a TV in it. There was also a telephone pole wedged in from one wall to the front door so no one could come in through the front door. The two bed-rooms were empty. The players came in the back door and the game was in the basement.

I had $400 on me, and by 10 pm, sadly, I was broke. I now had to wait for Danny to finish playing so he could take me home. So, I waited, and waited, and waited. (What's worse than sitting around a poker game after you've gone broke?) At about 2 am, I said, "Danny, I need to go. I've got to get back to Fort Knox today." He said, "OK, just a few more hands." At 3 am, I said, "C'mon, Danny. I really need to go." Finally, he cashed out and we walked up the stairs and started to leave.

Just as we opened the back door to go out, a guy flashed a badge at us, put his finger to his lips, pushed us to the side, and then at least 10 cops came in and raced down the stairs hollering, "Freeze! Freeze! Everyone freeze!" Busted.

One of the cops took Danny and me into the living room and

told us to sit on the couch. After 5–10 minutes, the boss cop came up the stairs, looked at Danny and said, "OK. Whose game is this?" Danny, obviously aware that no one downstairs had told him, said, "I don't know. We just stopped by to visit a friend. We weren't even playing." The cop then looked at me and said, "Who runs this game?" I said, "I don't know. I'm in the Army. I'm just in town for the weekend and rode out here with him."

The agitated cop then ushered Danny and me to the basement. He told us to join the other players who were all lined up next to the wall. Then, he said loudly, "OK. We can do this the hard way or the easy way. Whose game is this?" Nobody said anything for a minute or two but then Briar finally said, "It's my game." The cop said, "OK, you come upstairs with me. The rest of you have a seat by the wall. The paddy wagons are on the way." Paddy wagons? *WTF?* I couldn't go to jail – I needed to get back to Fort Knox.

One of the players then quipped, "Hey look. I know we're busted, but can we keep playing until the paddy wagons get here? I'm stuck." Everyone laughed.

Hearing the paddy wagons were on the way, Danny knew we didn't have much time and quickly summoned over the youngest cop in the room. He started talking to him, asking him if he grew up in Dayton, how long he'd been a cop, etc.

Danny discovered the guy was a part-time student at Wright State University and he quickly said, "I thought you looked familiar. I go to Wright State, too." (Danny had never set foot on the Wright State campus in his life.) He then said to the guy, "Hey, look. I'm in college and he's in the Army. We weren't playing poker. We weren't even downstairs when you came in. Can you go talk to your boss and see if there's anything he can do for us?" The guy said, "OK. I'll see what I can do" and went up the stairs.

A few minutes later, the boss cop came down the steps with Briar in tow. He walked over to Danny and me and said, "You two can go." Wow! I couldn't believe it. Danny's gift of gab and his ability to bluff kept us out of jail.

We jumped up, gave a thank you nod to the young cop, and as we started up the steps, Danny turned to me and said, "Watch this." He then leaned over the rail and bellowed out, "Hey Briar, what time does the game start tomorrow night?" I thought he was crazy to say that but the whole room cracked up – even the cops. As we walked out the back door, two paddy wagons were just pulling up. We were about a one-outer *not* to go to jail that night.

That story reminds me of a classic story that took place in Season 2 of the WPT at the LA Poker Classic at the Commerce Casino. I was talking to Bobby Hoff, an old school, Texas rounder who finished runner-up in the main event at the 1979 WSOP, but now worked as a prop player at the Commerce.

As we were talking, a guy came up to us and said, "Wow! Mike Sexton and Bobby Hoff – I can't believe it. Can I take my picture with you guys?" We said "sure" and he got someone to take our picture. Just after the guy took the picture, Bobby turned to me, chuckled, and said, "The last time I had my picture taken with regards to poker, I was fingerprinted at the same time."

Rent a Face

One night as I was walking through the Mirage, on my way to play poker, I heard someone call my name. He said, "Sexton, what are you doing?" I turned and saw that it was Mike Eakin. He played cards, pool, was quick witted and funny, and a guy whom I'd played a little golf. Eakin was cocky, loud, brash – and – to put it mildly, had a lot of balls. He was street smart and came from the school that believed if you're not doing something to them, they're doing something to you.

I told him I was going to play some poker and he said, "How much money have you got on you?" I said, "About $1,800, why?" He said, "That's perfect. I need to rent a face." Curious, I said, "Rent a face?"

He told me he had a pool game that he couldn't lose and needed someone to go with him who they thought might have a lot of money. He wanted me to pretend that I was his rich stakehorse. He said he had a contract for $500 a game with a three-game minimum, so $1,500 was all we would need because he had the nuts.

I'd never seen Eakin play pool in my life, and as you can imagine, I was somewhat leery about putting up my money to go to a pool hall. I wasn't much of a pool player, but I did know about "two brothers and a stranger" in pool halls.

He sensed my concern and said, "Look, I don't want you to stake me. We'll go 50-50 partners and I'll pay you back my $750 if we lose – which we won't." I asked, "Who are you playing?" He said, "The best player in the world."

I chuckled and said, "You're playing the best player in the world and you've got the nuts?" "That's right," he said confidently. "What's the game?" I asked. "We're playing nine-ball and I get the break and ball in hand", he answered. Not knowing how much of a spot that really was, I inquired, "And you can beat him with that spot?" He said, "Him, and anybody else in the world who wants to give it to me."

I don't know why, maybe because of his confidence, but it seemed like it would be fun to watch this, so I agreed to put up the $1,500 and go. We then headed over to the pool hall at Swenson and Twain.

As we entered, Eakin shouted out for all to hear, "OK, boys. I've got my man with me. Let's go!" Everybody started murmuring and it seemed like 40–50 people quickly gathered around the table to watch. Eakin spread the $1,500 out across the table and blurted out, "Here's our start money and there's plenty more where that came from" (which of course there wasn't). His opponent (Ishmael Piaze, aka "Morrow" who really was one of the best players in the world) put his $1,500 down and the game was on.

As I said, I'd never seen Eakin play pool and couldn't really believe he was good enough to beat one of the best players in the world, but I was impressed when he broke the balls. *Crack!* Two went in and the balls spread out all over the table. He put the cue ball on the table where he wanted it and proceeded to run the rack.

I thought to myself, *hmmm... this might not be so bad.* He collected $1,000 off of the table, put it in his pocket, and started the next game. *Bam!* Another good break and again he ran the rack. He picked up another $1,000. This was sweet!

In the third game, he made a ball on the break, made the next shot, but was slightly stymied, so he decided to play it safe. He played a perfect shot and hemmed the cue ball up behind three balls with the object ball clear on the other side of the table. Morrow got off the stool for the first time, studied the table, and then hit a three-bank shot that made perfect contact with the object ball. It was an incredible shot, but, luckily for us, the object ball hung in the pocket. My man got up, ran out the rack, and we collected the last $1,000.

His opponent then said politely, "Nice game. I'd like to keep playing, but we have to adjust the spot a little bit." Eakin got up, started unscrewing his cue stick, and blurted out, "Nope. No adjustment. This is our game. If you want to play any more, just give me a call. You've got my number." That was it. We left with our profit. It really was an enjoyable and memorable night at the pool hall.

Do You Have ID?

One time Stuey and I went to Palm Springs to play golf with two guys who had flown in on a private jet from Memphis, TN, to play us. We played PGA West, and after the round, Stuey asked where the best restaurant in town was and the four of us headed over there.

The place was completely jam-packed. We made our way through the crowd to the podium where the maître d' was and Stuey said to him, "We'd like a table for four." The maître d' asked, "Do you have a reservation?" Stuey said "no" and the maître d' said, "I'm sorry, we're all booked up. If you don't have a reservation, I can't help you."

Stuey then pulled out a $100 bill, gave it to the guy, and said, "The name is Ungar. In case a table becomes available, we'll be at the bar having a drink." The maître d' scarfed it up (a "for sure" sign that we'd get a table).

We weaved our way to the bar and the four of us squeezed in to order. The bartender said, "What'll you have?" The first guy from Memphis ordered a gin and tonic, the next a bourbon and Coke, I ordered a beer, and Stuey said he'd have a scotch and water. The bartender looked at Stuey (who was about 5'6" and 110 pounds soaking wet) and said, "I need to see your ID."

Stuey retorted, "ID? What are you talking about? I'm 35 years old!" The bartender said, "You might be 35, but you look young to me and if you don't have any identification, I can't serve you."

Stuey cocked his head to the side, quickly reached into both front pockets, pulled out two rolls of $10k each, banged them on the bar, pointed at them, and said, "There. There's my ID. Do you think any teenager would be carrying around that kind of money?"

The bartender nodded, smiled, and said, "You know, you've got a good point there. What'll you have?" About that time, the maître d' comes over and said, "Mr. Ungar, your table is ready." As we were following the maître d' to the best table in the house, Stuey turned to me and said, "I always let Benji make my reservations for me."

The Greatest Con of All Time

Before Jack Binion traded a piece of property in Laughlin for the Mint Hotel (one of the greatest deals in history), which was next door to the Horseshoe, the WSOP was played at the "old" Horseshoe in front of the bar next to the steps leading down to the coffee shop. They took out some slot machines to put in the poker tables. They were jammed in there with a rope around the outside of the tables where spectators could stand and watch.

I was playing in a $30/60 Limit Hold 'Em game, sitting next to a guy from Texas called Champ. We were at an outside table with the rope and spectators right behind us. Champ was a decent poker player but golf was his game. (He was a 2 handicap.) I knew him from golf as we both used to play in Jack Binion's Professional Gambler's Invitational Golf Tournament (you could write a book just on those). We were both winning in the game, having a good time, and talking mostly about golf.

A guy right behind us on the rail had obviously been watching, listening to us talk about golf, and said, "You guys play golf?" Champ turned around and said, "Yeah. Do you?" The guy said he played some, lived in Chicago, and was out here with a friend. He said he and his friend were staying across the street at the Golden Nugget, had played golf at Sahara Country Club yesterday, and that his friend had had tough luck on the tables last night. He added that his friend had just bought a new set of Ping irons (the hottest thing going at that time) the week before and might be interested in selling them to get some money.

Champ said, "How much does he want for them?" The guy said he paid $400 for them and would like to get $350 but would probably take $300 because he was broke. Champ said that was too much, turned around, and continued playing poker. The guy stayed and continued to talk to us and I could see that Champ was taking a liking to the guy.

After Champ had won a couple more pots, he said to the guy, "Do you think he'd take $200 for them?" The stranger said, "No. I don't think there's any chance he'd take that little. They're brand new clubs."

Champ then picked up eight green chips ($25 each), turned to the guy, and said, "Would you go show him the money, ask him if he'd take $200, and if he says yes, bring the irons back over here to me?" The guy shrugged and said, "OK. I'll ask him, but I don't think there's any chance he'll take it."

Champ gave him $200 in chips and the guy leaves. Stunned, I said, "Champ, do you even know that guy?" He said, "No, never seen him before but he seemed like an honest guy to me. Didn't you think so?" The whole table was shocked that Champ had given this total stranger $200. One guy laughed and said, "Champ, you're the biggest sucker in the world."

Incredibly, 20 minutes later, the guy returned and handed Champ back the eight green chips. He said, "Here. I told you he'd never take $200 for the clubs. He said he wouldn't take a dime less than $250 for them."

Champ, very pleased that the guy came back and that he was such a good judge of character, continued to talk to the guy. He won another pot, turned to the guy, and said, "Oh hell. What's the difference? Here's $250. Will you bring the clubs back over to me?" The guy said, "Sure, I'll be glad to." Champ gives the guy 10 green chips and the guy leaves again – *and he never came back!*

It was the greatest con I've ever seen. The guy brought back the $200 because he knew he could get another $50. If ever a guy deserved another $50, it was this guy. Champ might have gone for $250, but the story is priceless.

Move In On 'Em

While on a vacation trip to London (the same one Telly signed all the autographs on), a bunch of us poker players were going to the semifinals at Wimbledon. They had a nice little bus (about eight or 10 rows of seats) set up for us. I was in the first row and Amarillo Slim (1972 world champion and poker's biggest ambassador for 20 years), a talkative Texan, was standing up in the front of the bus, holding court and bullshitting as usual. Slim had a better gift of gab than Muhammad Ali and Minnesota Fats combined.

He turned to the driver and said, "Who we waitin' on, anyway?" The driver looked at his list and said, "Mickey Appleman." Appleman, a former soccer player at Ohio State, was an unusual character to say the least. He marched to the beat of his own drum.

Appleman was a very bright guy, a high-stakes poker player,

and an ultra-big-time sports bettor. But, he always looked messy and had a head of hair that looked worse than the entry of Don King and Harpo Marx. Slim quipped, "Oh, he must be up there blow-drying his hair."

A few minutes later, Appleman gets on the bus. The bus driver tells everyone, "Hold on!" and, out of the blue, starts making a U-turn right in the middle of all the traffic! No one could believe it. Cars were honking their horns and screeching to a halt from all sides. Slim, who was right in front of me, was holding that pole so tight that his knuckles turned white. It really was scary.

Finally, after completing the U-turn and not getting hit by any-body, Slim caught his breath, turned to the driver and said, "Pard-ner, if you ever want to quit driving a bus, just let me know. I'd love to stake you playing poker because you sure as hell aren't afraid to move in on 'em."

The Lou Groza Award

When I was living in Fayetteville, NC, I was playing golf one day with John Henry Reeves, who had come down from Virginia Beach, VA, to play golf and poker with us. He was a jovial, short, stocky, older guy, but was a very good golfer (a 4 handicap).

We were on the 16th hole at Gates Four Country Club, the shortest par 4 on the course. Henry had hit the longest drive but all of us were in the fairway. The three of us hit our second shots on the green and Henry had a simple wedge 75–80 yards away. He chunked the shot, bogeyed the hole, and lost the hole to everyone.

The next tee was around the other side of a lake and the other guys got in their cart and headed over there. I was driving our cart and John Henry got in and started stomping his feet on the floor. He was steaming, cussing himself out for missing that easy wedge shot. He hollered, "I can't believe it. I just can't believe that. I could have kicked that ball on the green!"

I had started going to the next tee but then stopped the cart and said to him, "What did you say?" He said again: "I could have kicked that ball onto the green from where I was."

"Henry," I said, "I'll give you 10 kicks to get a ball on the green from there and bet you $500 you can't get one on the green. You can kick it any way you like. You can punt it or put it on a tee and kick it." He said, "I'll take that bet." Luckily, there wasn't a group behind us, so I turned and headed back down the fairway to where Henry had chunked the wedge.

The other guys saw us driving back down the fairway rather than coming over to the next tee. They didn't know what was going on, so they drove back around the lake to see what was happening.

As Henry was dumping 10 balls onto the fairway, I said to them, "Henry thinks he's Lou 'the Toe' Groza (a famous kicker from the Cleveland Browns) and thinks he can kick a ball on the green from here. I'm giving him 10 kicks and betting him $500 he can't." They started laughing and told Henry they'd also like to bet $500 that he couldn't kick one onto the green as well. "You guys have got a bet, too", he said.

What made this bet even worse for Henry was that there was a bunker right in front of the green, meaning there was only a narrow gap to roll a ball up onto the green. That didn't stop Henry and he decided to punt the first ball. The ball hit on the bone just above his shoe and "down goes Henry".

He screamed in agony and was rolling around on the ground because it hurt. We started laughing uncontrollably because the ball went about 25 yards. He rubbed his ankle for a few minutes and that was it for the punting. He put the rest on a tee and started kicking them straight ahead and then went to sidesaddle, but to no avail. He only got one ball within 20 yards of the green.

That was the funniest thing I have ever witnessed on a golf course. He not only lost the hole to everyone, he lost another $1,500 by making one of the dumbest bets of all time. To this day, nearly 35 years later, I still smile every time I think about John Henry and that bet.

Flint to Saginaw

Years ago, I was playing in a $30/60 Hi/Lo split game at Dunes Hotel. As I got up from the table to go to the restroom, I saw Chip Reese (who was in a $200/400 stud game) standing by a $1–4 Seven Card Stud table. The players started screaming at each other, so I decided to stop and watch as well. On the river, one player bet and the other shouted, "Raise!" The original bettor then screamed, "Raise you back!" The other guy yelled back, "Raise you again!" The other then proclaimed, "I'm all-in" and was called.

The all-in player then announced, "Aces up." The other guy said, "Flint to Saginaw." With a puzzled look on his face, the all-in guy again said, "Aces up." The second player repeated, "Flint to Saginaw". He then proudly turned up three 10s out of the hole, spread them out, smiled, and said, "30 miles." Chip and I loved that story. Any time you get three 10s, be cool and say you've got "Flint to Saginaw."

Toilet Paper

David "The Devilfish" Ulliot was a legend in the poker world. He passed away in 2015 but was a high-stakes cash game player, a tournament champion with a WSOP bracelet and WPT title to his credit, and he didn't lack bravado. When you talk about unique characters in poker history, the Devilfish has to be near the top of everyone's list. If he's not, he should be.

Devilfish was tough, quickwitted, entertaining, and a hell of a poker player. I believe his win at the WPT in Tunica, MS, in 2004 was the most dominating win in the history of the WPT – which is saying something because Phil Ivey, who finished second, was at the table.

The Devilfish was from Hull, England (Northern England where they don't quite speak the Queen's language), so let's be polite and just say that he was hard to understand. But you could easily understand him whenever he was asked about the terrific young gun players of today. Devilfish would say, "I can out-fight 'em, out-fuck 'em, and out-play 'em."

A number of years back, there was a wealthy guy from Greece (George the Greek) who loved to play sky-high PLO. He played a lot in England and Paris and the game was always full when he was in it. The big boys loved it when he came to Vegas. He came out for the WSOP one year so the cash games were booming at Bellagio – really booming as the buy-in was $50k for this particular PLO game (extremely high stakes in those days).

PLO was the Devilfish's best game. He really wanted to play in that big game but lacked sufficient funding to get in. Finally, after winning a few days in smaller games and borrowing a little, the Devilfish had exactly the $50k buy-in and decided to risk it all in that game.

He got his seat, sat patiently for a round or two, and then picked up A-A-Q-10 double suited in hearts and diamonds. The blinds were $200/400 and George the Greek brought it in for $1,400, another guy called, Doyle called, and the Devilfish, on the button, then raised the pot to $6,200. Both George and Doyle called while the other guys got out.

The flop was J-6-3 with two diamonds. George checked, and Doyle bet $18k. The Devilfish moved all-in over the top. George folded but Doyle, who was doing well in the game, said to Devilfish, "Oh hell. I'll give you a little action" and called. The pot had over $100k in it!

They made a rule (George's rule) for that game that you couldn't run it twice so it was all or nothing for the Devilfish. The turn was the deuce of spades and the 4 of clubs appeared on the river. Doyle turned up 10-9-7-5 in diamonds and clubs and won the pot by hitting a gutshot straight on the river!

The Devilfish had waited days to try and get in this game, finally did so, and within 30 minutes was out as he lost a monster pot to Doyle when he hit a three-outer on the river. Everyone gasped when they saw what happened to Devilfish. I was afraid the Devilfish might turn the table over. But he just stared at the board in disbelief and to everyone's astonishment didn't utter a word – just slowly got up, turned, and headed off the balcony at Bellagio.

As he got to the bottom of the steps, he suddenly turned back around, walked back to the table, planted his hands firmly in the middle of the table, stared at Doyle, and said, "Doyle, have you got any more of those books of yours? I'd like to take one back with me so I'll have something to wipe my ass with when I get home." He then turned and walked out for good.

Be Careful What You Wish For

Twelve of us gambler–poker players went to La Costa in San Diego to play golf for a few days. These trips were always so much fun as there was action galore, especially if Doyle Brunson was there. He was the guy who always created the most action. This time, however, after two days, Ralph Rudd, a high-stakes poker player from LA, took over.

In all of Doyle's matches, he got the spot of getting to put his ball on a tee everywhere on the golf course. That was because he had a bad knee, a bad hip, played with a crutch, and didn't want to hurt himself worse by having to go down after a ball or play bunker shots – so everyone who matched up with him let him put it on a tee everywhere and matched up accordingly.

Ralph is normally an expert gambler on everything, including golf. On this day, however, Ralph started drinking before we teed off and was smoking whatever around the course all day. So, by dinner, he was feeling no pain.

I was sitting at the table with Ralph and Doyle that night when Ralph, who had been into the suds all day and was a little loser to Doyle, blurted out, "It's just not fair to let Doyle use a tee everywhere. It's too big of a spot."

Doyle, who was only a little winner over the two days, didn't say a word but Richie Sklar (who was my partner and who I staked

– and split bets with) said, "Ralph, how much of a spot do you think that is?" Ralph said, "It's worth at least six to seven shots a round. You get to hit a driver out of the fairway on the long par 4s and par 5s, you're never in the rough, and never in a hazard as going in the bunker means nothing."

Ralph then continued, "I've been giving Doyle one shot a side for two days, but I'd give him three a side if I could use a tee anywhere, and on top of it, I'll give him the strokes on seven, eight, and nine on the front nine, and 16, 17, and 18 on the back."

I couldn't believe my ears – strokes on the last three holes on each side? We play two-down automatic presses, so even if Ralph got ahead in this match, he could never win the finishing holes on either side, so it didn't seem possible to me he would have a chance in this match.

Richie then quickly said, "How much can I bet on Doyle with three a side on the last three holes each side and you getting to use a tee everywhere?" Ralph said, "How much do you want to bet?" Richie replied, "I'll bet $20k Nassau with one automatic press a side." Ralph said, "You've got a bet." Then Doyle said he'd also like to bet, but he wanted to up the bet to $30k Nassau. Ralph gave him the bet.

We were all in shock that Ralph made these bets, but he went a step farther, saying, "I love my bet. I'd like to bet I'm at least four up after six holes." That brazen statement was answered by Richie with, "You've got that bet. For how much?" Ralph, who as I said is normally a very shrewd gambler, bet another $5k on that. He was going off like a rocket ship.

Even if the tee helped a little in the fairway and bunkers, I didn't think Ralph would chip better using a tee, especially if he hadn't prac-ticed it. And he still had to make putts, which wasn't Ralph's strong suit.

Ralph grabbed a lot of extra tees the next day, but no amount of tees was going to help him. He lost the first hole, meaning he had to win the next five holes to win his additional bet. Not only wasn't he four up after six holes, he was four down! And the stroke holes were coming up. It was a homicide. Poor Ralph sailed off for nearly $300k that day.

The moral of the story – be careful how much you smoke and drink if you're going to make big bets. Life's a gamble, but recognize that a tee spot like Ralph's is not all it's cracked up to be.

We All Get Bluffed

I get asked from time to time, "What's the funniest thing you've ever seen on the WPT?" That's a tough one, but this story is certainly near the top.

It happened during the WPT Shooting Stars event at the Bay 101 Casino in San Jose, CA, in Season 9. I remember that event well because it was the first time I made a final table on the WPT. But, this story isn't about me.

With 12 players left in the tournament, there were six players at each table. I was at the table with the two huge chip leaders, Alan Sternberg and Vivek Rajkumar, who, to my dismay, were sitting directly on my left.

I'd never seen Alan before this tournament but I'd played with him a lot on the previous day and was wowed by how good he was. He seemed to win pot after pot without ever showing down a hand (the sign of an expert player). Vivek, an aggressive, terrific high-stakes player, was familiar to me. I've played with him in high-stakes cash games on numerous occasions and commentated when he won his WPT title at Borgata.

I was just trying to survive these guys (who, between them, raised every pot) and get down to 10 players. There, we'd all be at one table where I thought I'd have a good chance to make the televised final table of six.

A hand came up at 10/20k blinds where I was in the SB (with one of the shorter stacks), Alan (the chip leader with over 2m in chips) was in the BB, and Vivek (second in chip count with 1.4m) was the first to speak. He opened the pot for 45k. Everyone folded around to Alan in the BB.

Alan three-bet it to 110k and Vivek made the call. The flop came K-Q-8 rainbow. Alan led out for 115k and Vivek called. An offsuit 9 came on the turn and Alan checked. Vivek now bet 220k. After some thought, Alan check-raised it to 540k. Vivek's eyes now opened wide as he could obviously envision the possibility of getting eliminated by the chip leader. He went into the tank for several minutes and then folded.

The dealer started pushing the pot to Alan and, after the chips reached him, he started to muck his hand. In an instant, Vivek put his hand down on Alan's cards and said, "Wait a minute. I'll give you $300 in cash if you show me your hand."

Vivek quickly reached in his pocket and pulled out $300 in cash and put it on the table. Alan said, "You'll give me $300 to see my hand?" Vivek said, "Yes." Alan shrugged and said, "OK". He picked up the $300 and turned over the 3-4 of diamonds! It was a stone bluff.

Everyone was stunned. Vivek, in mild shock, smiled and said, "Wow! Nice play." He then turned to me and said, "Mike, I overpaid him to see his hand, didn't I?" I said, "You sure did. He would have showed it to you for a hundred." The table cracked up.

Vivek didn't care that the guy outplayed him. In fact, he admired him for it. But, it really bothered him that he paid $300 to see the hand when $100 would have got the job done. Such is the mind of a poker player.

I ended up finishing sixth in that tournament, Vivek finished fourth, and Alan Sternberg won $1,013,500, the title, and, oh yes, Vivek's $300. It was a well-deserved victory.

Some Real Characters in Poker

There have been some unique and colorful characters in the poker world over the years. Two of them include Jack Straus and Sam

Grizzle. They also had balls and regularly had 110% of their bankroll in action on a daily basis. They had one other thing in common. They were quite funny.

I was walking from the Golden Nugget to the Horseshoe for the WSOP one day. I bumped into Straus on the way. As we exited the Nugget, a guy comes running after us and said, "Jack! Jack! I'm in the best $3/6 game you've ever seen, but my luck has been awful." Before he could say any more, Jack reached in his pocket, threw the guy two $25 chips and said, "Here you go. Hopefully, you can turn things around. Good luck." The guy thanked him and we continued walking.

I turned to Jack and said, "Who was that?" He said, "I don't know. If I knew him, I'd have given him a hundred."

Another time, Jack told me a story where he once got a collect call from an old poker player he knew who was on death row. He took the call and talked to the guy for 30 minutes. The entire call consisted of Jack telling the guy about all the hands he lost the previous night in a poker game. He later said he felt horrible because all he did on that call was tell this guy his bad beat stories – *and that guy was on death row!*

Sam Grizzle is from Greer, SC. It was a rough town when Sam grew up there. After hustling around town for years, where you had to be tough to survive, he came to Las Vegas. Sam was one of the cockiest, brashest, and cold-blooded players you could ever meet. He was also one of the funniest.

Sam was one of the greatest parlay players of all time. By that I mean that he might start the day in a small game due to bankroll restrictions, but as soon as he got winner (and had the money for a buy-in to the next highest game), he would take his money and move up, and continue to repeat that until, by day's end, he was in the biggest game in the room. And when he was broke, he found stakehorses that liked that mentality, where they might lose a little, but could win a lot.

Sam was, however, rather crude in how he talked to people, and that included everyone. He was being staked in a $100/200 stud game one day and his stakehorse was also in the game. After his stakehorse lost a few pots, Sam would laugh loudly and say, "You're the worst fuckin' player I've ever seen. How in the hell do you stay in money?"

Another time, I was sitting right next to Sam at the Horseshoe during Binion's Hall of Fame poker tournament. It was held in a tent in the valet parking area. Our table was right next to the wall they had the pictures of the members of the Hall of Fame on. Sam was just staring at all the pictures when he said to me, "Sexton, they should take all those pictures down and put one big picture of me up there. I've busted everyone on that wall except Wild Bill Hickok."

I went to Bellagio one afternoon and walked up on the balcony where the higher stakes games take place. On the back table, I saw Grizzle was playing heads-up. For the previous few weeks, Sam was on a good run and when he had money, he feared no one nor playing any stakes. Every day for the past few days, he had been playing anyone who wanted to play heads-up. And they just kept coming. On this day, it was Annie Duke.

When I got to the table, I saw Sam had all the chips. Annie was down to a short stack and looked totally down-trodden. Grizzle looked at me and said, "Sexton, they should call me the barber." I inquired, "The barber?" And he said, "Yes, the barber. When anyone sits down, I clip 'em and holler, *next!*"

Grizzle was playing in a $1,500 buy-in half Hold 'Em, half lowball draw tournament at the Bicycle Casino in 1991. He made it to heads-up play and his opponent then asked, "Sam, do you want to make a deal?" Grizzle snapped back, "I sure do. I want the winner to get first and second place money both!" He then turned to the dealer and said, "Now deal the cards!" Sam won the tournament.

After pocketing over $70k for the win, at just about 2 am, he immediately went to the high-stakes cash game section and sought out the $400/800 game that was going on. He took a seat. At 7 am, he was in valet parking – dead broke. That afternoon, he was back at the Bike. While people were congratulating him for the previous day's win, he was looking to get staked in the $500 tourney.

10 Transition to the Business Side of Poker

All you can do in poker is get your money in with the best hand.

Johnny Moss

Becoming a Writer

My career as a writer began after I won the 1996 $5k buy-in, Four Queens Summer Classic championship – and it was because of that event that my career took an incredible turn. How I even got in that tournament is a pretty good story itself.

I was "between bankrolls" on the day of the championship event at the Four Queens. I went there on the morning of that event to play in a one-table satellite in hopes of getting in the tournament. It was the last satellite before the start of the tourney. With three players left, I was in second chip position and played a pot all-in pre-flop against the chip leader. I had jacks and he had the A-Q of diamonds. I lost the race and was headed out the door.

I walked by Scotty Nguyen and, thinking I was there to play in the championship, he said, "Good luck today, baby!" I told him, "Thanks, Scotty, but I'm not playing. I just lost a satellite and don't have the money to enter." He said, "Wha-wha-what? You're not playing?" I said, "No," and he said, "I'd like to take a piece of you. I bet others would too. What would you play for? Would you play on a freeroll for 20%?" I'd never played a tournament in my life for less than 50% but the tournament was about to start, I had nothing else to do, and it was a chance to make some money, so I said, "Yeah. I'd love to play."

Jack McClelland, Tournament Director, then made an announcement for players to start taking their seats. Scotty quickly turned to a small group of players that included Ron McMillan, Luis Santoni, Russ Hamilton, and Violin Joe, and said, "Hey, you guys. Mike Sexton isn't in the tournament. You can buy 20% of him for $1,250 or 10% for $625." Ron said, "I'll take a piece," and the rest of them quickly said, "I'll take a piece, too." In less than one minute, Scotty collected $5k, turned to me, handed me the money, and said, "You're in, baby. Good luck!" I was the last player to sign up for the tournament. (Late registrations weren't accepted in those days.)

I was juiced and excited about playing, even though there were only 56 players in the tourney and I was only playing for 20%. I was just about average in chips throughout the tournament, but with 12 players left, I was the short stack. I held on to make the final table (which I needed to do to make the money) and then won some pots to climb up in chip count. I made it to heads-up, but my opponent, Donny Kerr from Houston, TX, had a pretty good chip lead on me. Once we started, he was grinding me down by raising every pot.

As we took a break, Luis Santoni came over to me and said, "Mike, you've done great so far, but four eyes are better than two. Can I tell you something?" I said, "Sure." He then said, "This guy is running over you. You're getting whittled down. You're playing too tight. You've got to raise him back and slow him down. Don't be afraid to play a big pot." I said, "Thanks", and headed back to the table. I knew Luis was right.

The first hand after the break, Donny raised again. I looked down at the J-10 of diamonds and moved all-in over the top. He snap called with A/K. Oops, time to get lucky – and I did. I made a straight on the turn to win that pot and never looked back. I won the tournament! All my shareholders were delighted and, needless to say, so was I.

An interesting footnote to this story is that Scotty, like me, didn't have enough to enter the tournament either, but rather than ask those guys to stake him, he asked them to stake me and even bought 20% of me. (This was two years before Scotty won the WSOP main event.) Who knows what would have become of my career if those guys didn't take a piece of me on that day?

I learned a valuable lesson that day – *four eyes are better than two!*

Thank You Linda Johnson

After that win, the owner of *Card Player* magazine, Linda Johnson, asked me if I would like to write a story about my Four Queens win. I said sure. She liked my article so much that she asked me if I'd like to be a regular columnist for *Card Player*. I said I'd love to and my column "Inside Professional Poker" was born. I wrote that column for *Card Player* for 10 years. The exposure and platform *Card Player* provided me led me to numerous opportunities on the business side of poker, starting off with putting on my dream, the TOC of Poker.

The Tournament of Champions of Poker

I always wanted to put on a championship event in poker where you couldn't just buy your way in. Instead, you had to earn your way in by winning a tournament during the calendar year. I wanted to pattern the TOC of Poker after the TOC of Golf, where you had to win a PGA tour event during the calendar year to be eligible. I also wanted it to be a championship tournament that included multiple games, which had never been done before. It would be all champions, playing multiple games, to determine the ultimate champion – the TOC of Poker!

This wasn't going to be just another poker tournament. It was going to be an *event* – the greatest *event* in poker history! I wanted an international field where players paraded into the tournament area behind their country flags like the Olympic Games. I even had an international trophy for the country (outside the US) that performed the best. I wanted a player's lounge of no equal, with collages of all the great players, provided by my brother Tom. In addition, we displayed banners from participating casinos and flags from all nations, had lavish meals for players on dinner breaks and live music every night with a dance floor, awarded cars to all final table players, filmed the final table for worldwide internet broadcast, etc, etc. It was first class all the way.

The multiple games would consist of three limit games and No Limit Hold 'Em. The limit games were Hold 'Em, Seven Card Stud, and Omaha Hi/Lo. Levels for the limit games would be 90 minutes each with 25 minutes of Hold 'Em, 30 minutes of stud, and 35 minutes of Omaha Hi/Lo (to equalize the number of hands in those games as much as possible). When we reached 27 players, it would be strictly No Limit Hold 'Em until we crowned a champion.

A good number of players told me, "I don't see this working. Players won't play in a multiple game championship. Stud players won't play, Omaha Hi/Lo players won't play, etc." There is one thing I never doubted: that *if* someone qualified by winning a tournament during the year, they would *learn* the other games and play in the TOC. I felt sure I was right about that.

To become eligible to play in the TOC, players needed to win a poker tournament, with at least 40 players in it, anywhere in the world with a buy-in of $200 or more. The buy-in for the TOC would be $2,000 + $200, which was what I thought was affordable for those who qualified winning smaller tournaments.

So, I had what I thought was a great idea, but now I had to sell the idea to a casino to make it happen. I soon discovered that would be much tougher than I thought. I went to the Mirage first. It was the newest casino with the top poker room in town and the President of the Mirage, Bobby Baldwin, was a world champion poker player and a friend of mine. Bobby really liked the idea but couldn't or wouldn't commit to getting the Mirage involved.

I then went to the MGM Grand, Caesars Palace, the Commerce Casino, and the Stratosphere (which was just being built) with my pitch, but to no avail. I was close to landing the TOC with the Stratosphere. Lyle Berman co-founded Grand Casinos in 1990, the company that was brought on as an equity partner for the Stratosphere in 1995. (Bob Stupak ran out of money while building the Stratosphere, and Lyle bailed him out.) Grand Casinos' Native American casino holdings were spun off into a new company, Lakes Gaming, where Lyle was CEO. It was Lyle, thru Lakes Gaming, that later co-founded the WPT with Steve Lipscomb. To give you an idea of Lyle Berman's clout in the industry, he was the Gaming Executive of the Year in '96.

Anyway, Lyle liked the TOC idea and said that he would do it if his board of directors would approve it. He set up a meeting for me. I met with them and they *almost* went for it, but their concerns at that time were focused on opening their casino and not putting on a poker tournament, even though they knew it would bring a lot of players to the casino. They said they would consider the TOC at a later date, which I appreciated.

Everyone I met said they liked the TOC idea but were hesitant to get involved. That was primarily because casinos had never worked on a joint project with other casinos, not to mention them depending on an outsider – *me* – to handle everything. And, because their reputation would be at stake if something went wrong, they didn't want to risk it.

I was extremely disheartened that no one wanted to take a chance on the TOC. I was about to throw in the towel when I decided to make one more try, this time at The Orleans casino in Las Vegas. It wasn't a mega hotel on the strip like I had hoped for, but they put on the largest poker tournament in the world – the most entries at that time – with over 1,000 entries in their July tournament, and had the space and staff already in place. Logistically, it was perfect. It turned out to be the best venue I could have gotten. When The Orleans agreed to host the TOC, I was so happy. My dream of putting on the TOC was going to become a reality.

The first TOC took place in July '99 at The Orleans. To promote the event, I wrote about it in *Card Player*, did PR at every opportunity, and traveled to Europe to encourage foreign players who were qualified to come and play. I also knew that for this event to be a big hit, I had to get the high-stakes players in it. Players like Chip Reese, Doyle Brunson, Puggy Pearson, Billy Baxter, and Amarillo Slim didn't play many tournaments in those days, but I knew I had to get them to play in the TOC for it to be considered one of the, if not *the*, greatest event(s) in poker. The question was, how could I get them to qualify?

I came up with a solution. In addition to someone winning a tournament during the calendar year to be eligible for the TOC, I allowed anyone who had won a WSOP bracelet, in any year, to also be eligible for the TOC – and be eligible for life. This exemption into the TOC would strengthen the importance of winning a bracelet at the WSOP. To further ensure that the high-stakes players and Poker Hall of Famers would play, I asked Doyle Brunson to host my first TOC.

I called Doyle and said, "Doyle, I'm putting on the greatest event in the history of poker, the Tournament of Champions of Poker." I explained it all to him and then said, "If you host this event, Doyle, you'll be the biggest star in poker." He replied, "Mike, I'm already the biggest star in poker." Then, after a moment of silence and sensing my sadness, he said, "Mike, I'll do it under two conditions." I said,

"Great. What are they?" He said, "First, it doesn't cost me any money, and second, it doesn't take any of my time." I said, "Deal." It was now a sure thing that all the great players would play.

The TOC was on but I knew there was a lot of work to do. I met Karin Firmani, who did my event signage and ordered my merchandise. She loved my vision, was a great friend to me, and was a tremendous asset to the TOC. Chuck Humphrey, a lawyer, computer expert, and successful businessman, heard about the TOC and wanted to become a partner. His strengths were my weaknesses, so I was glad to team up with him.

The TOC was a smash hit. We had 664 entries in the first TOC — which may not seem like much by today's standards, but to give you an idea of how big it was, just two months earlier, the main event of the WSOP, won by Noel Furlong of Ireland, had 398 entries. The TOC was much bigger. In addition to being happy about that, I was really pleased that players loved the multiple game concept! And I'm sure The Orleans loved the TOC and all the Europeans that attended. Their roulette drop for the week was the highest in the casino's history — by a wide margin.

The French won the international trophy with five players cashing and two making the final table, and my host, Doyle Brunson, almost won the tournament! Doyle finished fourth. David Chiu was the inaugural TOC champion. David, a great player and ambassador for poker, has five WSOP bracelets and a WPT title to his credit. (He won the 2008 WPT championship event.) I was glad a player of David's stature captured the first TOC title.

The TOC was ahead of its time, before the TV explosion of poker. As special as the TOC was, there just wasn't a way to monetize it sufficiently, so we stopped putting it on after three years. They say everything happens for a reason. The TOC led me to other business opportunities that changed my life.

I played what I would consider a fairly substantial role in the development days of online poker, certainly with the rise and success of partypoker, and in putting poker on television via the WPT.

In a nutshell:

♠ partypoker.com was one of the most amazing business success stories in history.
♠ The WPT was the first poker show to be aired in prime time,
   each and every week. And that poker show, the WPT, changed
   poker forever!

partyp◆ker

11 The Story of partypoker

Are you a gambling man? Because I am..
Titantic Thompson

Partypoker was a combination of being the right product, in the right place, at the right time in history, and with the right combination of people behind it. The company, originally known as the iGlobalMedia group, later changing its name to PartyGaming, grew faster than nearly all of the largest companies in the world. Started from scratch by Ruth Parasol in 1997, with no outside investors, the company went public in 2005 valued at $8.5 billion, the largest float in five years on the London Stock Exchange.

Let's go back to the beginning and I'll tell you the story about how partypoker was developed and how I came to be involved. It's an incredible story.

The late 1990s was when online poker first started. Planet Poker was the first site to go live in '98, and then along came Paradise Poker in '99. Even though they were first on the block, Planet Poker had too many technical issues. They hired the highly respected Mike Caro to give them credibility, but Paradise Poker was far superior in features and stability and quickly dominated the market.

In December of 2000, I was at the Trump Taj Mahal playing in the US Poker Championship when I got a phone call from Michael Sacks, a friend from Toronto, asking if I was involved with an online poker site. I had met Sacks 18 months earlier when I put on the TOC. He owned Refund Management, Inc., which was a company that got tax refunds for Canadians and those from other countries where they took 30% off the top from gambling winnings in the US. I referred some international players who cashed in the TOC (where they took out 30%) to Sacks.

I told Sacks that I wasn't involved with an online site. In the summer of 2000, I'd spent much of my time in England working with a potential online site named Ace Poker, but after spending months there, having no contract, making no money, and not feeling at all confident about their potential for success, I came back to America. I figured I'd better get back to playing poker.

Sacks said he knew some people who had big money, who were already in the online gaming business, and who were developing an online poker site. They were looking to hire a "poker domain expert". That person would help them fine-tune development, as well as represent, and be the face of the site. He continued, "I think you're the perfect guy for the job and I'd like to be your agent." I told him I'd be glad to discuss the opportunity.

I got that call from Sacks in Atlantic City the Wednesday before Christmas 2000. I was flying back to Vegas the next day and a meeting was set up for me two days later at Bellagio with a lady from San Francisco. Her name was Ruth Parasol.

In 1997, Ruth had started her online casino business, and in 1998 she hired a software expert from India named Anurag Dikshit (yes, that's his real name – Dikshit) and later made him a partner in her business. Together they developed and operated several online gaming sites for blackjack, roulette, keno, and slot machines, and had launched some primitive poker tables without much success. However, by 2000, with more and more players talking about Planet Poker and Paradise Poker, they had begun to develop a similar poker table platform using the name partypoker as a testbed, but it was more difficult than anticipated. Vikrant Bhargava, a classmate of Anurag and the then hired "CEO" of the group, realized that, in order to finish the product and launch it, a poker expert was required – so Ruth got busy trying to find that poker expert, reaching out to associates far and wide, and one of them knew Sachs, who recommended me.

The meeting was to take place at Bellagio on December 22, 2000, at 2 pm, at the piano bar near the lobby. I arrived a little early, but Ruth was already there. She was 35 years old and a lawyer. I must say that she made an impact on me right away as she was very good-looking and dressed to the nines. And it didn't take me long to realize that she was also *very* sharp!

After a brief introduction, she took my resume material, set it to the side without glancing at it, looked right at me, and said, "Before we go any further, *if* we hire you, can you be in India within 10 days time? Our software company is in India and, if you take this job, you're going to have to be in India for several months and then go to the Dominican Republic, where our customer support is located, for several more months. You'll have to go down there to train our customer support people because they don't know anything about poker. Will all that work for you?" No bull – she got straight to the point.

I was single at the time and said, "Yes. *If* I take the job, I can go. But, what exactly is the job?" She said, "You're going to help our people develop the software, be the face of the site, and be our poker domain expert, meaning all poker questions will go through you." I said, "Ruth, I know poker, but honestly, I don't know anything about computers, software, or programming." She said, "Don't worry about that. Our people know all that stuff."

We talked a while longer and she asked me what I wanted/ needed if they accepted me for the position. I was expecting her to tell me what the job paid, etc, but instead, she put the ball in my court. I thought for a moment and then told her I wanted a salary of $15,000 per month, a piece of the company, perhaps a bonus if we did well, and $100,000 up front. If I was going to trek to India and the Dominican Republic for the next year, I wanted it to be worth my while. She took it all in and said, "Thank you for coming. I'll get back to you within a day or so."

Sacks called me back the next day. He said, "They went for everything except the cash up front. Ruth said nobody, and I mean *nobody*, gives cash up front in this business. You don't know if the site's going to work, you don't know what kind of problems you're going to have, and you don't even know if you're going to get customers. It may never get off the ground. So, no cash up front."

He did say that Ruth mentioned that she didn't mind paying me a bonus if it all worked out and things were going well, but again said, "They don't pay cash up front." I said, "Well then, there's no deal." I had just worked for months for nothing over in England and I needed money, so I was holding my ground. He said he would call her back and get back to me.

Sacks called me back later that day and said, "They'll go for everything except the $100,000 bonus. They'll give you $15,000 a month salary and 6% of the poker site, not the already existing casino sites." That sounded good but I still said, "Well, with no cash up front, tell her I'm sorry, but there's no deal."

I then told Sacks that if he helped me get the $100,000 up front, I would give him $20,000. He said, "Do you want me play hardball? Do you really want me to tell her there's no deal without the cash up front?" I said, "Yes. Play hardball. I need cash to take care of things before I go. I need the $100,000."

He hung up and called me back an hour later. He said, "You've got a deal if they can pay the $100,000 up-front cash bonus at $10,000 a month for the next 10 months, meaning you'll get $25,000 a month for the first 10 months. And FYI, they're planning on launching no later than September." I said, "Great. Tell them I'll take it. And thank you for your help." I gave Sacks $20,000 for helping me get the deal, and just over a week later, I was in India. Hello new world.

It really was quite a whirlwind experience – meeting Ruth, taking the job, and heading to the other side of the world – all within a week. And remember, I hadn't had a real job in 23 years! Talk about taking a gamble in life, 10 days after I had first met Ruth, I was in India to embark on a new career.

They flew me business class to India on Singapore Airlines. I must say, that impressed me – both the airline and that they flew me business class. I flew to Singapore and from Singapore to Calcutta, where I would then fly to Hyderabad, where the software part of the company was located.

The difference between Singapore and Calcutta was unbelievable! Singapore is one of the cleanest cities in the world (with a phenomenal airport that's so clean you could eat off the floor), while Calcutta was shocking, a truly eye-opening, or should I say eye-closing, experience. The number of people fighting to carry your suitcase at the airport for a mere 20 cent tip, the extreme poverty, and the massive population everywhere you looked, was all new to me. Calcutta was unbelievably grim.

Anurag, who made billions a few years later when the company went public, flew to Calcutta to meet me and escorted me to Hyderabad. He chuckled as he met me at baggage claim, "I could never let you fly into Calcutta cold turkey and then have you try to get to Hyderabad. I was afraid you'd get back on the plane and fly back to America. The poker site might never get going."

We had to take a bus from the international airport in Calcutta to the domestic airport. The bus was jam-packed. People were sitting with suitcases piled up to the ceiling and family members sitting on each other's lap. They crammed every person they could get on that bus to drive to the domestic airport, about a 45-minute ride. It was brutal. Although I wouldn't have flown back to America, I must admit that I was glad Anurag came to meet me. It would have been a much tougher trip going to Hyderabad by myself the first time.

While riding that bus, I looked out the window and was stunned. I saw hoards of people and witnessed their pathetic and depressing lifestyle: families literally living in cardboard boxes on the sidewalk, people pissing in the streets, etc. It was mind-boggling. If you ever travel to Calcutta, trust me, you'll appreciate your life and where you live a whole lot more. Hyderabad, although also very populated and poverty-stricken like all cities in India, is one of the nicer places because many overseas companies have call centers and tech development companies there.

After I checked into the hotel, Anurag took me over to the software company. He was anxious for me to meet the poker team. There were only about 40 people working in the software company in India at the time and none of them were 30 years old. The poker team consisted of five guys, headed up by Nitin Jain, who was a very bright kid. He was also engaged to Anurag's sister.

After talking to them for five minutes, it was apparent to me that none of them knew anything about poker. I couldn't believe a company was starting a poker site when no one in the company knew anything about poker. I said to them, "I have to tell you guys, I know poker but don't know anything about computers or software development." They told me, "If you tell us what to do, we can do it." I smiled and said, "Well, I can tell you what to do."

Naming the Site

While chatting with the poker team, I asked, "Do you have a name for the site yet?" It had been developed on a testbed with the name partypoker that Ruth had given it, but Vikrant and the guys didn't like the name as it sounded silly to them, pokerparty.com was owned by someone else, and there were many "P" sites (Planet Poker, Paradise Poker, and Poker Stars was in the works). They didn't have a name yet, but they brought out a list of six or seven other possible names they had locked up and asked "Which name do you like?" I scanned the list and within seconds I said, "Well, that's easy. It's a no brainer. I like partypoker.com." They said, "partypoker, are you sure?" I said, "Yes. partypoker, I love the name. It's simple, recognizable, a fun name, and easy to remember." As I was the "poker domain expert", they took my advice and kept the name partypoker.

From there, we rolled up our sleeves and started developing the poker site. They'd already designed the table, the chairs, and the little people who sat in them, but now came the time to create the games. I went through every game with them, starting with Limit Hold 'Em. I said, "Player 1 will start with the button; Player 2 will be in the small blind; Player 3 will be in the big blind; and Player 4 will have options A (fold), B (call), and C (raise). Player 5 and the other players will then have options A, B, and C, etc, etc."

That's literally how we did it. When we started out, it was all limit poker because that was pretty much all anybody played in those days. This was before televised poker and the No Limit era. It was also much easier to design limit poker software than pot limit and no limit software.

It was no accident this company became so successful. The work ethic – by everyone, starting from the top down: Ruth, Anurag, and CEO Vikrant Bhargava – was incredible. The poker team, and in fact everybody in the company, worked relentlessly and extremely hard. Everyone in the software company seemed to work at least 16 hours every day. They would sit at their computers working for hours. When they got tired, they would roll up their jacket, use it as a pillow and literally sleep on the floor. You would constantly have to step over people to get around the office. A short while later, they were right back to work at their computers. They were all happy to work there and massively incentivized as all the employees of the company were far better paid than the average person in India.

After the poker team understood Hold 'Em, I explained the other poker games to them: Seven Card Stud, Seven Card Stud 8 or Better, Omaha, Omaha Hi/Lo, and then a little later, No Limit Hold 'Em, PLO, and PLO 8 or Better. I went through all the games and explained to them how they were played. I also explained the difference between a one-table tournament and a multiple-table tournament (which was much tougher to develop the software for).

It took me about four weeks to go through all the games, explaining player options, antes, all-in situations, side pots, the features we needed on the site, etc. I wrote the rules for the site as they were developing the software. After a few months, the poker team got it and was doing well. It was time for me to go to the Dominican Republic to connect with the customer support staff.

What I really liked about joining this company was that it wasn't a start-up from scratch. They were already in the online gaming business, had affiliates established, customer support in place, banking connections, and their own software and servers. All of this provided a *huge* edge over others who were looking to start an online poker site.

Affiliates are people who send traffic to a site and get paid for it. They are your business partners. And this company was quite successful with its affiliate program and used affiliates richly. Affiliates might get a flat fee of $50 or $100 for sending somebody to the site, or they could get a piece of that player's action, for life! It was their choice.

If they chose getting a piece of that player's rake, they might start getting 15-20% of what that player contributed to the site and, depending on the volume of business that they sent to the site, have a sliding scale that went up to 30-35% of the revenue the site made from their players. I will tell you this – the top affiliates for partypoker made a lot of money, *a whole lot*.

As mentioned above, the CEO of the company, for both the

casino site and the poker site, was Vikrant Bhargava (one of the four who became a billionaire when the company went public). He was located in the Dominican Republic. Vikrant is a brilliant guy and, along with Anurag, attended one of the most prominent universities in India, the Indian Institute of Technology, in Delhi. (I was told that those who can't get in there, drop down and go to the Massachusetts Institute of Technology, an Ivy League school, Duke, or Stanford.) When poker was brought on board, they threw poker in Vikrant's lap as well. Lucky for all of us, he could handle it. Vikrant was a business guru.

I flew from Hyderabad, India, to Santo Domingo in the Dominican Republic – about a 30-hour trip. As soon as I arrived, I was immediately taken to the office to meet Vikrant. After a quick hello and a minor inquiry about how my flight was, the first question Vikrant asked me after my long trip, was, "Okay, now we've got the software. How do we get players to the site?"

Vikrant understood that you could have the best software and the best customer support in the world, but if you didn't have players, you didn't have anything. I admired that he was all business, smiled, and said, "Well, I've been thinking about that and I've got a few ideas." He said, "Okay. What are they?"

I began, "My big idea is that we launch the site with one-table satellites for the partypoker Million or PPM." He said, "The partypoker Million? What's that?" I said, "It's going to be a tournament where a guy can qualify on our site for $20, win a luxurious cruise for two, and then have a shot to win $1,000,000 in a live poker tournament on a ship." I paused for a moment to get his reaction and he told me to continue.

I said: "This will be a dream for poker players. It's an opportunity for them to go after the pot of gold at the end of the rainbow, and to do it for not much money. I think everyone will love it and come to our site." He was intrigued.

I continued, "Here's how it works: We launch the site with $22 buy-in one-table, 10-handed satellites – $20 will go to the PPM prize pool and $2 to the house. If a player wins that satellite, he'll go to the semifinals, which we will hold in late January. The second and third place finishers in those satellites get another entry into a one-table satellite, thus fueling the satellites.

"All the winners will then play in the semifinals that we'll hold over four days time, with players choosing which day they prefer to play. Each day, 25 players will qualify and advance to the finals on the ship. Those 100 players will win a luxurious cruise for two, get $500 in cash for spending money, and a $10,000 entry into the partypoker Million, which will be a Limit Hold 'Em tournament, with the winner getting $1m. We will guarantee a $1m first place prize!"

He looked at me and said, "Wait a minute. You're saying we're going to guarantee a million dollar first place prize?" I said, "Yes", and he said, "We're never going to do that. We don't even know if we'll get customers or the site's going to work."

I said, "Well, I know this, if we guarantee a $1m first place prize and a guy can win a cruise for two, put some cash in his pocket, have a shot to win a million dollars, and all he's got to beat is 100 players to do it, I can't see any poker player in the world who is not going to come on our site and try to qualify for $22."

I could see his mind whirring away and that he liked the idea. I told him that I was certain that I could get Card Player Cruises to host our event, as we would fill a cruise for them. Vikrant then said that he thought the partypoker owners would be very hesitant about putting up that kind of money.

Vikrant and I discussed the PPM idea with Ruth and Anurag, and they were somewhat hesitant, saying, "A million dollars is a lot. What about a half a million first place prize?" I said, "No. Our mission should be to create a *big* bang. To get players to the site, we need to create a real wow factor. $1m is wow. It needs to be a $1m for first place." Vikrant then said, "I think Mike's right. If we're going to do it, it needs to be $1m first place guaranteed." Ruth and Anurag weren't that convinced.

I went to Card Player Cruises (Linda Johnson, Mark Tenner,

and Jan Fisher) and told them about the PPM. I told them we'd fill a cruise for them (300 or more people). They would host our PPM championship and they would get the rake from the cash games. They liked the idea of the PPM and hosting the finals, but said they would only do it if the $1m in guaranteed prize money was put up in escrow.

I went back to the company with that and they didn't want to put up a million, at least by themselves. Vikrant said they wanted Card Player Cruises to partner with them as they were benefiting from the cruise and that, therefore, they should put up $500,000 of the guaranteed money.

I asked Vikrant, "Why would Card Player Cruises assume liability for a half million dollars? They don't know if the site's going to work. They are just hosting our cruise. They're not going to take a chance on damaging their reputation by promoting the PPM and hosting the event unless $1m is posted in escrow and the cruise costs are paid for well in advance."

Vikrant thought for a little while and then said he would make them a deal. If Card Player Cruises would guarantee half the $1m prize money, half the costs of the cruise, as well as half the $500 in spending money for each player, which was $625k in total, they would then get exclusive affiliate rights to not only the people they send to the site, but for every player who came to the site the first 30 days after we launched. And Ruth added this perk: that even if the company came up short where Card Player Cruises would lose money, that she would make them whole over time – meaning that over time they would be reimbursed for any losses associated with hosting the PPM.

I praised Vikrant for that idea and told him I thought it was a home run. I felt certain Card Player Cruises would go for that deal as they did understand "rake" and potential affiliate fees. They did go for it – and it was *the* smartest decision they ever made. The partnership was formed and the partypoker Million was a "go".

Launching the Site

On August 1, 2001, we launched partypoker.com, strictly with partypoker Million satellites. No cash games, just one-table, 10-handed satellites, with a $22 buy-in per player where $20 went to the house, $160 went to the PPM prize pool, and the winner advanced to the semifinals. The second and third place finishers got a free entry into another PPM satellite.

After about a week of nothing but one-table PPM satellites, which were going OK, Vikrant said to me, "What do you think about trying a cash game, say a $3/6 Limit Hold 'Em game on the site?" I said, "Great. Let's try it." Even though we hadn't gone through any proper testing, we basically just threw it out there to see what would happen. Boom! The table filled right up and the cash game was immediately going, with no software glitches. We were ecstatic, all high-fiving each other. And then we added a second game and a third game. Just like that, we had cash games going, as well as the qualifying single-table tournaments for the PPM. It was pretty cool.

I suggested to Vikrant that we put a few extra things into PPM qualifying that would not cost the company any money but would get players to play a lot more on the site. That was his kind of music. He was all ears.

We created extra starting chips that players could earn to add to their starting stack in the semifinals. It was a reward system for additional play on the site. If they won a qualifying satellite to get into the semifinals, they would start the semis with 1k in chips. If they qualified *and* played 80 hours of cash games on the site prior to the semifinals taking place, they got double the starting chips for the PPM semis (2k instead of 1k). And the amount of extra starting chips were scaled down according to the number of hours they played on the site. For example, if they played 40 hours in cash games, they would start the semifinals with 1.5k in chips.

This gave players incentive for playing extra hours in cash games and/or extra tournaments on the site, because they would receive extra starting chips in the semifinals for doing so, thus giving them a better chance to make it to the ship. And remember, they could qualify four times for the semifinals, meaning they needed to play 320 hours of "live" play to get maximum starting chips in each semifinal. Vikrant loved that the company didn't have to pay any bonus money or rakebacks out of its pocket to get players to play more hours. The extra starting chips for the PPM semis was a clever idea and it worked beautifully.

In the first month after launching, we had some technical glitches where the site would crash. Obviously, nobody liked that – not the players, Card Player Cruises, nor us. Card Player Cruises was upset as they recommended their database of players (over 3,000) to play on partypoker. Fortunately, our players were extremely loyal and stuck with us. One thing is for sure – without the support of Card Player Cruises and their customer base, partypoker may have never gotten off the ground, or certainly not had anywhere near the success it did.

Mike O'Malley also deserves a shout out, as he hired and ran our props (players who used their own money to play but would get paid $15 an hour to play x hours a day and help start cash games). We never used bots, so utilizing props were a key ingredient to maintaining successful cash games in the early days.

I was the one who convinced everyone at partypoker and Card Player Cruises that the PPM would be a huge success and bring thousands of players to our site. In early October, however, Anurag, who had come to the Dominican Republic for the launch, called me into his office and said, "Mike, I'm sorry, but we've got to cancel the PPM and shut down the site."

Shocked and bewildered, I said, "What are you talking about? You can't do that!" He said, "Well, I put the pencil to it and it looks like if things keep going like they are, we're only going to take in about $650,000 by the time the semifinals go off. That means we're going to lose $600,000 on this promotion. We can't afford to lose $600,000. It's not worth it to us. We're making money on the casino side so we're just going to scrap the poker site."

Trying to maintain my cool, I said calmly, "Anurag, we can't do that. We've guaranteed the people who have already qualified for the semis the chance to possibly win $1m and make their dream come true. Our reputation, our name, and Card Player Cruises' as well, is on the line. And we promised the Card Player Cruise people a cruise that they've already booked." I didn't mention Card Player Cruises would absorb half that predicted loss or how much the company would make in rake from the satellites and extra starting chips idea.

Again, he said, "I'm sorry, Mike. We're just going to lose too much money on it." I looked him right in the eye and firmly said, "Anurag, let me tell you something. I understand that right now, today, the bread and butter of your business is the casino games. But I promise you that one day poker will be far and away the bread and butter of this company." He sort of scoffed at what I said. He certainly didn't believe that.

Anyway, he, Vikrant, and the poker team had a meeting and they decided not to scrap the partypoker Million (the smartest move they ever made). Anurag was right in that we did lose nearly $600,000 on that first PPM in terms of what we took in from the qualifying $22 satellites, but putting on the PPM gave the site credibility and an extensive, loyal, customer base.

The PPM qualifying continued and then, wham, a few days before the semifinals, the software guys told me that we were going to have to postpone the semifinals. *WTF?*

We had scheduled our semifinals on January 27-30, 2002, and the cruise was scheduled for early March 2002. The players had only one month after qualifying to make plans to go. The cruise had been booked and paid for, and now the software guys were saying they needed to postpone the semifinals because they needed to do more testing.

The problem: they were not sure the semis would work with that many players, about 1,000 per day, on the site. They hadn't tested a multiple table tournament, which is what they would play in the semis, with that many live players and were afraid it might not work.

I inquired, "You've known about the semis for months, and now, you're not sure the semis are going to work?" And they said, "No. It's a multiple table tournament with a lot of players. We haven't tried it with that many people. We need more time to develop it. The whole thing could easily crash." I said, "Well, let me tell you something: *if* the whole thing crashes, we're out of business, and *if* we don't run the semifinals as scheduled, we're also out of business. It doesn't matter. Either way, we're dead in the water if you can't make it work."

I went to the head of the tech guys, the one I trusted the most. I knew he would be honest with me about the situation. I said, "I need a number. Give me a percentage of what you think it will be for the semifinals to *not* crash." He thought a minute and said, "Probably 75% to 80% at best." I said, "Well, that's good enough. We've got to gamble. We have no choice."

I then told Vikrant and the owners, "Look, we've got to hold the semifinals as scheduled. Everybody has been playing for months to get their extra starting chips, they've spent all their time on our site, we promised them this $1m guaranteed tournament, a luxurious cruise, the semifinals on these dates, and that's what they've planned for. People have taken off work to play in the semis. If we don't hold them as scheduled, we lose all credibility, and nobody will trust us again. I don't see anybody coming back to our site if we move these dates. Besides that, we can't change the dates of the cruise."

I then told them what I told the tech guys, "If we don't hold the semifinals as scheduled and/or the site crashes when we hold them, we're out of business. Period. We've got to roll the dice." Fortunately, they agreed. And we really were rolling the dice for partypoker's life.

Everyone in the company, every technician, software person, and customer support person, had to be available during the semifinals. The tech guys would hopefully prevent anything from going wrong and the customer support people had to be ready to soothe player issues such as getting logged out during the tournament where they would be blinded off. We'd never tested these multiple table tournaments with near that many real people. Nobody seemed to know for sure if we could handle that much traffic. Nevertheless, we had to roll the dice.

Fortunately, we didn't seven out. We got through the semifinals on Day 1 without crashing and no mishaps. Whew! The software worked to perfection. The tech guys were heroes.

I'll never forget the celebration we had after that first day of the semifinals. We didn't finish until 5 am in the morning and I personally called all the winners and congratulated them. They were all over the moon. Then, the poker team and I drove to a gas station that was open 24 hours, bought some cold beer, sat in the car, and celebrated the success of making it thru Day 1 of the semis. I can never remember a beer tasting better.

We held the semifinals – all four days – without a crash. The money we lost on a shortage of qualifiers turned out to be an advertising fee because everybody who was on the ship for the PPM, and most everybody in the poker world, knew the company took a bath by guaranteeing that kind of prize money. They knew that we didn't take in anywhere near $1.25m, so there was a big overlay for them. No one ever mentioned the extra revenue we took in as a result of players playing more to get the extra starting chips.

To get additional money for the PPM prize pool so it wasn't just a million dollar, winner-take-all tourney, we invited anyone who wanted to put up a $10,000 entry fee and pay for the cost of the cruise, to come on the cruise and play as well. To my amazement, considering the value, we only sold 35 additional seats. The extra prize money covered second through ninth place. So, as you can imagine, it was a totally top-heavy tournament in terms of prize pool payout. There was a *huge* difference between winning $1m and finishing anywhere else in the money (top nine places).

About a week after the qualifying field was set for the finals, I got a phone call from Steve Lipscomb, a lawyer turned TV documentary guy. I'd met Steve a few years earlier at the WSOP, where he was filming a documentary on the series. I did an interview with him for that documentary. He said, "Mike, I think I can get your partypoker Million tournament on television and it won't cost you any money. I went to the Travel Channel with an idea to film it and they approved the budget. They will put it on the Travel Channel as a one-hour special." I said, "Wow! That is fantastic! Thanks so much, Steve!" I knew this would not only excite the players, it would be a big shot-in-the-arm for the site as it would give partypoker tremendous exposure.

There was really a buzz on the ship. Everyone was excited because the PPM was going to be on TV. Putting the PPM on television was not only huge for the company, it turned out to be *huge* for the entire poker world – for several reasons. First, Kathy Liebert was the PPM winner. She became the first woman poker player ever to win a $1m first place prize. (But truth be known, they made a deal six-handed.) It also helped the TV show that players who bought in and made the final table included two former world champions, Phil Hellmuth and Chris Ferguson, long-time pros Ken Flaton and Mel Judah, as well as Kathy.

A month after the cruise, the documentary, called *The partypoker Million*, started airing on the Travel Channel. It was a smash hit! It quickly became one of their highest rated shows ever. Steve Lipscomb did a *great* job in producing the PPM, much to the delight of all of us at partypoker.

The PPM did so well in the ratings on the Travel Channel, I'm certain it was the primary reason that the Discovery network took a chance a year later on putting a poker show on the Travel Channel in prime time each week. That show was the World Poker Tour, created by Steve Lipscomb.

The credibility that the partypoker Million gave us was enormous and the site started to grow. Ruth and Vikrant recognized that if we stayed in the Dominican Republic we would have growth problems. We had to expand the company, increase customer support, and get people who spoke English, not the easiest thing to do in a Spanish speaking country. Bottom line – extensive growth for the company would not be possible in the Dominican Republic.

They knew that in India everybody spoke English and you could get the help, and smart help, there, a lot cheaper. Putting the software people and customer support people together only made sense. So, in a very clever and quick move, Ruth started making plans for the company to leave the Dominican Republic, even though they still had another year on their lease. They decided to move the customer support to India and move the company headquarters to Gibraltar, where Ruth was familiar with a few other operators licensed there. I went back to India for six months to train and work with the all-new, customer support staff, as well as the fraud and security teams.

Russ DeLeon, who went to Cal Berkeley and Harvard Law School, and had just left a San Francisco-based software company that had IPO on NASDAQ, was Ruth's boyfriend and joined the company in 2001 as a consultant to help with legal and finance. In January 2002, the company was approached by investors about joining a multi-company consolidation. Following substantial negotiations, Russ was able to get them to agree that at the time partypoker, although a loss-making start-up facing intense competition, was worth at least $5 million, which was double what they were initially willing to pay.

Knowing I would not be happy selling the site, Russ told me, "Mike, I've got them up to $5 million for partypoker. What do you think of that?" I said, "Do you really want to know?" He said, "Yes", and I said, "I think it's a great deal – for them." It was clear to me after the PPM that partypoker was just going to get bigger. I told him that I believed the buyer was getting *way* the best of it at that price. Lucky for all of us, by the time investors were requiring binding commitments to sell, the company was beginning to generate significant profits from a revamped casino and a steadily growing poker site. Russ and Anurag flew to Australia to discuss and consider the potential deal with the investors and other target companies. Russ and Anurag simultaneously agreed before beginning the second day of meetings that they didn't want to sell and backed away from the deal. The investors were furious and started increasing their offer, going as high as $30 million, but it was too late. I was greatly relieved when I heard the news, as things were really taking shape.

After we moved the customer support back to India, Vikrant was trying to figure out how we could get more business. He said to me, "Mike, what do you think about advertising partypoker on television?" No online gaming site had ever advertised on television up to that point. I said, "Wow, that's a great idea!"

At that point in time, the WPT had filmed some events but the show hadn't launched on television yet. I said to Vikrant, "Look, if we're going to advertise on TV, we should advertise on the show that I'm going to be on, the WPT. Nobody really knows if the WPT will be a hit or not, but I know this, everybody that watches it is going to be a poker player, so you're going to have a built-in audience. Plus, they'll see me on the show and then see me doing the ads, which will give partypoker instant credibility to potential new customers." He agreed and said, "Maybe I'll try to buy a couple of ads." I looked at him and said, "Buy as many ads as you can buy."

Vikrant negotiated a deal with the Travel Channel that is surely one of the all-time greatest advertising values for a company in history. You could only buy two ads per show and Vikrant bought all the ads he could for the WPT regular season *and* the re-run season. And because he opted to pay them cash up front (something new to them), he got them at a very nice discount.

Within 30 days after the partypoker commercials aired during WPT shows, we multiplied our business by 10 and never looked back. The power of television was amazing. The rest, as they say, is history. We went on to become the number-one online poker site in the world – due primarily to those TV ads.

With the success of partypoker, they began to launch additional casino sites: PartyCasino, PartyBlackjack, PartySlots, etc. In 2004, along with the relocation of the company headquarters to Gibraltar (within the EU), the company's name was changed from iGlobalMedia to PartyGaming. The business was growing fast and professional management from London was hired and relocated to Gibraltar, with an eye to obtaining financing from UK institutions for the distant long shot of going public. Russ (who married Ruth in 2003) took the lead in the IPO dream for the group.

In June 2005, the company went public, when founders and a number of senior executives hired to help take PartyGaming Plc public sold 23% of the company shares for £1 billion, valuing the business at $8.46 billion. However, due to unmet demand in the US, the first trade during unconditional dealing was over $10 billion. It was the largest float in five years on the London Stock Exchange and one of the largest tech IPOs in history at the time. PartyGaming was immediately added to the FTSE 100 index, and was larger than British Airways and MasterCard.

Within a month, the rising share price saw the company's value go up to $13 billion, but by September 2005, the share values settled back to the original initial public-offering value.

When the Unlawful Internet Gaming Enforcement Act (UIGEA) was passed by Congress on September 29, 2006. PartyGaming made a decision (although reluctantly) to suspend real money games to US customers. Hearing the news, the stock dropped 60% in 24 hours. Compounding things, after UIGEA, the company came under investigation by the Department of Justice for the Southern District of New York as to whether they violated US law prior to the passage of UIGEA. In April '09, the company made a settlement with the DoJ agreeing to pay a penalty of $105 million over the next four years as part of a "non-prosecution agreement".

PartyGaming merged with bwin Interactive Entertainment AG to form bwin.party digital entertainment plc in March 2011. In September 2015, bwin.party's board of directors recommended an offer from GVC Holdings PLC valuing bwin.party at $1.5 billion. That transaction was completed on February 1, 2016.

Ruth, Russ, Anurag, and Vikrant together cashed out a few of billion dollars from the June 2005 IPO and a secondary share sale in May 2006. They were all on the Forbes List (and the under 40 Young Forbes List) when the company went public in '05. So why not me? Why didn't I make hundreds of millions? Simply put, I sold my shares 18 months before the company went public.

By the middle of 2003, partypoker had become the number-one online poker site. During 2004, the company rebased from the Dominican Republic to Gibraltar, which is part of the European Union, and Ruth and Russ relocated to Gibraltar as full-time residents away from the US and were in the process of relinquishing their US citizenships, as Ruth was born a multinational and they had both already been working out of the US for many years. In early 2004, the owners were in Las Vegas for a convention and asked me to meet with them at the Venetian. They said, "Mike, Would you be interested in selling your shares?"

Up to this point, partypoker had not paid out any dividends (since all the profits had been reinvested in the business) and who knew what was going to happen in the future. I also knew I'd be rich – very rich – so I said, "Yes, I'm interested in discussing it." They said "Okay. What do you think your shares are worth?"

Well, I didn't honestly know the value of the company, but I did know that I didn't want to tip my hole card first, so I said, "You tell me what you think my shares are worth." They said, "We want to hear what you think they're worth first." After thinking for a moment, I said, "Well, how about this? We'll both write down what we think my shares are worth on a piece of paper and we'll see how far apart we are." They agreed to that and then they left the room for 10 minutes to discuss it. I started calculating what partypoker took in daily, monthly, and the growth rate over the last year. I then came up with what I felt my shares were worth.

They came back in and we both revealed what we had written

down. They wrote down $10m on their piece of paper. I had written down $15m on mine. They said, "$15 million is too much. They might pass laws that will prohibit us from operating. Anything can happen and we think $10m is fair." As much as I was thinking about what I could do with $10m, I held firm and said, "No. I really think $15m is fair." They said they wanted to think about it.

A week later they called me from Gibraltar and said, "Okay, we're going to agree to $15m under these conditions: You get $5m now and you get $2m a year for each of the next five years. We'll pay you $20,000 per month and $440,000 each quarter for five years, but you have to continue working for and representing partypoker. You can't work for any other online gaming company. If you do, or if you quit, or if we have cause to fire you, we don't have to pay you the $2 million a year anymore." I was *thrilled* with that deal – and proud of myself for holding out for another $5m – but I wanted to stay cool and maintain my poker face, so I calmly said, "That's fine with me. Thank you."

I once heard Ruth say, "I've negotiated deals with some of the smartest business people in the world, but the toughest guy I ever dealt with was a poker player."

The company went public in June 2005. On the day it was announced, I went to Bellagio. As I was walking onto the balcony of the high-stakes area, Mike Matusow saw me coming, stood up, and hollered out, *"What's it feel like to lose $500 million?"* The whole room cracked up, including me.

Honestly, it never really bothered me. I never second-guessed myself for making the decision to sell when I did. I always looked at it like playing a hand of poker. Suppose you hold a 7-5 and the pot is raised and re-raised in front of you. What do you do? You fold. You shouldn't be angry and upset if the flop comes 4-6-8 and both opponents flopped a set where you would have tripled up if you played the hand. At the time, you made the right decision to fold. I was thrilled when I sold my shares – at the time I did – for $15m. I went from basically being broke to rich!

Obviously, in looking back at what my shares would have been worth 18 months later, I *wish* I would have waited to sell them. But, suppose I didn't sell them and the UIGEA would have happened a couple years before it did? Then, my shares would have not been worth much. I would have kicked myself forever for not selling my shares for $15m when I had a chance to. I always remembered what Puggy Pearson told me years ago, "It's easy to play the red board."

After selling my shares, I was happy to continue to work for the company, that it continued to grow, and that the owners became so successful. When the company went public, a Gibraltar trust established with a small percentage of PartyGaming shares in 2004 (to benefit PartyGaming employees, consultants and local communities) gave me a gift of an additional $15m — which they didn't have to do. I was extremely appreciative and happy to get it.

It was an amazing run for partypoker. To go from a start-up poker site to the largest float on the London Stock Exchange in five years is incredible. I've done seminars at Harvard Law and Business Schools, and the Fisher School of Business at Ohio State, and have spoken to grad students at New York University Business School and others. I briefly tell them the story of PartyGaming and how it grew so quickly to become one of the most amazing business success stories of all time. It gets their attention. And it's a story that, outside the gaming world, not that many people even know about.

Ruth, Anurag, Vikrant and Russ are no longer shareholders or involved with the company in any way, nor have they been for a number of years. As of this writing, I'm still a consultant for partypoker.

Black Friday

On September 29, 2006, Congress passed the UIGEA. It didn't make online poker illegal, but it made the funding of online sites in the US illegal. It was attached to the Safe Ports Act and was passed without discussion or debate. Sadly, because of that law, partypoker was "forced" to leave the US, which was 73.4% of their business at the time.

Partypoker was making over $2m a day when UIGEA was passed. Nobody wants to give up a business like that, but the company was a public company with an independent board of directors accountable to its shareholders, and its lawyers were clear that with this change the company needed to stop transacting with US players. If they didn't, they could face prosecution and public shareholder lawsuits.

When partypoker left the US in '06, it had 58% of the total online poker market – far more than all the other sites combined. As one analyst said, "partypoker is the Coca-Cola of online poker." It was a sad day for the company and our players when we left the US market. I call it the "Original Black Friday". I am proud to have been a part of helping create the largest online poker site in the world and proud that I'm still there, even though the dynamics of the market have changed dramatically.

All the online sites that were connected to publicly traded companies left the US market when UIGEA was passed. Like PartyGaming, they felt they had no choice. The online poker sites that were not publicly traded continued doing business in the US. PokerStars became the largest online poker site in the world, with Full Tilt in second position. On April 15, 2011, the US Government shut down all online poker sites in the US. It was deemed "Black Friday" by the poker community, but it will always be "Black Friday number 2" to me.

Full Tilt collapsed in disgrace as they didn't have funds to pay players back when they were shut down. That was a black eye for the industry. A little over a year later, PokerStars bought its former competitor Full Tilt for $731 million. It was a deal to settle a civil lawsuit with the Department of Justice.

A little over two years after Black Friday number 2, Nevada was the first state to offer legalized, regulated, online poker. Currently, as of this writing, three states have legally sanctioned online poker

– Nevada, New Jersey, and Delaware. Partypoker returned to the US in force, relaunching in New Jersey with the number one network (including Borgata). Hopefully, many more states will follow suit so we can once again play the game we love in our own homes.

12 The World Poker Tour

*It's better to live one day a lion
than your whole life a lamb.*

Jack Straus

It was March, 2002, when we held the first partypoker Million. A short while later, Steve Lipscomb, who filmed the PPM for the Travel Channel, took Linda Johnson and myself to lunch during a poker tournament in Costa Rica. He wanted to tell us his idea about putting poker on television. He introduced us to his idea of the WPT. Well, of course, Linda and I loved it. We thought it was a phenomenal idea. He was trying to do something that had never been done before, and that was to bring competing casino properties together for the first time working on a common project.

Life's a Gamble

His plan was to hold WPT events at different locations, essentially creating the PGA Tour of Poker. Poker on TV on a weekly basis – wow! But, he said he wouldn't do it unless he could get Audrey Kania (development/marketing) and Robyn Moder (production) to agree to do it with him. Luckily for the poker world, they both agreed to do it.

Steve had vision and a 10-year business plan – but no money. He estimated it would cost $3.5m to fund the WPT for two years. He wanted to know if we knew anyone that might be interested in funding the WPT. I told him I could get him a sit down meeting with two people who had big money, clout, and loved poker. Those two were high-stakes poker player and entrepreneur Lyle Berman, and Jerry Buss, owner of the LA Lakers.

Steve was adamant about a couple of things. Number one, he wanted to be a 50/50 partner and wanted the final say on anything to do with the television program, and number two, he was absolute in that it was going to be a two-hour show, where you would have a start and a conclusion to each episode. He was also adamant about "the WPT hole cam", the camera on the rail of the table that would show the players' cards, something without which he knew the show could not survive.

I decided to contact Lyle first. I knew he wanted to buy television rights to the WSOP from Jack Binion in the early '90s. I called Lyle, explained briefly what Steve had in mind and, shortly after, Steve and I went to Lyle's condo in Vegas for a meeting. Typical Lyle, he immediately brought out his television proposal for the WSOP he had from years earlier.

Lyle had learned that networks turned down his WSOP proposal because they didn't want a once-a-year program. They wanted a season of events leading up to a championship, which is just what Steve was bringing to the table. Steve explained his concept of the WPT and Lyle was clearly interested. He wanted us to come back a couple of days later with more details of how Steve would be able to get casino partners on board.

Linda Johnson, owner of *Card Player* magazine and the most

respected person in the poker world, went with Steve and me to the next meeting. Linda told Lyle she thought she could help in getting card rooms on board. Lyle listened intently and told Steve he'd get back to him in short order.

The next day I got a call from Steve. He said, "Mike, Lyle called and said he would do it. He said that his company, Lakes Gaming, would fund it, but that they would only do it if Lakes would get 70% and the WPT would get 30%. But, I can't go with Lyle as I'm not doing it for less than a 50/50 deal."

I said, "Steve, I think you're making a mistake. Lyle is the perfect partner. He's smart, successful, knows poker, and who else do you know that can pick up the phone and get Donald Trump on the line? Lyle can. Very few have the respect he does in the casino industry. He was the Casino Man of the Year a few years ago. You have an opportunity here to fulfill your vision and make your dream become a reality. If it works, you'll be a millionaire, regardless of the 70/30 split, and worse case scenario, if it doesn't, you'll have a job for the next two years and at least have had a shot to make your dream come true." He ended the call by saying he wouldn't do it for a 70/30 split.

The next day Steve called me back. He said, "Mike, I've decided to take Lyle's offer. We're going to do the WPT." I was so happy to hear that Steve had changed his mind. It turns out that Lyle went to his buddies Jack Binion and Doyle Brunson, and offered them a chance to be 1/3 partners each. Surprisingly, they turned him down. But Lyle still wanted to do it. He then went to his board of directors at Lakes Gaming and they agreed to do it. Doyle later said, "Just another dumb move that cost me millions."

Steve's first task was lining up casino partners. The first stop Linda recommended was Foxwoods – the largest casino in the world at the time. She knew Kathy Raymond (poker room manager) well and knew she would be excited about it. Steve flew to Connecticut and had a meeting with Kathy and the Foxwood executives. They said they would get back to him.

Before Steve got out of the building, Kathy called him on his cell phone and said, "Foxwoods is in." Next, Bellagio came on board, and then the Commerce Casino – three of the largest poker rooms and most prestigious casinos in the country were on board – and the rest followed quickly. The WPT was happening.

When we put on the last TOC in 2001, we wanted to produce a televised broadcast. We hired Steve Lipscomb to film it for us. And because it was my tournament, I did the commentary. When it was over, Steve came up to me and said, "Mike, that was the best job of poker commentary that I've ever heard." I said, "Thanks!"

A year later, when he was going to start the WPT, Steve came to me and said, "Mike, I've got good news and bad news for you. The good news is that I want you to be a commentator on the WPT. The bad news is that if you take the job you can't play in any WPT events." I had played the tournament circuit for 15 years and this was a new challenge for me, so I was thrilled with the opportunity.

Lyle Berman was shocked that Steve had selected me to be one of the commentators. He said, "What? Mike Sexton. You've got to be kidding. He's just a poker player. What does he know about commentating on television?" Steve held his ground and said, "I want Mike." Lyle said, "I don't see him lasting more than one show."

Incredibly, as of this writing, we are now finishing Season 14 of the WPT. Most TV shows don't last anywhere near that long. It's been a dream job. I still love working with Vince Van Patten and everyone at the WPT. They're great people and real pros at their jobs.

Vince and I have been with the WPT since Day 1. I've never missed a WPT final table (although twice I was a player and not a commentator). Vince has only missed one, and that was only because a tournament in Florida added one more day to their event just a couple of weeks before the tournament and Vince had a previous commitment. He promised that he would be the master of ceremonies (MC) for a charity event in Texas months prior to finding out our final table would be moved back one day. He, and everyone at the WPT, felt he should honor his obligation as MC of the charity event. And he did.

Vince and I are life-long poker guys who became poker commentators, not commentators who were slotted into a poker show. We really do love playing poker and love our job. After all these years, we still really enjoy watching the final table action at every event. It's still fun for us. What a ride. I can remember that first show like it was yesterday.

The first WPT event was held at Bellagio in July 2002, and I was petrified. I'd never been in a high school play, and here I was going on national television. Vince grew up in television and movies, so I was glad he was there with me. But, Vince didn't really understand what the WPT was all about. He thought this was a one-day gig, so he drove in that morning from Palm Springs. He was so tired, he was out of it by midnight and the final table lasted until nearly 4 am! With the way Lyle felt about "a poker player in the booth" and with Vince dozing off, it's amazing either one of us survived after that show.

Lucky for all of us, that first show was one of the greatest final tables ever on the WPT. Some of the biggest names in poker at that time, including Scotty Nguyen, John Juanda, Freddie Deeb, and John Hennigan, were at that final table. Basically, the only poker unknown at the table was Gus Hansen. He was a world-class backgammon player, but had no poker resume to speak of. But Gus had the looks (he was voted one of *People* magazine's 50 sexiest men in 2004), style, and poker creativity that was wowing. Gus won that tournament and soon became the biggest star on the WPT, winning two more times. His three titles tie him with Carlos Mortensen, Anthony Zinno and Chino Rheem for the most wins in WPT history.

Because of gaming regulations, Vince and I, or anyone else except one guy in a locked room, aren't allowed to see the players' down cards during play at the final table. We can only speak about players' cards when they are shown at the end of a hand or when players are all-in and they are turned up. We don't guess what they have as we're pretty close to the table and we don't want to influence play in any way.

A few weeks after our final tables take place, we go back to a studio in LA and watch the final table again, this time seeing the cards. They splice our commentary from the studio with the final table footage and, *voilà*, you have the magic of television.

When Vince and I got back to the studio in LA after that first show and saw what these guys were playing, especially the garfunkle hands the ever-aggressive Gus Hansen was playing, we looked at each other and *knew* this show would be a hit. Watching him play these junk hands was riveting television.

That Bellagio tournament would be the pilot show for the WPT. Lipscomb worked on editing that show for months, finally put it in the can, and then started shopping it to the major networks. Steve was telling them all that he had the next biggest sensation for television – the newest sport – poker. But, they all turned him down. He then went to ESPN. They wanted to do it but they'd only do a one-hour show. Steve insisted on it being a two-hour show, so ESPN was out.

Finally, after all the big boys turned him down, Steve went to Discovery (the Travel Channel). They had a history with Steve with the production of the highly successful partypoker Million. Because of that, they were willing to take a chance on the WPT.

They told Steve, "We'll advertise it and put it on in prime time every Wednesday night from 8 to 10 pm." Wednesday night became poker night in America. The WPT was the highest rated show on the Travel Channel. It was their number-one-rated show all five years that it ran!

Without the first partypoker Million, without the successful history that Lipscomb had with Discovery (the Travel Channel) in putting on that one-hour PPM documentary, there's a possibility that the WPT would have never made the airwaves with any network. But, luckily, that didn't happen. Because of television, the WPT changed poker forever.

As to why the five-year contract wasn't renewed by the Travel Channel, they said they didn't want to be known as "the poker network". I have a different theory, though.

During Season 4, to prevent competition from beating them to the punch, WPT enterprises decided to start a Professional Poker League (PPL), where 100 invited pros would compete in a season long series of events. The problem was they made a deal and were going to put that show on another network, which didn't please the Discovery people. They felt their contract with the WPT had been violated. Discovery threatened a lawsuit (feeling the new PPL would compete with the WPT). Both parties settled by agreeing to televise the PPL on the Travel Channel for one year. The PPL lasted only one season.

The WPT has evolved over the years. Under the guidance of Adam Pliska (President since 2009) and his executive staff, the WPT has really expanded globally. It's also become much more financially stable, and in June 2015 it was acquired by Ourgame International Holdings Ltd, for $35 million.

Once the WPT hit the air and poker came to television, the poker world was never the same. Prior to the WPT, nearly every casino across the country was shutting down poker rooms at that time. But, within a year's time after the debut of the WPT, they opened them up again. Business was booming because of the popularity of poker on television. And No Limit Hold 'Em, a game you couldn't find on a regular basis in any card room in the country prior to the WPT, is now the prominent game – by a wide margin – in every poker room.

I often get asked, "Is poker a fad? Why is poker so popular on television?" My answer is, "The WPT is reality TV at its finest. It's real people, who have put up real money, where life-changing money is at stake on the turn of a card. That is riveting television." And the best part is that nearly everyone at home watching the WPT says the same thing, "I can play as well as that guy. I should be at that table playing for a million dollars."

I believe that everyone in the poker industry – players, card room owners and employees, people who work with media or any poker related occupations, including those involved with online poker sites – owes Steve Lipscomb (and Lyle Berman) a debt of gratitude for creating the WPT.

Make no mistake about this: it wasn't online poker or the "Moneymaker effect" that caused the poker explosion. The primary reason – without question – was the WPT. The WPT literally changed the poker world forever.

13 The WSOP (the First 30 Years)

My favorite chip trick is to make everyone's chips disappear.

Amarillo Slim

Many of you may be too young or simply not know what it was like at the WSOP back in the day. Hopefully, this chapter will give you a better idea of what the WSOP was like prior to the television era. You will also get some insight into the poker pioneers that made it all happen.

In the old days, there was an ambiance about the WSOP that's hard to describe unless you were there. Binion's Horseshoe put on the largest poker event in the world and didn't even have a poker room in their casino. During the WSOP, they took out slot machines to put in poker tables. Nearly all who came were comped hotel, food, and beverages. And they put on a lavish buffet every night for the players in the back of the coffee shop, complete with ice sculptures daily. Players actually left their poker games to eat together at the buffet!

I have witnessed some extraordinary things at the WSOP. I'll cover some of my favorite stories over the first 30 years until the television era of poker started after the turn of the century. There will be things that will surprise and entertain you from that era.

To my knowledge, the first-ever poker tournament was held in Reno, NV, in 1969. Tom Moore, part-owner of the Holiday Casino, invited several big-time poker players including Johnny Moss, Doyle Brunson, Puggy Pearson, and Amarillo Slim as well as celebrities Benny Binion, Jimmy "the Greek" Snyder, and "Minnesota Fats" (Rudy Wanderone) to what he called the Texas Gamblers Reunion. It turned out to be the event that fueled the original WSOP.

The WSOP in the '70s

As Moore passed on having a second reunion in Reno, Benny Binion recognized the potential of hosting this and asked Moore if he could take the event to Las Vegas. Moore was fine with that. Benny called it the World Series of Poker.

The WSOP was started by the Binion's not necessarily because of their love for poker, but because they were looking to get some high-stakes gamblers to their casino. Poker was the bait. The WSOP evolved as an annual reunion of gamblers, primarily from Texas and the southwest in the '70s. It was the pit action that accompanied the poker that made the WSOP so attractive to the Binion's. The PR and media attention was a bonus.

In that first WSOP in 1970, there wasn't even a tournament. After several days of high-stakes cash games, Johnny Moss was elected the best all-around player by his peers. It wasn't until 1971 that a "freeze-out" tournament was introduced. The buy-in was $5,000. Moss won that winner-take-all event (six entries) to retain his title.

The Years 1972 to 2001

1972

In 1972, eight players posted up a $10,000 entry fee. It came down to Doyle Brunson, Puggy Pearson, and Amarillo Slim (Thomas Austin Preston, Jr.). Doyle and Puggy have both told me that neither of them really wanted to win it (back then, the WSOP didn't mean anything to them – it was all about the money) as they didn't want the publicity nor any Internal Revenue Service (IRS) problems. Slim, on the other hand, did want to win. He recognized the potential and opportunity for him.

They took a timeout and went into the back room with Benny. They made a deal three-handed where Puggy and Doyle got over twice as much money as Slim, and they all agreed to let Slim take the title. It was a PR jackpot for poker and the WSOP as Slim loved the limelight and had a gift of gab second to none – and wasn't afraid to spew it.

Amarillo Slim was poker's premiere ambassador for the next 20 years. He parlayed that WSOP "win" into a personal bonanza. His Texas drawl, his story-telling ability, and his willingness to promote the WSOP and Binion's Horseshoe bode well for him. He appeared on the *Tonight Show* 11 times, wrote a best-selling book, and hosted Amarillo Slim's Super Bowl of Poker, the only other poker tournament in the world until '85, for a dozen years, starting in '79.

Once, on the *Tonight Show*, Johnny Carson asked him, "Slim, what's the population of Amarillo?" Slim said, "Well, I'm not sure of the number, but I know the population never changes." Johnny took the bait and said, "Really, why is that?" And Slim quipped, "Every time a girl gets pregnant, some guy leaves town."

In addition to his poker skills, Amarillo Slim was one of the best pool players in the world. He was also famous for his gift of gab, his all-round athletic talent, and his prop bets. These are some of the quotes Slim was most noted for:

I never go lookin' for a sucker.
  I look for a champion and make a sucker out of him.
You can sheer a sheep 100 times,
  but you can only skin him once.
My favorite chip trick is to make
  everyone's chips disappear.
I don't believe in hunches.
  Hunches are for dogs making love.

1973

In 1973, the WSOP expanded to five events (Seven Card Stud, razz, 2-7 draw, and a preliminary No Limit Hold 'Em event, in addition to the main event). Jimmy the Greek got CBS to film the WSOP main event for the first time. (I highly recommend you go to YouTube.com and watch it. It's very good. It's fun to see what the players were wearing back then and witness all the smoking that was going on, especially cigars.) Puggy Pearson was king that year, as he not only won the main event (13 players), but two other preliminary events as well.

1974–'77

In '74, Moss won his third title (16 entries) and in '75, Sailor Roberts, former Texas road partner of Doyle Brunson and Amarillo Slim, took the crown (21 entries). In '76 and '77, Doyle became poker's biggest name by winning back-to-back titles (22 & 34 entries).

1978–'79

The 1978 main event at the WSOP was historical for two reasons. It was the first time the main event was not a winner-take-all tourney. Five places were paid. It was also the first time a woman, Barbara Freer, played in the main event. And let me add, it was the first time a

Texan didn't win. A high-stakes gambler from Tulsa, OK, Bobby Baldwin, got the win (42 entries).

Baldwin made a name for himself the year before, during the '77 WSOP, by winning both the $10k buy-in No Limit 2-7 draw tourney and the $5k buy-in Seven Card Stud tourney. He also won the No Limit 2-7 draw event in '79. Bobby's main event win in '78 was the launching pad for him to become a business legend in Las Vegas, working first for Steve Wynn at the Golden Nugget, Mirage, and Bellagio, and later heading up the development of City Center, the largest building project at one time in US history, for MGM, and as of this writing, he is the President of Aria Resort & Casino in Las Vegas.

In 1979, an amateur won the WSOP for the first time (54 entries). Hal Fowler from Oregon upset Bobby Hoff heads-up by outdrawing him several times along the way. Incredibly, Fowler was "one and done" at the WSOP. He never played again and, basically, just faded into oblivion.

Every champion in the 1970s, with the exception of Hal Fowler, has been inducted into the Poker Hall of Fame.

1980-81

Stu "the Kid" Ungar from New York was the talk of the town in 1980–81. Stuey dropped out of school in the tenth grade and played gin rummy for the Mafia at 16. He was a gin rummy superstar who came to Vegas in the late '70s looking for gin action. He took on all comers, including poker's elite. Those guys were all excellent gin players, but it wasn't long, even with the numerous spots he would give them, until no one would play him any more. Everyone – and I mean everyone – considered Stu Ungar the best gin rummy player of all time.

So, lacking gin action, Ungar turned to high-stakes poker. He entered the main event of the WSOP for the first time in 1980, playing in only the second poker tournament of his entire life. Because of his lack of experience, nobody gave him a chance to win. But Stuey was cocky, confident, and bet on himself to win, changing the odds from nearly 80-1 down to 20-1. There were 73 entries in the tournament. Although raw, he knew how to move his chips to the center, battled his way to the final table, and defeated two-time champion Doyle Brunson heads-up to win. He made more in side bets by betting on himself to win than he got for winning the tournament, which was $365k.

Incredibly, in 1981 (75 entries), he successfully defended his title – back-to-back wins in the main event of the WSOP his first two times out. Wow!

Stu Ungar was the most aggressive and fearless player anybody had ever seen. Most thought he was lucky the first time around but, after successfully defending his title, he became a legend in the poker world forever. He captured a third WSOP main event title in 1997. Think about it, he won the world championship the first two times he played it, and the last time he played it. Stu Ungar was inducted into the Poker Hall of Fame in 2001.

1982

This was the year that 6'6" Jack "Treetop" Straus took down the WSOP championship event. This became known as "the chip and a chair" tournament. Jack was a renowned bluffer and on the river one hand halfway thru the tournament, he pushed his chips in the pot. His opponent said, "Call", and Jack said, "Nice call. You got me. I was bluffing." As he stood up to leave, he picked up his Coke and, as the napkin came up with his drink, there was one $100 chip left. It was the intent of Jack to move all-in. The questions were, "Did it play?" and "Should Jack be out?"

They called the floorman over. Because Jack pushed his chips forward rather than saying "All-in", and his opponent said, "Call", they ruled it didn't go in the pot and that he could play his remaining chip. Amazingly, he came back and went on to win the tournament and the slogan "A chip and a chair" was created and immortalized. Jack Straus was inducted into the Poker Hall of Fame in 1988.

1983

This was the first time in history that a satellite winner (winning a smaller buy-in tourney, in this case $1k, to get an entry into a bigger tournament) won the main event. Ironically, the final two participants, Tom McEvoy and Rod Peate, had both won their way into the tournament via satellites – which were the brainstorm of Tournament Director Eric Drache.

It was also the first time – and the last – that network TV would cover the main event live. Jimmy the Greek had convinced CBS that they needed to cover the largest prize pool event in sports live. Their plan was to film the final table, possibly witness the final hands live, hopefully by two well-known big-time gamblers, and then show it on the 6 pm news.

Well, McEvoy and Peate were playing in their first-ever main event, so they were not big names – nor were they in a hurry. They played a marathon heads-up battle, much to the dismay of CBS. The 6 pm EST news came and went, as did the 11 pm news. Tom and Rod were still playing. The lengthy final table, production costs, and boring television, as no whole cards were shown, were more than CBS could stand. They never came back.

Tom McEvoy, from Grand Rapids, MI, eventually won that heads-up battle and captured the title. He was inducted into the Poker Hall of Fame in 2013.

1984

The first time I went to the WSOP was in 1984. I remember how excited I was to be there. I played in three events and made two final tables. It was a life-changing experience for me.

A guy from Philadelphia named Jack Keller had an amazing WSOP that year – far more amazing than mine. Jack, who served in the Air Force prior to becoming a poker pro, was primarily a stud player, as most east coast players are, or were back then, but he became an expert at all games. There was a $5,000 buy-in Seven Card

Stud tournament that year that Jack wanted to play in. A guy from Salt Lake City by the name of Dale Conway, a regular at the WSOP, decided to stake Keller in the $5k Stud event.

Keller won the tournament for $167k and, after they split the money, Dale said, "I'm going to take $10,000 out of my share and enter you in the main event." Jack didn't play a lot of No Limit Hold 'Em at that time, but was more than happy to play the main event. And you guessed it – Jack Keller won the tournament (140 entries). It was quite a parlay.

After that win, an interviewer asked, "What's it feel like to be the greatest poker player in the world?" Jack looked at the interviewer, chuckled, and said, "Are you kidding? I just got lucky and won a No Limit Hold 'Em tournament." He continued, "I'm not the best Hold 'Em player in the world by any means. I just got lucky in one tournament." It's not often you hear a newly crowned champion say something like that after he or she wins, especially someone who just won the main event at the WSOP.

In the 1980s, Jack was a fearless, risk-it-all, high-stakes player. He had balls – big ones – and a lot of gamble to him. Unfortunately for Jack, as he got older, he got into drinking and drugs.

He spent the latter part of his life in Mississippi playing in smaller games and I heard he was drunk most of the time. It was a rather sad ending for him. He died in Tunica, MS, in 2003 at age 60. But, back when he won the world championship and throughout the 1980s, he was as high-stakes a player as there was, I can tell you that. Keller was inducted into the Poker Hall of Fame in 1993.

1985-86

I didn't enter the main event of the WSOP until 1991, but 1985 was the first time I was there for the main event from start to finish. I was on the rail, watching it all, and I mean right in the front row. I'll never forget watching the final table of the '85 WSOP. I was sitting three feet from the table, at the center of the table, and right next to Berry

Johnston's wife. Although Berry was playing, his wife seemed a little nonchalant about the whole thing and only seemed to look up at the table every once in a while. I found that a little unique.

The tournament came down to Bill Smith and T.J. Cloutier, both from Dallas, TX, and Berry Johnston, from Oklahoma. Smith, who was drinking beer all day, and smoking using a cigarette holder, was a good size chip leader with three left. T.J. and Berry had about the same amount of chips.

A hand came up between Berry and T.J. where all the money went in before the flop. Berry had A/K and T.J. had A/J. Basically, whoever won this hand would play Bill Smith heads-up for the title. The flop came A-7-2. Berry was way ahead with the A/K. On the turn, off comes a Jack! T.J. was now well out in front with aces and jacks.

Berry winced slightly when the Jack hit on the turn, but he didn't moan, didn't whine, didn't complain, didn't say a peep. From a big favorite, he now had to catch a three-outer to stay alive. The river card was a baby. T.J. barely had him covered and Berry went out in third place. He stood up, shook both players' hands, and said, "Good luck, guys."

Berry then walked around the table to where we were sitting. His wife looked up at him and said, "Oh, hi, honey. Are you out now?" He said "yes" and she said, "Oh, good. I'm hungry. Can we go get something to eat now?"

I was stunned. Berry just took a bad beat to get knocked out of the main event in third place, and all his wife seemed to care about was getting something to eat! Berry looked at her and simply said, "Sure, honey. If that's what you want to do, we'll go get something to eat." They then headed to the coffee shop.

The next time I saw Berry, I went up to him and said, "Berry, I was sitting next to your wife when you took that horrible beat and finished third. I heard her ask you if you wanted to go get something to eat, and you said, 'Sure, honey, if you want, we'll go get something to eat.'" He laughed and said, "Can you believe that? I just wanted to go throw up. I sure didn't want to go get anything to eat."

Life's a Gamble

My dad (Ray) and mom (Gloria)
on their wedding day (1945)

My favorite picture - me and Tom

With my sister Loni, and my brother Tom

My mom with her husband Elmer and
her three kids: Loni, me and Tom

Paratrooper in the 82nd
Airborne Div (1970-72)

My gymnastic days at Ohio St (1965-'69)

With two Olympic gymnasts (both Buckeyes):
Paul Hamm ('04 All-Around champion)
and Raj Bhavsar ('08 bronze medalist)

Little League Coach - Honeycutt
Pirates, Fayetteville, NC (1979-84)

Life's a Gamble

Golfing with Carl McKelvy and Jack Straus

Marsha Waggoner and Stu Ungar

Congratulating Phil Ivey after
he won his fourth WSOP bracelet

Winning my first WSOP bracelet (1989)

On the cover of CP -
the first player to be sponsored

Amarillo Slim, me, Bob Stupak, and Puggy
Pearson (note Slim picking Stupak's pocket)

Stuey after winning the
'97 WSOP, with Jack Binion

With Linda Johnson -
The First Lady of Poker

Life's a Gamble

Wondering "Where did all my chips go?"

With Tom, our sister Stephanie
and Tom's daughter, Kim

Kathy Liebert and Phil Hellmuth joining me
in the commentary booth at the first TOC

The inaugural TOC in 1999 with host
Doyle Brunson, and winner David Chiu

My golf swing (I must have posed for this picture as I don't take it back anywhere near that far)

Doyle Brunson and I celebrating our win over Howard Lederer and Huck Seed (top left)

Me and Vince - together on the WPT since Day 1

Nolan Dalla, Stu Ungar, Puggy Pearson and me just a few weeks before Stuey died in '98 (bottom left)

My dad with the boys: Lance, Tom, Jeff, Rodney and me

Life's a Gamble

WPT founders and talent:
Robyn Moder, Steve Lipscomb, Shana Hiatt, me, Audrey Kania and Vince Van Patten

Five Hall of Famers celebrating the launch of the WPT on television:
me, Chip Reese, Lyle Berman, Doyle Brunson and Bobby Baldwin

With Vince, three-time WPT champion Gus Hansen and Shana

Getting the first-ever
Poker Ambassador Award (2006)

Winning the WSOP TOC in 2006 ($1,000,000)

New Year's Eve party at Chip Reese's house

With Bobby Baldwin at the first-ever airing
of the WPT at Bellagio (March 30, 2003)

Life's a Gamble

On the cover of CP after being
inducted into the Poker HOF

Dancing with my niece Ashley

With Karen Sexton and Irish pal Padraig Parkinson

With Tom at my
HOF induction in 2009

The happiest day of my life!

My man - Ty Michael Sexton

Life's a Gamble

Winning the $20k buy-in
speed tourney 'Down Under' (2005)

O-H-I-O – with friends Chris, Darcee
and Boston Romero #GoBucks

Playing poker with Ben Affleck

Doyle Brunson winning the WPT
Legends of Poker (2004)

With Vince, Tiger Woods and Mark Cuban at the
WPT Foundation Tiger Jam poker tourney (2015)

Before a WPT final table

With Lynn Gilmartin and Vince on the WPT set

I'll never forget the class that Berry showed in losing that tournament. He didn't bitch or moan after taking that beat and agreed to go eat with his wife when he just wanted to go puke. He was class with a capital "C". Incidentally, two hands after Berry was knocked out, T.J. was all-in pre-flop with A-3 of diamonds against Bill Smith's two 3s. The two threes stood up and Bill Smith became the 1985 world champion.

But here's the best part of the story: the very next year, in 1986, Berry Johnston came back and won the main event! To me, if there was ever justice in the poker world, that was it. Johnston, the guy with the most cashes in the main event in WSOP history (11), the ultimate player and gentleman, took that bad beat in '85 to go out third, and then came back and won in '86. Amazing!

Berry Johnston was inducted into the Poker Hall of Fame in 2004.

1987-88

The next year, 1987, was the first year that Johnny Chan, the "Oriental Express", went on that incredible run in three consecutive years in the main event of the WSOP – a streak that will never be matched or duplicated in the history of poker. It's how it happened and what happened between his WSOP streak that wows me.

Most poker players know about Chan's WSOP main events, first, first, and second place finishes from 1987–89. What people probably don't know is that Chan won back-to-back $10k buy-in events at Bob Stupak's America's Cup tournaments in 1982–83 and back-to-back wins in the $5k championship event at the Hall of Fame poker classic, also held at Binion's Horseshoe, in 1988–89.

Think about that: of the five biggest tournaments in the world between 1987 and 1989, Johnny Chan won four of them and finished second in the other! It was far and away the most incredible run in poker of all time.

The first win by Chan in that incredible run, the '87 main event, has me talking about what I witnessed to this day. With five tables left, I was standing right behind Chan, watching the action.

He raised the pot and everybody folded except Richard Klamian, who was in the big blind. Klamian was a pretty good poker player but was primarily a sports handicapper and sports forecaster, and a very good one, and he had more chips than Chan did.

The flop came 2, 3, 4 with the deuce and three of hearts. Klamian checked and Chan then moved all-in. Klamian quickly called and turned up the A/5 of hearts! He flopped a straight with the straight-flush draw. Chan turned up an A/J offsuit. He stood up and started to put his jacket on, getting ready to walk away. The 8 of spades came on the turn and the 5 of clubs appeared on the river. He made the same straight and they split the pot! It was a miracle for Chan – and he sure took advantage of it.

It was remarkable to me that a guy who should have been out of the tournament and was lucky to stay alive, not only won that tournament, but then went on the greatest streak in poker history. Chan defended his title the next year and came in second to Phil Hellmuth in '89. He won two Hall of Fame titles in '88 and '89 as well – truly remarkable. Johnny Chan was inducted into the Poker Hall of Fame in 2002.

1989

In 1989, Hellmuth, at 24 years of age, became the youngest player to win the main event. He has since become the all-time bracelet winner at the WSOP (14), and also has the most final tables and the most cashes in WSOP history, both by a wide margin. Without question, Hellmuth is the best all-time performer in WSOP history.

My favorite story of Phil Hellmuth came in 2012. A month or so before the WSOP, I was at a WPT event, in the bar with some young guns. A few started bad-mouthing the old school players, saying they were all past their prime and, essentially, over the hill. One of those old school guys they spoke about was Phil Hellmuth.

I'm not always a fan of Hellmuth's behavior at the table, but I've always been a fan of his play. There's one thing I do believe, and that is that nobody fights for bracelets harder than Hellmuth. So, I said to the group, "I'll tell you guys what I'll do. I know you don't think much of Hellmuth's play. If you lay me $12k–10k, you can pick any player or as many players as you like to win a bracelet vs. Hellmuth winning one." I said nobody pays if one guy wins two bracelets and the other wins one. I also said that if they both win one, they didn't have to pay juice.

One after the other said they would take the bet. I told them, "You can take as many unique players as you want to bet, but two or more of you can't take the same player." Well, they started compiling their list. They came up with a total of 10 players to win a bracelet vs. Hellmuth winning one laying 6-5. (I would have bet them even money, but they jumped on laying 6-5.)

I loved my bets. I figured at worst I would lose $20k–30k. In my mind, there was no way more than two or three of those 10 would win a bracelet. On the other hand, *if* Hellmuth won one, I figured to win $100k or so.

Well, it couldn't have worked out better for me. Hellmuth snapped off a bracelet in the $2,500 Razz event. The guys on their list won zero bracelets. I won $120k by betting on Hellmuth. Put me down as a member of the Hellmuth fan club.

Phil Hellmuth was inducted into the Poker Hall of Fame in 2007. Every main event WSOP champion in the '80s has been inducted into the Poker Hall of Fame with the exception of Bill Smith.

1990

In 1990, Monsour Matloubi from England became the first foreign player (non-US citizen) to win the main event of the WSOP (194 entries). Although I didn't play in that event, I've got a good story about it.

An Irish bookmaker named Terry Rogers, who incidentally was the first person to bring foreign players to the WSOP, came to the US to play in, as well as to book, the main event. He would put up prices on players to win and then make new lines at the end of each day

– and they were very fair prices. I, and most everybody else, loved Terry and loved that he put up prices on players that you could bet on. It really added extra excitement to the tournament.

At the end of Day 1 in '90, Hans "Tuna" Lund from Reno was in second chip position with about 60 players left. I loved the way Tuna played No Limit Hold 'Em. He was a beast and I felt quite sure that with his chip count he would make it to the final table.

To give you an idea of how good Tuna was, up to that point in his career, he had cashed 30 times in tournament poker. He finished in the top three 23 of those times with 12 wins, including winning Amarillo Slim's Super Bowl of Poker and a WSOP bracelet.

His number-one dream in life was to win the main event at the WSOP. He was obsessed with winning it. Knowing all that, I went up to Rogers and said, "What price can I get on Tuna to win the tournament?" He said, "Oh, Mike, you're a good man and a good customer. I'll give you 17 to 1 on Tuna."

Frank Henderson, the runner-up to Johnny Chan in the '88 WSOP, used to say when he was broke, "I'm between bankrolls". I love that phrase. Well, I was pretty much between bankrolls at the end of the WSOP in 1990. I had $2,000 in the entire world – and I had it on me. I took it all out and said, "I want to bet $2,000 on Tuna to win." Rogers took the money and said, "You've got a bet, Mike. Good luck!" Life's a gamble, right?

Tuna played great and made it to the final table with a way-above-average chip stack. I loved my bet! He battled his way down to play heads-up against Monsour, a well-known high-stakes gambler. It would prove to be a *very* tough match between two extremely determined players.

Tuna had the chip lead and a hand came up where it was raised by Tuna on the button and re-raised by Monsour. Tuna called. The flop came 9-4-2 rainbow. Monsour led out and bet, Tuna raised, and then Monsour went all-in. Tuna thought for quite a while before he called. They turned up their cards: Monsour tabled 10-10, and Tuna showed an A-9. The crowd, nearly all of whom were pulling for Tuna, oohed and aahed. Monsour was well out in front with the two 10s. On the turn, however, an ace came off, giving Tuna aces and 9s and the lead! The crowd went wild.

My heart was pounding because if Tuna could dodge a two-outer on the river, I was getting $36,000 – which was like a million to me back then. I was standing three-deep behind the final table next to a friend of mine named Tab, who was a high-stakes poker player and we played a lot of golf together. As quick as Tuna spiked the ace on the turn, I turned to Tab and said, "I'll bet $200 on Monsour to catch a 10 on the river and I'll take 15-1 on it."

Tab was a very smart gambler and knew that Monsour was a 22-to-1 dog to catch a 10 on the river. He said, "You want 15 to 1 for $200?" I said, "Yes," and he said, "You got it. You got it." No sooner than he said, "You got it," they turned and burned. *Bam!* A 10 comes off on the river. The crowd was stunned and my heart dropped to the floor. I was sick. Tuna was so close to fulfilling his dream – and I was so close to having $36k!

Tuna kept his cool, though, and fought back from the short stack to almost pull even in chips, but Monsour prevailed to become the first foreign world champion. I collected $3k from Tab, so at least I had a little bankroll again. Even though I had the worst of it, I thought it was ingenious on my part to bet Tab, and to do it that quickly.

That was one of the two most dramatic river cards in WSOP history. Chris Ferguson spiking a nine on the river to beat T.J. Cloutier in the 2000 main event, when it was A-Q vs. A-9 and they were about even in chips, was the other. Monsour spiking that 10 on the river is certainly a memory I'll never forget, and I'm sure Tuna never forgot it, either... one card away – a two-outer that cost him the world title.

To give you an idea how tough Tuna was at No Limit Hold 'em, after his runner-up finish in '90, he finished 19th in the '91 championship event and third in '92. That was quite a three-year run for Tuna Lund – one of the best No Limit Hold 'Em players of all time.

1991

In 1991, Tuna Lund's best friend, Brad Daugherty from Reno, NV, won the main event (215 entries). It was the first year Jack Binion guaranteed a one million dollar first place prize. That created quite a buzz among poker players. I had a buzz that year myself because it was the first time I entered the main event. I won a satellite to get in and cashed, finishing in 24th place.

Here's something I'll never forget. When that tournament was down to six players, I was watching the final table alongside Stu Ungar. Brad didn't even have average chips at that time. The chip leader was "Tucson Don" Holt. Tucson Don – obviously from Tucson, AZ – was a high-stakes Seven Card Stud player. He had never played a No Limit Hold 'Em tournament before in his life. Just for kicks, he decided to enter the main event. The advice somebody gave him was "Just keep betting." So, that's what he was doing throughout the tournament. And that strategy was paying off in spades for him. He was the chip leader at the final table with six players left.

Don Williams was also at that final table. Williams was known as the "World's Best Unknown Player", which didn't make sense to me because Don had a lot of success in tournaments. Anyway, a hand came up where Tucson Don raised the pot pre-flop, which he was doing quite a bit, and everyone folded to Don Williams, who was in the big blind. He made the call. It was here that, to me, the worst play in poker history was made. *Yes, the worst!*

The flop came 8-8-2. Williams then moved all-in out of the blind. Tucson Don thought, stalled for a while – obviously not knowing what to do – then shrugged his shoulders, showed the A/J of spades, and pitched it into the muck. Instead of quietly folding his hand, Don Williams now laughed and turned over a pair of 8s! He flopped quads and moved in on the flop!!! *WTF?* I, like everyone else, was shocked.

I was standing next to Stu Ungar, and I said to him, "Can you believe that? That's got to be the worst play of all time in poker history! The worst!" And in one second, Stuey said, "That wasn't the worst play. The worst play was showing it!"

He was right. Had Don Williams quietly mucked his hand, no one would ever have known what he had, but once he showed the four 8s, it was there for the world to see – and for my money, the dumbest play in poker history.

Chances are very, very good that Tucson Don would have made the continuation bet had Williams checked the flop. And even if he hadn't bet on the flop, with quads, you *have* to give him a chance to bet later. When Williams was later asked about the way he played that hand, he shrugged and said, "If Don had an over-pair, I know he's gonna play and double me up." *Hello!*

If Tucson Don had an over-pair, he's not going to check the flop. He's going to bet and get his money in the pot. If he had nothing, he's still probably going to bet. Even if he didn't bet the flop, he might hit an ace or jack on the turn. For a guy who had all the success that Williams did in tournament poker, to this day, I'm astounded that he moved all-in on the flop with quads. Stuey's instant quip, though, was a classic.

1992

This was the second year that I played in the main event of the WSOP. Again, I won a $200 super-satellite seat to get in and, again, was thrilled to play. It was the first time in 22 years that the main event had fewer entries than the year before (201 compared to 215 in '91) but needless to say, it didn't matter to me, I was just excited to get to the starting gate.

They paid 27 players, but because Jack Binion was guaranteeing a $1 million first place prize, it was a totally top-heavy payout. The winner got $1m, but ninth place only paid $15k. Can you imagine making the final table of the main event at the WSOP and only making $5k? Think about that payout variance at the final table – from $15k to $1m. Tenth through 18th paid $10,100, and 19th through 27th paid $8,080, meaning you could make the money but get back less than the buy-in. It was a different time.

I played conservatively back then and was hovering around average chips most of the time. As we neared the bubble with four tables left, I was still alive with just under average chips. We get to the bubble with 28 players left and then start dealing hand-for-hand. I was confident I could hold on to make the money because I'd pretty much decided I wasn't going to play a pot unless I picked up aces or kings, and I didn't get them. Getting in on a $200 satellite, I just wanted to cash and make sure I made a score.

I was sitting to the immediate left of Hamid Dastmalchi, an excellent high-stakes cash game No Limit Hold 'Em player. With 28 players left, Hamid had slightly above average chips. Tournament director Jack McClelland would say, "Shuffle up and deal," and the four remaining tables would play a hand. Everybody would throw their hand away and look around at the other tables hoping somebody would go broke, but nobody did. Hamid immediately saw what was going on, decided to take advantage of it, and started raising every pot – and I mean every pot.

We played for two and a half hours with 28 players. It was so agonizing. Whenever somebody was all-in, they would win the pot and on we'd go. I'd make a good wager that in the history of poker, of any tournament held anywhere in the world, the one that took the longest to go from 28 players to 27 players was the main event of the '92 WSOP.

I knew Hamid was stealing every pot, but I didn't want to go against him because I really wanted to make the money, so, like everyone else, I just continued to let him steal. He increased his chip stack substantially before we finally lost a player and reached the money. Hamid Dastmalchi went on to win the tournament.

I'm convinced that because it took so long to knock the bubble out, it allowed Hamid to win. To this day, I believe that had somebody gone out in five or 10 minutes, from 28 players to 27 players, Hamid Dastmalchi would most likely never have won that tournament. I salute the guy, though, because he recognized what was happening, took advantage of the situation, and became world champion because of it. As for me, I went out 23rd, but was content to make the money the first two times I played in the main event.

Another thing I'll remember about that tournament is that on every break down the stretch, Hamid would kick up to a handstand next to a wall and then do handstand push-ups. As a former gymnast, I appreciated that.

1993

The 1993 main event was extremely unique. Nearly half of the 220 entrants won seats in a satellite, including me. Three tables were paid and I made the money again, finishing 24th. (I made the final three tables the first three times I played the event – not bad.) But it was the domination by one player, John Bonetti from Houston, TX, that this tournament should and will be remembered for. He dominated it perhaps more than any player dominated any other tournament in the history of poker.

From the start of the tournament, Bonetti was raising nearly every pot, intimidating players. He was playing well and running well. In those days, you got 10,000 in chips for your $10,000 buy-in. At the end of Day 1, Bonetti had $240,000 in chips – more than 10% of the total chips in play! The second place guy had $80,000, and nobody else had $50,000. It's the most dominating chip lead at the end of Day 1 in WSOP history.

Bonetti continued his ways and was the big chip leader at the end of Day 2, and at the end of Day 3. No one had ever seen anything like it. He completely dominated the entire tournament up to the final table. Sadly, though, he's remembered for a blunder he made with three players left in that tournament, one that will never be forgotten by anybody who was there watching it.

Bonetti probably prevented WSOP history from being made as Marsha Waggoner could well have been the first woman to make the final table of the main event, but her problem was running into red-hot Bonetti. With 19 players left, Marsha was nicely above average in chip count. Bonetti, of course, was the massive chip leader. He raised the pot and Marsha three-bet him. Bonetti then moved all-in. After some thought about Bonetti's massive all-in bet, Marsha called. Bonetti turned up an A/8 offsuit and Marsha turned up the A/K of spades. He spiked an 8 and won the pot, devastating Marsha and preventing potential WSOP history.

First place was $1m, second place was $420k, and third place was $210k. Monsour Matloubi, the 1990 champion, went out fourth, and with three players left, Bonetti and Jim Bechtel of Arizona, who was doing quite well at the final table, were reasonably close in chip count, about $1m each. The third player, Glenn Cozen from Pasadena, CA, was extremely short-stacked.

Truthfully, I don't remember Cozen playing one hand at the final table until he was forced to go all-in from the big blind with three left with a K-J, where he doubled through Bonetti's two 9s to stay alive. The guy came in second in the main event essentially without playing a hand at the final table!

With blinds at 6/12k, Bechtel raised it to 30k and Bonetti just called with A/K in the small blind. Cozen, with $95k left in the BB, pondered for a pretty good while and then also called. The flop came K-6-4 with two spades. Bonetti checked, Cozen checked, and Bechtel bet 60k. Bonetti check-raised to 180k. Cozen folded but Bechtel called.

The jack of spades came off on the turn. Bonetti, with no spade in his hand, moved all-in! Bechtel snap called him with three 6s. Bonetti was drawing dead! Much to the shock of the crowd, and the delight of Cozen, Bonetti went out in third place.

Bechtel was a quiet guy from Gilbert, AZ. He was also highly respected by pro players. He had placed 11th in the '86 main event, sixth in '88, made the money again in '89, and finally captured the title to become the 1993 world champion. But the guy everybody talked about throughout that tournament, and long after, was John Bonetti.

Bonetti, originally from New York, often said, "Fuggedaboutit". Well, those who were there will never "fuggedabout" Bonetti's domination of the '93 main event – or the way it ended.

1994

This was the Silver Anniversary of the WSOP, and in addition to the $1 million first place prize, Jack Binion was awarding the winner of the main event his weight in silver. The final three guys were John Spadevecchia, Hugh Vincent, and Russ Hamilton. Neither John nor Hugh weighed 150 pounds, but Hamilton tipped the scale at 330 pounds.

Jack Binion, known to be a little on the tight side, appeared to be sweating bullets at how much this would cost him if Hamilton won. And, yes, Hamilton took the title. Sadly, years later, Hamilton became disgraced in the poker world because of a major cheating scandal at UltimateBet.com, an online site in which Hamilton was part-owner.

1995

This was the year that the first woman made it to the final table of the main event. Barbara Enright was a very aggressive player and could always hold her own against the guys. And believe me, very few of them played more aggressively than she did.

As Barbara neared the final table, a buzz was going on throughout the casino and the crowds increased. Everyone was pulling for her to make the final table – and she did. The next day, she came to the final table dressed to the nines and was the overwhelming crowd favorite.

With five players left, Barbara was still there but on the short stack. Action folded around to Brent Carter, who was in the small blind. He was sitting in fourth chip position with not that many more chips than Barbara. Brent limped in and Barbara, in the big blind, then moved all-in. Brent looked around at the other stacks, thought for a few moments, and then called.

They turned up their cards. Barbara showed two 8s and Brent turned up the 6-3 of diamonds! Wow! I was stunned. Brent didn't move all-in with the 6-3 from the small blind in an effort to steal the BB and take the pot; instead, he called off a lot of his chips with a 6-3 after Barbara raised all-in. Like me, the crowd was shocked at Brent's call but was thrilled to see Barbara so far in front.

Unfortunately for Barbara and for the poker world, a 6 and a 3 hit on the flop. Brent flopped two pair and they held. The hopes of a woman winning the main event of the WSOP that day were dashed by that horrendous beat – by what nearly everyone thought was a horrible call by Brent.

Barbara Enright has three WSOP bracelets to her credit and to this day, as of this writing, she is the lone woman to make the WSOP main event final table. Enright was inducted into the Poker Hall of Fame in 2007, the first woman to be inducted. Since then, Linda Johnson (2011) and Jennifer Harman (2015) have joined her in the Poker Hall of Fame.

Dan Harrington was on a heater in '95. He won the $2,500 No Limit Hold 'Em tourney right before the start of the main event and then won the main event! Harrington has a terrific resume in the main event. In addition to his win in '95, he was sixth in '87, 17th in '96, third in '03, fourth in '04, and cashed in '09 as well. Dan also has a WPT title to his credit.

As good a player as Dan is, especially for a guy who doesn't play many events, he may be better known as a noted author who wrote three phenomenal poker books called *Harrington on Hold'em*. Harrington was inducted into the Poker Hall of Fame in 2010.

1996

Huck Seed, a phenomenal young talent, took the main event title in 1996. It was his seventh attempt at this event, entering every year since being 21. Ironically, Seed was the last player (of 295) to enter the tournament.

Huck was an electrical engineering student and star basketball player at the California Institute of Technology. He took a leave of absence from college to play poker. We all saw Huck's potential as a player when he finished runner-up to Stu Ungar in the Four Queens championship event in 1991.

Seed's poker resume is very impressive. He's a long-time high-stakes cash game player, has four WSOP bracelets to his credit, and the best record of any player (14-4) in the NBC Heads-up Poker Championship Tournament, winning that title in 2009. He also finished sixth in the '99 main event and won the WSOP TOC in 2009.

As great a poker player as Huck is, he may be an even better athlete. He was an all-state basketball player in high school in Corvallis, MT, a basketball star in college, he runs like a deer, and he's an excellent golfer. Huck is known for making some amazing prop bets – for big money! Here are some of them:

- ♠ He bet $100k he could break 100 on a golf course four times in one day using only a five-iron, sand wedge, and putter – and do it on foot carrying his own clubs. He did it.
- ♠ Having never done one in his life, he bet that within 30 days he could do a standing back flip. (Huck is 6'5".) He did it. This one impressed me.
- ♠ He bet $50k he could stand in the ocean in shoulder deep water for 18 hours. Oops! He quit after three hours but only after they called the bet off fearing Huck might die.
- ♠ He bet Doyle Brunson $50k he could run a 4:30 mile. He ran 4:32.
- ♠ He wanted to bet $100k that no woman in the world could beat him in both the mile run and 18 holes of golf. No one found a woman they wanted to bet on.

Huck certainly understands that life's a gamble, but I think most of his opponents are gambling more than Huck when they make a bet with him.

1997

1997 will forever be remembered in poker history. That's when Stu Ungar captured his third WSOP main event title, a feat duplicated only by Johnny Moss, and Moss won them three out of the first five years of the WSOP, where 15 players was the most he had to beat. Ungar's third win in the main event was certainly one of the most memorable wins in WSOP history.

I saw Stuey right before the '97 main event started and he looked horrible. It looked like he was completely strung out on drugs, like he hadn't been to sleep, hadn't showered, and he was in scruffy, dirty clothes. He looked pathetic. He was looking to get staked and wanted me to help him find somebody to do that.

The way he looked, I couldn't imagine anybody would stake him in that tournament. He went to Tommy Fisher, then gambler extraordinaire Billy Baxter, but Tommy and Billy told him to look around for someone else.

Billy certainly knew Stuey's talent, but he had a history with him, having staked him in the main event in the past, and it wasn't good history. Once, when Billy was staking him in the main event, Stuey was one of the chip leaders at the end of Day 1, but he didn't show up for the rest of the tourney and Billy lost his $10k.

Because of his scraggly condition in '97, no one wanted to get involved or stake Stuey. Everyone knew he was strung out on drugs. But just as the event was starting, Stuey continued to beg Baxter, and Billy reluctantly staked him on a 50-50 deal. He did it on the condition that Stuey would have to agree that he wouldn't ask Billy to ever stake him again. Stuey agreed.

The breaks were every two hours, and I saw Stuey on the first break. He said to me, "Mike, I can't do it, I can't last. I'll never get through the day." I grabbed him by the shirt, firmly told him it was a miracle he'd found somebody to put him in the tournament and, because he was dead broke, that he couldn't blow this opportunity.

I looked him in the eyes and said, "Stuey, wake up! You've got to get a hold of yourself. Somehow you've got to get through the day and then go get some sleep tonight. You'll be fine by tomorrow." Well, Stuey not only got through the day, he got through it as second chip leader. And he did get rest that night, and plenty of it.

The next day, Stuey came in cleaned up and ready to go. He looked like a new man – showered, shaved, enthused, and eager to play. He was one of the chip leaders at the end of Day 2, and on Day 3, with three tables left, he was at a table with four other previous champions (Doyle Brunson, Bobby Baldwin, Berry Johnston, and Phil Hellmuth) as well as other tough players including Billy Baxter and Chris Bjorn from Sweden. It was an amazing table, perhaps the most difficult tournament table of all time, and the one everybody was watching.

I had told Chris Bjorn for a long time that, when he was straight, Stu Ungar was the best player in the world. This was the first time that Chris had a chance to play with Stuey and, on one of the breaks, he came up to me and said, "Mike, you're right. Stuey is amazing. He's in a class by himself." Stuey dominated that table and was the chip leader going into Day 4, the final table.

That year, only six made it to the ESPN-televised final table. Gabe Kaplan was doing the commentary. Like Stuey, he was from New York. The final table, for the first time ever, was set up outside on Fremont Street between the Horseshoe and the Golden Nugget. It was at least 110 degrees out there, but they had a tent over the table and a mist machine that sprayed water into the massive crowd. Most were there expecting to see Ungar make poker history. He didn't disappoint.

The night before the final table, Baxter said to me, "Go out and bet all you can bet on Stuey to win. Lay up to -140 against the field." Now, there were five other players at the table, so if you had average chips, you'd be a 5-to-1 underdog to win the tournament. Yet, Baxter, one of the shrewdest and most successful sports bettors of all time, made Stuey the favorite against the field and told me to bet all I could on him to win.

Stuey loved it when he heard this because it showed him the

confidence that Billy had in him. He also loved that his man wasn't happy just winning the million, he wanted more. The confidence Billy showed in Stuey really psyched him up for the final table, and nothing but the win would do. The problem I had was that *everyone* thought Stuey was going to win and didn't want to bet against him. Incredibly, even laying -140, I could only get $4k worth of action.

Stuey pulled out a picture of his daughter Stefanie and put it in front of him as the final table got under way. He told her he was going to win it for her. Peter Bao and Bob Walker went out pretty quick. Ron Stanley, who was wearing a tuxedo in all that heat, was second in chips and figured to be Stuey's biggest hurdle. Then, on a board that read A-9-6-8 with two spades, after both checked on the flop, Stanley bet $25k and Stuey raised $60k, which Stanley called. The king of diamonds fell on the river and now Ungar bet $225k.

Stanley thought for a while, showed the 9-7 of diamonds, and mucked. Stuey then showed a Q-10 – a complete bluff – and the crowd went crazy. It was straight downhill for Stanley from there. He picked up two kings, and John Strzemp had 10s but caught a 10 on the turn to double-up; and a short while later and still steaming from getting bluffed by Stuey and outdrawn by Strzemp, Stanley moved all-in on Strzemp holding a J-8 on a board of K-7-2. Strzemp had aces, quickly called, and Stanley was out in fourth place.

Stuey eliminated Mel Judah in third place to take a big chip lead going into heads-up play. It was Ungar vs. Strzemp for the title. Stuey closed out the match in six hands. In his interview with Kaplan, Stuey said, "There's nobody that can beat me playing cards except myself because of my bad habits." It looked like Stuey was back in a big way, but '97 turned out to be Stuey's last time ever to play the WSOP.

1998

The night before the '98 main event started, I was at the bar at the Horseshoe with Todd Brunson. Bob Stupak came up to us and asked if we knew where Stuey was. I told him he was up in his room. Stuey had been at the Horseshoe the entire month but had not come down-stairs yet. I was one of the few that knew it. Stupak and Todd were very surprised Stuey was in the building. Stupak wanted me to take him to his room.

Todd, Stupak and I went up to Stuey's room, knocked on the door and, after inquiring who it was, Stuey let us in. To put it mildly, he didn't look good. He was unshaven and had blackened fingers, meaning he'd been doing crack. Stupak said he wanted to talk to Stu privately and that he'd see us back down at the bar.

Todd and I went back downstairs and discussed Stuey's drug problems and how we could help. Todd was visibly upset. He said he wanted to kidnap Stuey – he didn't care if it was illegal – just take him somewhere where he couldn't get access to any drugs. He really did want to kidnap him – and I thought it was a good idea!

I suggested we take Stuey to Doc Earle's place in Nova Scotia, Canada. To put it mildly, Doc was unique. He was quite a physical specimen, strong as an ox, and extremely intellectual. He was a re-nowned player from Houston, a WSOP bracelet winner, and he really loved Stuey. I knew he would be happy to help us. Stupak came back down and told us Stuey would be OK. He said that after the WSOP was over he was going to help him, meaning look after him and stake him. We aborted our kidnap plans.

When Stuey didn't come down to defend his title the next day, Baxter, who had put up the $10k to enter him, went up to his room. He came back down extremely disappointed saying Stuey would not be playing, and got his $10k entry fee back. It was very disappoint-ing news.

Stuey had told me for a year how much he was looking forward to defending his title. Yet, even though he was broke and getting staked, he refused to come downstairs and play. I couldn't believe he wasn't going to play. I was angry and confused. A buzz went all around the room when it was announced Stuey would not be playing.

Stuey later told me that he had to make a choice. He could play the tournament and hear the whispers from everyone as to how bad he looked (he knew how fucked up he was), or he could not play – and save the dignity of not embarrassing himself in front of everyone. He chose not to play.

Thanks to a one-table satellite that Mike Matusow put him in, Scotty Nguyen did play and won the tournament. Scotty knocked out two players on one hand at the final table, the first and only time that's ever happened. He played Kevin McBride heads-up for the title, and on the last hand of the tournament, with the board showing 8-9-9-8-8, a full house, Scotty moved in and uttered that famous line: "If you call here, it's all over, baby." McBride called, hoping for a split pot, but Scotty had a J-9 for a bigger full house. It was all over.

Scotty's story is pretty amazing in itself. He was one of the Vietnamese boat people, lucky to escape from there, came to America when he was 14, learned the language, worked hard, and found poker like a number of other Vietnamese have. He has five WSOP bracelets and a WPT title. He's also the only player in history who's won the main event of the WSOP and the $50k buy-in Player's Championship, which is a multiple game tournament. And what's a little weird about that is that, after Scotty won Stuey's title, Stuey died the next year and, after he won Chip's title in the $50k HORSE tournament (five different games: Hold 'Em, Omaha Hi/Lo, Razz, Seven Card Stud, and Eight or Better Stud), Chip died the following year.

Although Scotty has made a lot of money playing poker, he has been in and out of money his whole life. Many in the poker world have made bad choices and pissed off huge amounts of money (something I can relate to), but through it all, Scotty, a very prideful guy, remains real in that his personality stays the same – with or without money. And let me add that Scotty is a fan favorite, and for good reason. He always signs autographs and never turns down a picture request from fans, even if it means missing some hands after a tournament break.

Scotty Nguyen was inducted into the Poker Hall of Fame in 2013.

On a fun note regarding the '98 main event (350 entries), I was with Linda Johnson and Jan Fisher when Erik Seidel offered us a proposition bet. The night before the event started, he said we could pick any 60 players to win the main event and that he'd take the field. We took the bet. We gave him our list the next morning and it turned out to be a good one. We had five out of the final six players, including champion Scotty Nguyen.

1999

The '99 main event had a record 393 entrants. It turned out to be the Year of the Irish. Incredibly, given the fact that probably only eight to 10 Irish guys entered, there were three players at the final table from Ireland! They came in first – Noel Furlong, who finished sixth in the '89 main event, third – Padraig Parkinson – who's been in the money three times in the main event, and eighth – George McKeever, who has finished in the money six times in the main event.

With six players left, former champion Huck Seed was still in, as were former runner-up Erik Seidel and the eventual runner-up in this tourney, Alan Goehring, who is a two-time WPT champion. It was a *very* tough final table.

Noel Furlong, a successful businessman and big-time horse bettor, is from Dublin, Ireland. He's called Noel because he was born on Christmas Day. Noel was aggressive before aggressive became cool. He may have been more aggressive than Stu Ungar and John Bonetti put together, and that's saying a lot.

Furlong may not have been known in the US, but he was well known in Irish poker circles. He won the Irish Poker Championship twice – and believe me, it's no easy feat to win the Irish Poker Championship. Furlong was also the last player over age 40 ever to win the main event. (Greg Raymer was 40 when he won in 2004.)

I know that because, over the past five years, I've taken 10-1 that someone 40 or over would win the WSOP main event. No one in those years has come close. (Yes, I know 61-year-old Neil Blumenfield came third in 2015, but he really never came close to winning.) I've done my money every year – but I'm going to keep trying. I'll be taking 10-1 on that prop as long as I can find the young guns (or anyone else) who will keep laying it. Hey, life's a gamble.

How about raising your glass and toasting the Irish's performance at the WSOP main event in 1999. It really was remarkable.

2000

The 2000 main event was the first time they guaranteed $1.5 million for first place and, as a result, had the largest percentage jump in entrants in WSOP history, from 393 in '99 to 512 in 2000. I remember it well because it was my deepest run ever in the main event. I finished in 12th place in that tournament and I still think about what might have been.

As the final table was getting closer, I felt like I had a good shot to win it. I'd played the main event eight previous times and had finished at the third table on four occasions prior to 2000, so I felt I was ready for the pressure that accompanies going deep in the main event.

Back then, when you bought in for $10k, you got 10k in starting chips. I was above average in chips with 485k, I felt good about the way I was playing, and, truthfully, I felt comfortable. I liked my chances.

There were six players at each table and a hand came up where I'm in the big blind with A-9. The blinds had just gone to 15/30k with a 2k ante. The first man to act limped in, so did the next guy, as did the button and small blind. It was five-way action and there was $162k in the pot now. It looked to me like a good spot to try to pick up the pot, so I raised 170k – just over the size of the pot.

I didn't move all-in because there's a slogan in poker, "Beware of the Limper", and it especially applies to the guy under the gun. I didn't really think someone would be limping in under the gun with a big hand at this stage of the tournament, but in this case, if the guy under the gun ("Captain Tom" Franklin) moved in over the top of me, I was going to throw my hand away where I'd still have 285k to play with. Well, it goes fold, fold, and then Jeff Shulman, who was the son of Card Player owner Barry Shulman and playing in his first-ever main event, who was also the big chip leader at the time, sat there for a few seconds and then announced, "I'm all-in." Yikes.

Everyone on the rail jumps up and gathers around the table because it's now a monster pot. I stayed calm on the outside, but on the inside my stomach felt like a washing machine on full throttle. I thought to myself, *What could this guy possibly have, not to have raised previously?* I then said out loud, "What could you have here but two 4s or two 5s?" Although I was hoping for an A-5 or similar hand, after some thought, I said, "I call." And sure enough, Jeff turned up two 4s. Needless to say, he won the race.

In poker, you always play the "what if" game after losing a big pot. *What if I'd played the hand differently? What if I'd moved all-in instead of raising 170k? Would Jeff have called? What if I'd just knocked the table, seen the flop, and then thrown my hand away?* In hindsight, I don't fault the way I played the hand. Jeff made a bold play and I needed to win a race. I didn't.

With seven players left, Chris Ferguson, who has a PhD in math and computer science from UCLA and was the backbone of starting FullTilt a few years later, was still left. He was second or third in chips, but had less than half as many chips as Shulman. He and Jeff played a big pot which, after a raising battle, got all the money in before the flop. Ferguson had two 6s and Shulman had two 7s. Ferguson hit lightning and made three 6s to double-up. So now he had nearly as many chips as Jeff had.

On the very next deal they got into another raising battle, and again, all the chips went in the pot. This time, Shulman had two kings, but Ferguson picked up two aces! He doubled through Jeff one more time, leaving him on the respirator in terms of chip count.

Only six made it to the televised final table and Shulman, who had a *huge* chip lead with seven left, went out in seventh place. As a footnote, Shulman made it back to the final table again in 2008. That year, he played a monster pot where he got it all-in pre-flop with jacks vs. Joe Cada's 3s. Cada flopped a 3 to knock him out. Shulman was extremely unlucky both times he made the main event final table, losing two giant pots with pair over pair.

With six players left in 2000, Chris Ferguson had a big chip lead. Jim McManus, an English professor and writer from Chicago, finished fifth in the tournament. McManus had come to Las Vegas on assignment to write about Ted Binion's murder for *Harper's Magazine*. He took his fee and entered a one-table satellite in an attempt to win an entry into the main event.

He won that satellite and subsequently wrote what I think is as good a book on poker reality as you will ever read. It was about his experience at the 2000 WSOP called *Positively Fifth Street*. It's great!

The heads-up battle came down to Ferguson and T.J. Cloutier. At that time, T.J. was by far the most successful guy in tournament poker history. In addition to his six WSOP bracelets, Cloutier finished second in the main event in '85, fifth in '88, third in '98, and here he was playing heads-up for the title in 2000.

In addition, Cloutier also won Amarillo Slim's Super Bowl of Poker in '90 and the Diamond Jim Brady championship event, now called the Legends of Poker, at the Bicycle Casino three consecutive years, from 1990 to 1992! That is truly remarkable.

Although Ferguson had a big chip lead when heads-up play started, no one was counting Cloutier out. T.J., who at one point was a 10-1 chip underdog, kept fighting and chipping away, and finally they were about dead even in chips. The final hand was raised by Chris and re-raised all-in before the flop by T.J. Chris thought for a moment and called. The cards were turned up: Cloutier had A-Q and Ferguson had A-9.

The flop came K-4-2. Another king came on the turn. With one card to go, Ferguson had to catch a 9 to win. He could have split the pot if a 4 or 2 would have come on the river. Sure enough, as you know, a magical 9 for Chris appeared on the river, and Chris "Jesus" Ferguson became the world champion of poker. T.J. was extremely gracious in defeat and uttered the famous words heard around the world: "That's poker."

Everyone knows about that final hand, but few know about the hand that took place right before that. They were about even in chips and T.J. raised on the button with A-7 of hearts. Chris moved all-in from the big blind with A-2 of spades and T.J. called. The board rolled out K-10-3-Q-9 and they split the pot. So it was not once, but twice that T.J. had the best hand with all the money in the pot, but lady luck wasn't shining on him. In dice terms, he seven'd out.

T.J. Cloutier was inducted into the Poker Hall of Fame in 2006.

Sometimes, things are just meant to be. To become world champion, Chris Ferguson had to outdraw Jeff Shulman with 6s vs. 7s for all the dough with seven players left to stay alive, pick up aces when Jeff had kings to double-up again, and then spike a 9 on the river with one card to go to wear the crown. It just shows you how luck and fate play a role in determining tournament winners, including the WSOP main event. When it's all said and done, to win any tournament, the poker gods have to be smiling on you.

Ferguson was a founder and primary shareholder in the online site, Full Tilt Poker. When Black Friday occurred on April 15, 2011, online poker was shut down in the US. Full Tilt didn't have the funds to pay their players. It was a big black eye to the poker industry and Chris was deemed one of the responsible parties. It was a very sad state of affairs for Chris and the poker community. PokerStars later bought FullTilt for $731m to settle a civil lawsuit with the Department of Justice and a portion of this money was designated to pay the FullTilt players back.

Trivia question: There are three former WSOP main event winners whose pictures have been removed from the Ring of Honor during the World Series of Poker. Who are they?

- ♠ Russ Hamilton (cheating scandal on UltimateBet)
- ♠ Chris Ferguson (Full Tilt scandal)
- ♠ Bill Smith (his family wanted money from the RIO to put Bill's picture up or have it removed – so they took it down).

2001

Carlos "The Matador" Mortensen from Spain won the 2001 main event (613 entries). He's the only Hispanic main event winner. He parlayed a win from the Bay 101 Shooting Stars Tournament two months earlier, where the winner received an entry into the main event of the WSOP, and then won the WSOP main event as well. That was *very* impressive.

Carlos, with two WSOP bracelets and three WPT titles (which is tied for the most all time with Gus Hansen, Anthony Zinno and Chino Rheem), is the only person in the world who's won the main event of the WSOP and the main event on the WPT. He's one of the biggest winners in tournament poker history with $11.5m in earnings. He's also one of the most renowned chip stackers in the poker world – and, invariably, he has a lot of chips to stack.

I hope you've enjoyed some of the stories of the WSOP prior to television and the "poker explosion". From the next year on, the poker world changes forever.

Poker Comes to TV

The WPT started in 2002. The televised WPT events started airing on March 30, 2003. And make no mistake about it, the WPT is the primary reason for the "poker explosion". I get upset when I hear otherwise. It's something I feel passionate about and feel everyone should know. The first poker show on in prime time weekly – the WPT – was the primary reason for the "poker explosion".

Combine that with the fact that online poker was picking up steam and that, in 2003, Chris Moneymaker, an accountant from Tennessee, parlayed a $40 online satellite (and he didn't even know that he was playing in a WSOP satellite, he just thought he was play-ing in a tournament for cash) into winning his seat into the WSOP main event – and then won! His win, two months *after* the WPT started, brought many more to the online world, to say nothing of many more who came to play in the main event of the WSOP the years after. There is no doubt that the "Moneymaker effect" was real.

Moneymaker's win became historic. His "average man" status gave everyone the idea "If he can do it, I can do it", and from there, because of the combination of televised poker, which was so popular, and online poker, which was growing like crazy, the main event at the WSOP just exploded and continued to grow in numbers.

It tripled the entries in 2004 (with 2,576), increased by over 3,000 in 2005 (with 5,619), and then set the all-time record in 2006 (with 8,773 entries) when Jamie Gold took the title and won $12 million. That 2006 main event was the largest prize pool in the history of sports until the One Drop tournament at the WSOP in 2012.

But let's not forget those poker pioneers who played the WSOP in the 1970s that made it all possible.

14 Gamblin' on the Golf Course

When betting on golf, you need to have a brain or a game.

Harold Henning

Gambling on the golf course is as good as it gets. It doesn't matter your skill level, there are numerous ways to handicap golf where everyone is equal – giving strokes, spotting distance off the tee, using fewer clubs than your opponent, giving someone an extra tee shot or extra putt, one guy scrambles two balls vs. another scrambling three balls, etc, etc. I could play Tiger Woods, Rory McIlroy, or Jordan Spieth even up, meaning it would be 50/50 as to who would win, if the spot was right.

A smart gambler once said, "Matching up is the key to success in golf as most outcomes are won or lost on the first tee." In the big matches I used to watch in Las Vegas, it seemed like it took forever for players to make a game. They would start negotiating at breakfast in the clubhouse, then go to the driving range, then hit chip shots and bunker shots, and then go to the putting green, all the while proposing (and negating) bets. Even after all that, many times they still didn't have a game. But, as frustrating as it seemed at times, most seemed to relish in the negotiation process.

From my experience, I've discovered that you're far better off making a game in advance of getting to the golf course. That way, once there, you just warm up and tee off without hassling. And many times, we put in an attachment to a wager made prior to getting to the course: "Anyone that doesn't show up pays off one bet."

I've also discovered that the more that people and groups meet at the golf course the tougher it is to match up and get a game. People knock bets or other players, or immediately want to bet on one side or another as soon as they hear a proposal, thus scaring the other guy out of the bet; "the more the merrier" isn't always the best way to get action at the golf course. An old gambler once told me, "If just two people meet at the golf course, they never have a problem making a game."

In matching up, you must first know what you can shoot at the game you're playing, plus have a good idea of what your opponent will shoot. For example, suppose you are a 90 shooter and are playing someone who says they are also a 90 shooter. If you shoot 98, you are supposed to lose. If, on the other hand, you shoot 86, you should win. If you don't, you made a bad game.

You Need a Game or a Brain

One of my best friends was Harold Henning. He was a professional golfer who played on the Senior Tour. He once said to me, "Mike, when gambling on golf, you need a game or a brain, and you don't have either." Ouch! He was right. My swing is weak and I'm an action guy – a bad combination. I remember the first time I ever played golf with Puggy Pearson. As soon as he saw my golf swing and watched me tee off on the first hole, he looked at me and said, "Son, I promise you one thing. I'll never quit you."

I met Harold in '89 one Friday night in the fall while playing in a $30/60 Limit Hold 'Em game at the Golden Nugget. He was sitting on my left and J.C. Pearson (Puggy's brother) was sitting on his left. J.C. said to me, "Mike, do you know who this is?" I said, "No, I'm sorry I don't." He said, "It's Harold Henning and he's in town playing in the Senior Tour's golf tournament." I nodded and said, "Nice to meet you, Harold."

We kept playing and J.C. then said, "Harold, Mike likes to play golf, too." And Harold, just being nice, looked at me and said, "Maybe we can play sometime." Most golfers would love to play a round with a pro, but I replied, "Harold, don't take this personally, but I don't play golf for fun. I like to gamble when I play golf." He lit up like a Christmas tree, laughed, and exclaimed, "I don't want to play for fun, either!"

A little later in the game, I noticed Harold was looking over a sheet from the Sportsbook with all the football games on it. He said to me, "Do you like anybody this weekend?" I told him I spoke to a handicapper earlier in the day and he liked three games. Harold said, "Who does he like?" I gave him the three teams and he checked them off. He said, "Do you like anybody else?" I said, "Harold, I like a lot of games but I'm like the worst picker of all time." He said, "Give them to me." I gave him nine other teams I liked.

Incredibly, 11 out of the 12 games I gave Harold won! I went back to the Golden Nugget on Monday and the floorman said, "Mike, I've got something for you." He brought out a bag with three-dozen golf balls and two golf gloves in it, along with a note from Harold. It said, "Mike, thanks for the picks! Please call me this week."

It turned out that Harold, a great golfer from South Africa, loved to play cards, bet on sports, and play in the casino. He was pretty much an action junkie. Because of that, we bonded immediately. I called him every week with picks, but I don't think we ever had another winning weekend. We did, however, become great friends. He came to Vegas as much as possible, where we gambled and played golf together, and I went to tour stops with him whenever I could. We were two peas in a pod – and lovable losers betting on sports.

Getting It Up and Down

Harold would come to Vegas and we would play golf with poker player gamblers, usually Puggy Pearson and Tommy Fisher, both good golfers who would shoot in the high 70s. He would spot each of them 20 yards off the tee and give them four shots a side. We would also play a team bet where I would play the red tees and Harold and I would give them two a side. It was a tough match but always fun to play.

We played at Spanish Trail once and, on this particular day, Puggy shot 75 – but did it hitting only three greens in regulation! He literally got it up and down on every hole. It was the most amazing chipping and putting display you'll ever see.

Harold lost $7,000 to Puggy that day. We got back in the clubhouse and as Harold was writing out his check, he said, "Puggy, let me tell you something. I've played with the greatest golfers in the world for the last 40 years – Arnold Palmer, Jack Nicklaus, Lee Trevino, Ray Floyd. I've played with all of them. And there's not one of them – not one – who can chip and putt as good as you do." Puggy wiggled that cigar, broke into a big, wide grin, reached out and grabbed that check from Harold and said, "You should have seen me 10 years ago."

Greatest Putter Ever?

Once, while I was sweating the high-stakes game, a discussion came up about who the greatest putter in the world was. A question was asked, "If you had a 10-foot putt and you had to pick someone to putt it where you'd be shot and killed if they missed it, but you got to live if they made it, who would you have putt it?"

The first guy said Ben Crenshaw, the next guy said Tom Watson, the next said Jack Nicklaus, and then it was Doyle's turn to answer, and he said, "Puggy Pearson". They all turned to Doyle, laughed, and someone said, "Puggy Pearson? You've got to be kidding." Doyle emphatically said, "That's right! Puggy Pearson. Puggy's the greatest pressure putter I've ever seen. I'll tell you one thing about Puggy. He won't dog it. He might miss it, but you'll get a good roll for your life."

Speaking of Putting

In the gambling world, Stu Ungar became a bigger legend on the golf course than he was at cards. That's because he couldn't play and gambled sky-high. He was a thing of beauty on the golf course. He wore two golf gloves (which I do, having picked that up from Stuey) and always got to put his ball on a tee – whether in the fairway, rough, or bunker. He even had a 3-foot tee in his bag in case he went in the water, where he could tee it up and play it. Some of those who played with Stuey for the first time were shocked by him getting to tee it up everywhere, but nobody really minded because he was such a fish.

Stuey grew up in New York, had never played golf, and didn't know anything about the game, including how to hold a club. Well, for a long time, Jack Straus kept telling Stuey that all the high-stakes action was on the golf course, which it was, and not in the poker room. He knew Stuey was an action sicko, and if he could get him to the golf course, he thought he could win a lot of money off him.

Finally, one day in the mid '80s, Jack got Stuey to go with him to Las Vegas Country Club. Once there, he said, "Stuey, before anyone can gamble at golf, they have to develop some skill at hitting the ball, but the most important thing in golf is putting. You've got to learn how to putt." So, he took him to the putting green and started showing Stu how to putt.

The next thing you know, Jack set Stuey's ball about 3 feet from the hole and put his 10 feet away and said, "Let's bet $500 and see who can get the ball in the hole in the fewest strokes." Stuey grinned and took the bet. After Jack got ahead, Stuey wanted more spot. So, Jack adjusted the bet – he started spotting him a stroke a hole where they were the same distance from the hole. Then, as Jack kept winning, he backed his ball up and left Stuey's in the same place and made the same bet.

It wasn't long before they upped the bet to $1k a hole, then $2k a hole, and then $5k a hole. In just over two hours time, Stuey lost $68,000! I would make a bet that, in the history of America, no one else has ever gone to the golf course for the first time and lost $68k – without even making it to the course!

A One-Sided Scramble Match

One time, Stuey and I had a match in Las Vegas against two guys who had flown in from Memphis on a private jet to play us. We were playing a scramble match at Canyon Gate. It was a $20k Nassau with one automatic press a side, meaning we could win or lose $100,000. This was quite a high-stakes bet back then (1990). I was betting $5k Nassau and Stuey was betting $15k.

In a scramble, you both hit a shot and you play the best shot between the two of you, so when you reach the green, you take the closest ball to the hole and putt two balls from there. If two guys can play mediocre golf, when they're scrambling their ball, they should be able to shoot par without much difficulty.

In this match, Stuey was on the red tees, I was on the white tees with the rich guy from Memphis, and the other guy was on the blue tees. It only took a few holes for me to see that these guys were way better than us. They birdied 1 and 2 and we pressed, which was automatic, but I knew we were in trouble. They birdied 4 and 5. We were four down, but Stuey insisted we press again. They birdied 7 and 8. We were even par, not that bad for us, but we were six down going into number 9!

We had a very bad game. It was obvious they were way better than us, and although I tried hard to talk him out of it, Stuey told them, "We press again." They hit their usual perfect tee shot and I hit a pretty good tee shot. My approach shot was about a foot off the left edge of the green, about 15 feet away from the flag. They hit their second shot to within 6 feet of the hole. Luckily, I knocked our putt in from off the green to birdie the hole, but it goes without saying, they birdied the hole also. We lost three bets on the front nine and were lucky we didn't lose four bets.

In gamblers' rules, you have a chance to quit after nine holes. You have to pay off the Nassau (the 18 hole bet) but you don't have to play the back nine. So, in my mind, we were going to pay off the Nassau and lose four bets – enough punishment for one day.

We go in to grab a quick sandwich and Stuey ducks into the bathroom. When he comes out, he had powder on his nose – not good. He said to me, "We're going to double them on the back nine." I said, "Stuey, are you out of your mind? Can't you see this is the most one-sided match in the history of golf? If we don't make that putt on number 9 from off the green, we'd have lost seven-up in nine holes, playing a scramble! It's unheard of. And we didn't play bad. We shot one under par!"

Stuey was totally on tilt and said, "No, we're going to gamble. We're going to double on the back." I said emphatically, "Well, I'm not. I'm paying off my $20k and I'm done." Stuey said, "No. No. No. Come on, you've got to play. I'm going to stake you on the back nine." Shaking my head, I reluctantly said, "Stuey, I'll play, but you're just giving your money away – giving it away!"

So, we get to number 10 tee and Stuey announced, "We're doubling." Now the rich guy from Memphis howls, "Oh no you're not. You're going to get out of this trap like you got in it. We're not taking any doubles." Hearing that, Stuey went ballistic. He started screaming and hollering, cussing them out. He went over to his bag and grabbed a club out of it like he wanted to hit the guy with it. I stopped him but then I started laughing.

The guy from Memphis said, "What's so funny?" I answered, "What's so funny is that you guys have got the greatest stick-up match in the history of golf against a guy who's looking to sail off like a rocket ship, and you guys won't take the double. I can't believe it." The guy said, "I'll tell you what. If you pay off the Nassau, we'll play some other bet on the back nine." The chances of us winning that Nassau against these two guys in the same game we just played, were probably more than 10,000 to 1.

Stuey and I couldn't believe what we heard – they wouldn't take the double! As a gambler, in your wildest dreams, you couldn't find a better match than this – if you were them. And for them not to take a double when they were six up and essentially four bets ahead, well, to me, it was bizarre – just off the board. To this day, it's still impossible for me to contemplate they didn't take the double. I told them, "You guys are good and know how to match up, but you sure don't know how to take it off."

So, after I got Stuey to calm down, we negotiated a new bet. The adjustment: I went up to the ladies' tee with Stuey, and their good player, who was on the blue tees, went all the way back to the championship tees. This was a much better game for us. It was a far worse game for them. Even after getting trounced like we did on the front nine, I liked our side of this bet and thought we might get some of our money back.

Can you imagine? Rather than play us the same game they crushed us at for $40k with one automatic press, they went to this game for $20k w/1 press. On the back nine, we made two 20-footers and a 15-footer, shot 3 under, and won 1-up. We won back $20k, but still lost $60k for the day.

This gives you an idea of how action-oriented Stuey was. That he was going to double that match with the same game where we lost 6-up, and could have lost 7-up had I not made the putt from off the green on number 9, in nine holes *scrambling*, is mind-boggling.

The kicker to the story is that, when we got back to the clubhouse, we negotiated the same match we played on the back nine for the next day. Stuey and I got out to the course early and were feeling good. We knew we had a game we could get some of our money back. Then, we got a call from the rich guy telling us his A player, who had no money and was getting staked in this match, was up all night playing blackjack, hung over, and couldn't play. Damn!

Needless to say, Stuey went crazy when they didn't show. This is why many gamblers have a forfeit bet where you have to pay off one bet if someone doesn't show up after a match has been made. It's definitely a good idea and one that I'm in favor of, but when Stuey was your partner, I was fine without the forfeit bet. It was far more likely that Stuey would be the one not to show up.

A Seven Handicap?

Jack Binion used to host an annual Professional Gambler's Invitational golf tournament, where he'd invite gamblers from all over the country to play. He charged $5k a person to enter. It was a three-day golf tournament where each day Jack would match you up with somebody else with the same handicap you had. It was mandatory that you played a minimum $500 Nassau each of the three days, and if you wanted to bet more with a guy, you and he negotiated the extra stakes, and nearly always everyone bet more. Jack took out $500 from the entry fee for green fees, food, drinks, hotel rooms, running the tournament, etc.

Gamblers from all over the country would come to Las Vegas to play in Jack's golf tournament. One year, it was held at Angel Park, which is not a tough golf course. They had Puggy listed as a seven handicap. He was matched up with some guy from Georgia and they bet an extra $2k Nassau. I finished and was in the clubhouse when Puggy came over to our table shaking his head, saying, "I can't believe that guy they matched me up with today. There's *no way* that guy's a seven handicap. He's way better than that." And I asked, "How did you do?" Puggy said, "Do you know that I had to shoot a 69 to beat that son-of-a-bitch?" And the whole table cracked up.

I was standing next to Puggy one day at the WSOP when a reporter was interviewing him. The reporter said, "Puggy, I know you're a champion poker player, but I hear you play pretty good golf as well. Just how good do you play?" Puggy looked at him, broke into a big grin, wiggled his cigar, and said in his W.C. Fields voice, "I shoot whatever it takes to get the money." And he could. Puggy was one of the few players that I've ever seen, that the more money he bet, the better he played. You can put Doyle and his high-stakes partner, Dewey Tomko, in that category, too. Puggy could really play for the dough.

Should I Sandbag?

Not long after I came into big money, my partypoker money, I was in LA playing poker and golf. A bunch of us agreed to play golf one day at Rio Hondo golf course near the Bicycle Casino. I teamed up with Richie Sklar, a guy I had met a couple years earlier at a golf tournament at La Costa in San Diego. We made a number of bets. Richie was a very good player but was broke, so I staked him in our matches. We had a good day and won $20k.

I gave him his $10k, and after the round, he asked me what I was doing next. I said, "I'm going back to Vegas." I asked him what he was doing and he said, "I'm following you!"

After we got back to Vegas, I set up a best ball match at Shadow Creek for Richie and me vs. Phil Ivey and Matt Othick. Ivey and myself were on the front tees and Richie and Matt were on the back tees. At the time, there were only two sets of tees at Shadow Creek. Matt, a former basketball player at Arizona, was a great athlete and an excellent golfer. But, at that time, I was better than Ivey – meaning I thought I would help in the match much more than Ivey would, thus giving us an edge.

On the driving range as we were warming up, Richie said, "I'm going to lay down and sandbag a little. We don't want to lose Ivey." I said, "Don't lay down. Play as hard as you can. We're playing for a lot of money." Richie asked, "How much?" I said, "$40,000 a hole!" The look on his face was priceless. He exclaimed, "Wow! $40k a hole?"

The sandbag plan was out the window.

On the first hole, Richie hit a perfect 300-yard drive down the middle and then hit a wedge in the leather for a birdie. Sweet. On the par 4 second hole, he hit another good drive, which was good because I hit a bad one. But, he hit a bad second shot. He was long and left and had a very tough third shot. Matt was on the green 25 feet from the hole. I was out of the hole so it was up to Richie. He was at least 50 feet away and on a steep hill. The green slanted way back toward the fairway and the ball was going to break at least 20 feet to the right. Getting it within 12 feet of the hole would be a terrific shot.

Richie hits the ball great from tee to green, but is not a good chipper or putter. He doesn't ever chip around the green if there's any way he can putt. So, he got out his putter and putted his ball higher up the hill to allow for the huge break. It started curving around, reached the green, and started tracking the hole. Somehow, even though it was going fast, it hit the flagstick dead center and went in! It was a miracle. Matt missed his putt and we were 2-up. We finished the day 6-up, winning $240k. Richie, a Californian all his life, never left Vegas. He stuck to me like glue.

Lesson Learned?

Tommy Fisher and I were playing Puggy Pearson and Billy Walters one day at Canyon Gate. As we came to the 18th tee, the team was 1-1 and I broke even with Puggy on the front nine. I was 0-2 with Puggy, with another press coming. Number 18 is a very tough par 4 and all the money was on the line. There is water all the way down the right side of the hole as well as in front of the green. There's also a long bunker guarding the water on the right.

I hit a poor drive. I dubbed it down the middle, so there was no chance I could go for the green in two. I just choked. Puggy then sliced a ball to the right and I felt sure it went in the water. I went from despair to joyous because I felt sure he hit it in the water. We drove over to the corner of the water and couldn't find Puggy's ball. Sweet.

I went over to my ball and laid up. Then, I heard Puggy screaming, "I see it. I see it. There it is in the middle of the bunker." Well, there was a ball in the bunker, but it couldn't have been Puggy's ball, nor Tommy or Billy's because they were on the left side of the fairway, because it was at least 50 yards farther than I knew he hit it. I knew Puggy was putting in a false claim.

Puggy drove up to the ball in the bunker, which was 175 yards out and all carry across the water, and hit an amazing shot out of the bunker to the middle of the green. He then started racing up to the green. I quickly hit my third shot and raced to the green as well. I wanted to see the ball Puggy hit. We both jumped out of our carts and I got to his ball first. It was a cut up Titleist (which really made his second shot that much more impressive) – and Puggy *always* played with Ultras. I said, "Puggy, that's not your ball. You always play with an Ultra. You lose the hole." He countered, "It is my ball. I just changed balls on the 18th tee."

After everyone putted out, Tommy and I got back in our cart and I said, "I know that wasn't Puggy's ball. Let's go back and find it." He agreed. As we turned around to head back down the fairway, Puggy started screaming, "Hey. What are you doing? Where are you going?" I shouted back, "Puggy, we're going to go find your ball."

We drove back to the corner of the water with Puggy following us, who was still screaming that it was his ball in the bunker, and we started looking for the ball. We spotted what looked like a new ball about 6 feet out in the water. Tommy got a club and I held his hand as he fished out the ball. "Voilà", it was an Ultra ball with a La Costa logo on it – just where we played three days earlier! I picked up the ball, tossed it to Puggy, and said, "Here's your ball, Puggy. It's an Ultra with a La Costa logo." He didn't say a word. Tommy and I got back in the cart and headed toward the clubhouse.

As we were ordering lunch, I was still complaining about Puggy trying to pull a fast one on us. I said, "Puggy, I can't believe you did that." Blushing, he said, "What could I do? That ball was just sitting there in the trap." Billy then said, "Puggy, I hope you learned a lesson today." Puggy said, "I sure did. I'll never use another logo'd ball again as long as I live."

All the high-stakes gambling golfers knew that Puggy was one you had to watch. He would always want his own cart and would tip the cart boy $100 to give him the fastest cart they had. After he teed off, he would jump in his cart and race down the fairway to get to his ball first. Whenever he hit it in the rough, in the trees, or over a hill, somehow, he always had a shot. He never seemed to have a bad lie. I'm sure it was just a coincidence.

Doyle used to invoke the "Puggy Rule" when he played with him. The "Puggy Rule" meant that any time Puggy got ahead of you on a hole, he automatically lost the hole. Doyle is a clever man.

At least on this occasion, justice prevailed.

Maybe You Should Warm Up

When Phil Ivey first started playing golf, it was a reincarnation of Stu Ungar. He couldn't play and loved to bet high – the perfect combination for the lions looking for the limping gazelle.

One day, after we played the previous day, about eight of us were waiting for Ivey to show up at TPC Summerlin. He was over an hour late, but he was "it" and nobody wanted to tee off without him. Finally, Doyle said, "OK. Forget about Phil. It looks like he's not coming. Let's make some games and go play." So, we made matches and went to the first tee.

Doyle's group teed off first and just about as they were ready to drive off, here came Ivey racing around the corner, hollering, "Wait! Wait for me! I want to play." You have to know Doyle to appreciate this, but he shouted back, "Sorry, Phil. You're too late. We've already made our games. We'll see you tomorrow." Ivey, having reached the tee by now, protested, "No! No! I really want to play."

Doyle snarled back at him, "Well, let's go then. Hit the ball. If you want to play, hit it and let's go. You can put your golf shoes on after you hit. I've got the same bet with you as yesterday, $20k a hole." Ivey didn't play Nassaus. He always bet by the hole.

Phil got out of the cart, headed to the tee in his street shoes, and said, "OK. You got it." I then said, "I'll play you the same bet as yesterday for $10k a hole". Others quickly followed, "I've got you for $5k a hole", another said, "I've got you for $2k a hole", another said for "$1k a hole", and Phil said OK to everybody.

There's a small set of bushes about 2 feet high at the end of first tee box, about 5 yards away from where we were teeing off. Phil dubbed his first shot right into the shrubs. Everyone tried not to laugh. He then hit his second shot into the same bushes. Disgusted, he said, "I can't play like this. I've got to warm up. I'll catch up with you guys on the course after I warm up." He then got in his cart and headed back toward the practice range.

I hadn't hit a shot, hadn't even gotten out of the cart yet, and was up $10k. Phil came driving back up when the first group reached the par 3 fifth hole – and all bets continued. He stepped on the tee and hit it in the rocks short of the green. Again, he lost the hole to everybody. He "X'd" (didn't finish the hole) four holes out of the next five after he came back out to play. He quit after number 9. He only played six holes out of nine, but lost $200k." I beat him for $40k. Those were the days.

Unlike Ungar, Ivey didn't stay a sucker on the golf course for long. He teamed up with Danny Dotson, who may have been the best amateur player in the country at one time, practiced a lot, and got *way* better before too long. And Dotson didn't let Phil make any matches without his OK – which meant Phil became nearly impossible to match up with.

How to Rank Players

It's surprising, and pretty amazing, to most good golfers when they see bad players bet so much money on the golf course. It really is mind-boggling to the average person. But in the gambling world, everything is relevant. What's a big bet to some might not be to someone else. To high-stakes poker players, it's only natural to bet high on the golf course, regardless of your skill level.

We went to a golf outing once with 16 players. We were going to make up four teams and play a scramble format. There was a lot of commotion as to who would be an "A", a "B", a "C", and a "D" player. "A" players are the best, "B" the next best, and "D" players the worst golfers.

As the bickering continued, Stuey said to everyone, "Why is this so hard to figure out? It's easy. Here's how you rank players: regardless of how they play, anyone that's over $1m winner in his life playing golf is automatically an 'A' player. Anyone who is plus in their life at golf is a 'B' player, those who are even or up to $1m loser in their life are 'C' players, and anyone who is over $1m loser at golf is automatically a 'D' player." Everyone laughed, but Stuey was serious. He felt players should be rated on how they've done financially over the course of their life, not on how good or bad they played.

What's the Catch?

I was a member of Spanish Trail in Vegas and Richie and I were heading over to the course to practice one day. As we were reaching the first tee, around the corner came Russ Hamilton and Denny Mason. They had just finished playing nine holes and Russ, who was laughing, said to me, "Hey, Mike. Come join us. We're playing for $25k a hole, but you can play cheap if you like – for $5k a hole. And you won't believe how horrible we're playing!" Denny seconded that. Richie whispered to me, "These guys are a better team than Dean Martin and Jerry Lewis."

I knew Russ had been away from golf for quite a while. He was an owner of the poker site UltimateBet, and was trying to put together a televised blackjack tour called Ultimate Blackjack. Still, I was always leery when it came to betting Russ.

The first time Russ played at Augusta National, the home of the Masters, he made a hole-in-one on number 12 and did something on number 18 that I'd wager has never been done before or since. He parred number 18 hitting driver, driver, driver, driver. Yes! He hit two drivers to the green and whenever Russ's ball would break left to right, he preferred putting with his driver rather than his putter. Thus, he two-putted number 18 with his driver to make par on the hole using nothing but his driver.

Years ago, when I first started gambling with Russ on the golf course, a bunch of us went to St George, UT, to play golf for a few days. Russ acted like he was a 90 shooter, and although he shot that the first few days, it seemingly happened by him making an 8 or a 9 on two holes a side, but he played the rest of the holes well. On the last day there, Russ upped his bets substantially with everyone. He started out with a bogey on the first hole and then made eight consecutive pars. He busted everybody.

The point is, I knew he was a golf hustler. So, even though he'd been away for a while, I was skeptical about playing him. But, because he hadn't played in a long time, I thought I would try it for a few holes just to see what happened. Well, I won the first four holes with bogeys (I don't think he finished a hole) to go up $20k. Rather than being upset or mad, he was laughing at how bad he was. He then wanted to double the bet to $10k a hole. I said "OK".

I won three of the next four holes while only making one par. I was up $50k going into the last hole! I kept trying to figure out what the catch was, what he was up to. I couldn't believe he was this bad. We got to the tee on the last hole, a par 5, and he said, "Let's play this hole for $50k." Extremely suspicious and not wanting to give it all back, I said, "I'll play this hole for $30k if you like." He said, "OK. That's fine."

I made a par and won the hole. I couldn't believe it. He then went to his golf bag, got out $80k in $5k Bellagio chips and gave them to me. He laughed again and said, "I told you how bad we were." I kept waiting for the hustle but it never came. I just went out to practice a little, ran into Russ, and won $80k. That was the last time I ever saw Russ.

Looking back on it, I'm guessing that the $80k I won that day came from some of the losers on the online poker site UltimateBet. For those who may not know, there was a cheating scandal on UltimateBet where someone in the company could see the players' cards on the website – while they were playing in the game!

UltimateBet made refunds to certain players when the scandal was uncovered. One of those players to get a refund was Bobby Hoff. When he got a check in the mail for $22k, he was quite surprised. He chuckled and said, "I know I've been cheated a number of times in my life playing poker, but this is the first time anyone ever gave me anything back."

Ha! Ha! Ha! Ha! Ha!

Watching Doyle Brunson, Jack Straus, and Stu Ungar play golf together was like going to the circus – a three-ring circus at that. It was truly a spectacle to behold.

Jack was 6'6" and Stuey was about 5'6" and weighed 110 pounds soaking wet. Doyle weighed well over 300 pounds. These guys were the farthest thing from your average-looking golf group. Jack and Stuey would team up to play Doyle. They would scramble their ball against Doyle playing one ball. It was Mutt and Jeff vs. Goliath. And they would bet big money!

They were playing one day at the Las Vegas Country Club on what was certainly one of the hottest days of the summer. On this day, Doyle had a surprise for his counterparts. He brought a "laughing box" with him to the golf course and snuck it on his cart. Every time Jack or Stuey would hit a bad shot, which was often, Doyle would hit the button on the box and it would go "Ha! Ha! Ha! Ha! Ha!"

Doyle crushed them on the first 18 holes, winning $120k, and the laughing box got quite a workout. But, Jack and Stuey weren't finished. They were stuck and wanted to play more. Doyle said it was too hot to play any more, but when they said they wouldn't pay him unless he played more, he headed back to the tee for another 18 holes.

Well, the heat started getting to Doyle. Because of that, he started playing worse. Jack and Stuey were winning the second round. As the holes were going by, Doyle was becoming visibly fatigued. It took him longer and longer to hit a shot. On the 16th hole on the back nine, Doyle, now losing back all he won on the first 18 holes, just slumped in his cart overcome with heat exhaustion. Having no sympathy, Straus snuck up to his cart and hit the button, "Ha! Ha! Ha! Ha! Ha!" It was just another fun day at the golf course – or should I say the circus?

15 David "Chip" Reese

Why did I choose poker over law as a profession? I decided to choose the more honorable of the two professions.

Chip Reese

Chip Reese is a legend in the poker world. If you talk to any of the high-stakes poker players who were around Las Vegas in the '70s or '80s and asked them, "Who do you think is the best all-round poker player of all time?", I'm fairly certain that every one of them would say, "Chip Reese".

Chip was inducted into the Poker Hall of Fame in 1992, the youngest player to be honored in this way. They later incorporated the Chip Reese Rule which states that no one under the age of 40 (younger than Chip) can ever be inducted into the Poker Hall of

Fame. It's a great rule.

Up until his untimely death at the age of 56, on December 4, 2007, Chip was probably the most successful cash game player of all time, certainly in Las Vegas casinos. In the old days, the cash games were much bigger than what you could win in most tournaments, so Chip didn't play many tournaments. Nevertheless, he still captured three WSOP titles, including the inaugural $50k buy-in HORSE tournament in 2006, good for $1,784,640. At the time, it was the biggest buy-in tournament in history.

The David Reese Memorial Trophy was inaugurated in 2008 and would go to the winner of the WSOP $50k HORSE tournament. In 2010, the name of that tournament was changed to the Players Championship, but the winner still gets the David Reese Memorial Trophy, one of the most coveted prizes in poker.

Chip grew up in Centerville, OH, a suburb of Dayton. He was sick as a kid and, during his elementary school days, stayed home for nearly a year with rheumatic fever. While at home, his mom taught him board games and card games, including poker. He was a whiz at board and card games, and also in school.

In high school, he played football and was on the debate team. He was such a good debater, he won the Ohio State Championship debate title and competed in the National Finals. He went to Dartmouth, majoring in economics. He was accepted to Stanford Law School, but a successful trip to Las Vegas, the summer following his college graduation, with his buddy Danny Robison, changed his career plans.

I was standing next to Chip once when he was being interviewed at the WSOP. The reporter asked, "Chip, I know you were considering Stanford Law School after graduating from Dartmouth. Why did you choose poker as a profession rather than law?" Chip answered, "I decided to choose the more honorable of the two professions." It was classic.

At Dartmouth, Chip became a member of Beta Theta Pi fraternity. While there, he had tremendous success playing poker, bridge, and other card games. He also taught his fraternity brothers how to play and then extracted some inheritance money from them. Upon graduation, the fraternity named their chapter card room the David E. Reese Memorial Card Room in his honor.

As you learned in Chapter 8, I met and became friends with Chip on my first trip to Vegas in 1977. I stayed at his and Danny Robison's house. Danny was one of my best friends growing up. I noticed there was paperwork spread all over the living room as soon as I entered. It was Chip's notes for his chapter on Seven Card Stud that he was writing for Doyle Brunson's book *Super System*. I couldn't believe the effort Chip put into writing that chapter. That book is still considered to be the Bible of the poker world.

Many players wonder, "Why was Chip such a good poker player? How did he do it? Why was he so much better than everyone else?" First and foremost, he was blessed with a great deal of intelligence. He was simply smarter than just about everyone. Chip also knew the gambling world inside and out. He was an expert at all forms of poker, as well as gin rummy, blackjack, backgammon, and other games. Sports betting was also a passion of his.

Guys that bet like Chip and Doyle, meaning bet big, were known as "line movers" in the sports betting world. That sparked an idea between Chip, Doyle, and Dewey Tomko. Tomko is an excellent golfer and member of the Poker Hall of Fame. They came up with an idea to start a sports tout business, where people would pay a fee to get picks from the poker icons, sharp gamblers, and highest rollers in Vegas, which they were. Their primary selling point: they would bet on the same picks they gave out.

The threesome formed a company called The Line Movers. They promoted and advertised the business strongly before they launched. The first week of football season, they went like 2-12. The next week it was something like 4-8. Not only did they lose a fortune betting on their picks, the phones quit ringing. So much for The Line Movers.

I thought The Line Movers was a great idea so, naturally, I was a customer. Who wouldn't want to be in with these Las Vegas legends?

I'm sure it would have worked very well had they given out winners. With their record, however, people wanted to book them, not follow them. For me, it was just a normal two weeks of betting.

Chip found another answer to success in the sports betting world, betting baseball. One summer, while building a new house at TPC Summerlin, he had a computer guru work for him. The guy created a program where he ran possible line-ups through his computer thousands of times prior to the game starting. This gave Chip a predictable percentage of one team winning over the other. If the bookies betting line was different than what their computer thought it should be, Chip would bet the game at up to $100k a pop.

He was having a great summer betting baseball. It was so good, in fact, that he told his wife, Norlene, that she could go and spend whatever she wanted on the interior of the new house. As the house was going up, Chip told me that it was a good thing he was having a winning baseball season as his wife was spending money like crazy. Every day, he said, she would order some imported Italian tile for $80k, buy some antique for $50k, get a custom fireplace for $200k, etc. I've never forgotten what Chip said about that: "I gave her an unlimited budget, and she exceeded it!"

One thing I really admired about Chip was how close he was with his children, especially his son Casey. Once Casey started playing baseball, aged about 6 or 7, Chip was there at most practices and all his games. No matter how good a poker game was, Chip would leave to go to Casey's games. I don't think he missed one of Casey's games from Little League thru high school. In addition, he provided Casey, who was a good pitcher, with tutorage and private workout sessions with top coaches. He also took him to the World Series nearly every year. (If you were as successful as Chip, you could do that, too.)

Poker Tip – be Like Chip

Here's something that I find pretty amazing. For over 25 years, Chip always played in the biggest game in the room, regardless of the type of game being played. It was always the biggest, never the second biggest. In my opinion, that fact alone should qualify one for the Poker Hall of Fame. Another thing that jumped out at you when you watched Chip play was his conduct at the table. We may never play as well as he did, but we should all strive to "Be Like Chip" at the table.

In his entire career, I never saw or heard about him criticizing an opponent, moaning about a bad beat, throwing cards, or blaming the dealer after losing a pot. He was the epitome of class. He was the gold standard for how one should behave at the poker table. Even though he was so good, because of his courtesy, friendliness, and professionalism, tourists loved playing with Chip. If they ever start a Conduct Hall of Fame for poker, I'm certain that Chip Reese would be the first inductee.

It has always baffled me how players can get angry at a dealer when they lose a pot. Some verbally abuse them and others wing the cards back at them, or just leave the cards in front of them, forcing the dealer to stretch clear across the table to get them. Dealers are simply trying to make a living. They just deliver the mail. I always wondered this about those who abuse dealers when they lose a pot: when the mailman brings bills to their house, do you think they throw them back in his face?

Where's the Edge?

There are two things in poker that separate the good from the average, and the great from the good. The first is the "steam factor" (go on tilt) and the second is the fortitude to take it off (not be afraid to win). Chip never steamed and could well be the greatest take-off man in history.

I once asked Chip, "The guys you play against are tough. What separates you from them?" He said, "You're right, Mike. They are tough. In fact, when they play their A game, I'm really no better than they are. The difference is that they also have a C and D game, whereas I don't. They become weak players when they steam and just about all of them do. My edge is that I don't steam."

When gambling, whether in the casino or in a poker game, most people, when they win a little, quit and run. On the flip side, when they're losing, they go off like a rocket ship. That formula for gambling is just the opposite of what they should be doing. I call this "the human element" and it's really why casinos do so well. You should press (bet more) when you're ahead and playing on house money, and bet less when you're losing. But, not many do it.

Chip had an edge playing poker in that he wasn't afraid to win. You're probably wondering, "Who's afraid of winning?" Read on. If others are losing, they're probably steaming or playing badly. *Regardless* of how much Chip was winning, he would stay and play with them if they wanted to play. He always accommodated the losers if they wanted to continue playing.

Once, I was sitting in Bobby's Room at Bellagio when a man from Beverly Hills came up to Chip and said, "Hi Chip, how are you doing?" I didn't know him, but Chip did. He was a successful businessman who Chip had played with on occasion. Chip said, "Hi. I'm doing fine. How about you?" The guy replied, "Fine, thanks. Do you want to play some $1,000/$2,000 Stud?" Chip said "Sure".

They ordered chips. Chip introduced me and then asked the guy if he minded if I watched for a while (a polite gesture), and the guy said, "No. Not at all." So, they started playing and I sweated Chip.

The guy got on a heater right off the bat, and in only 20 minutes he was up $30k. He folded a couple hands and then started looking at his watch. He said "Chip, I'm sorry, but I just remembered that I've got to meet my wife for lunch." Chip said, "Sure, sure, go ahead. Don't worry about it. We'll play some later. Thanks for playing."

Most guys would have started screaming, *What are you talking about? We just started playing. I can't believe you're quitting!* Chip was just the opposite. He thanked the guy for playing and said he'd see him later. As soon as the guy left, Chip turned to me and said, "That's why I've got all the money."

I looked at him quizzically. The guy just beat Chip for $30,000! Chip then said, "Most players are just like he is. They play for a while, win a little, and then get up and quit. But, when they get stuck, they stay and play until they go for their lungs." He told me that guy would have played all night had he gotten behind. Then, he smiled and said, "He'll be back."

Nightmares

One February in the late '80s I got a call from Chip. He said, "Doyle and I are going out to play some golf. Come out and play with us. You'll have the nuts. We haven't hit a ball since last summer." I quickly said, "Thanks! I'd love to play, Chip, but I haven't got any money." He said, "Don't worry about it, we'll play cheap, just a $500 Nassau. And you can owe if you lose."

Now, if you're broke and sitting around the house trying to figure out your next move, getting a phone call like that is like hitting the lottery. I quickly said, "Thanks! I'd love to play. I'm on the way." I gathered my clubs and headed to Las Vegas Country Club.

Chip was the kind of golfer who didn't play well after a long layoff. He was pretty good, an 80-82 shooter, if he played every day for a month or so, but might not shoot 100 if he hadn't played in a while. And Doyle figured to be pretty rusty after this long layoff. For these guys, a $500 Nassau was cheap, meaning they probably wouldn't put forth their best effort, which would give me a decent chance to win.

It was fun playing with these guys. There was a lot of laughter, a lot of needling, and a lot of prop bets around the course. It was also fun to watch Chip hit the ball. He stood over the ball and then would flex his knees and bounce up and down a few times before he would hit it.

On this particular day, he wasn't bouncing too well. He played horribly and Doyle didn't play much better. But, rather than be mad or upset about how they were playing, they were laughing all the way around the course at how bad they were. They were just happy to be outside. The money we were betting meant nothing to them. I, on the other hand, was playing for my life.

I beat both of them for two bets on the front nine. Even after playing badly, and not even finishing at least five holes on the front nine, Chip said he would double on the back if I gave him a stroke. Doyle said the same thing. I was happy to accommodate them.

It didn't get any better for Chip on the back nine. I beat him for two bets. He owed me $3,500. I beat Doyle for one bet on the back. He owed me $2,500. I was ecstatic! I had a bankroll again.

Then, as we were driving back toward the clubhouse, Chip said, "Let's play some more!" Doyle said it was OK with him, and even though I was happy to quit winner, I was fine with playing more. (It was extremely rare to catch these guys on a day like this.) On the second 18 holes, I played Doyle the same but gave Chip another shot a side. I played them both for a $1,000 Nassau.

The extra stroke didn't help Chip. I beat him for a bet on the front nine and closed him out for two bets after number 17 on the back nine. He said, "I'm done. I'll just ride in and watch you and the tall Poppy play number 18." Thus, Chip owed me $7,500. Sweet.

I beat Doyle one up on the front and was one up on the back nine going into number 18. That meant the worst I could do with Doyle was win two bets from him on the provisional 18 holes, for a total of a minimum $4,500 from him. If I tied or beat him on number 18, he would owe me $5,500. What a great day – from zero money to $12k–13k (which was like $100k to me at that time)!

Number 18 at Las Vegas Country Club is a par 5 with water in front of the green. Long hitters can easily reach the green in two, but if I hit two perfect shots, I'd be 100 yards out. And that's what I did. Doyle hit two good shots as well and was just in front of me. As I stepped up to hit my shot, Chip said, "Wait a minute. I want to bet you can't get down in three from here." I stepped away from my ball.

It was a perfect wedge for me and the flag was in the center of the green. No tricks. I'm not good off the tee, but with a wedge and putter, I'm a pretty good player. I felt I could, should or would make a three from where I was in the fairway *at least* eight times out of 10. I asked, "You want to bet I can't get down in three strokes from here?" And Chip said, "Yes." I said, "OK, I'll bet you $3k I can." He said, "No. It's all or nothing. I want to bet everything I owe you, the entire $7,500."

Well, I knew I was a big favorite to make three from there, and even if I didn't, I was going to win at least $4,500 from Doyle, so I said, "You've got a bet." Doyle now chirped up, "I want the same bet. I'm betting all my money, too." I didn't really want to hear that. I'd played all day (36 holes), but now I knew that if I messed this hole up, I would go home with the same amount I started the day with: zippity-doo-dah.

Doyle continued, "You gave Chip the bet. You've got to give it to me, too." I said *fuck it* to myself, and then said to Doyle, "OK. You can bet all your money, too!" I couldn't help but think about how much money I would have ($26k) if I could just hit one simple wedge shot. And for me, it was a simple shot. I stepped up to the ball, but then backed off. My heart was pounding and, suddenly, I felt very nervous. I just wanted to take a deep breath and clear my mind.

I stepped back up to the ball, rubbed my hands together, said *you can do this* to myself, swung, and hit the ball. I immediately started screaming, "Go! Goooo!", but to no avail. Splash! The ball barely got halfway across the water. It was 100% choke. I was devastated and dropped my head so they wouldn't see the tears in my eyes.

Chip and Doyle laughed so loud, I'm sure people could hear them all the way over in Caesars Palace valet parking. After his hysterical laughter subsided, Chip then roared, "I knew you were a poopy dog. I just wanted to see how big a poopy dog you are!"

He was right. To this day, I've never grabbed the handlebars on a golf course worse in my life! I went up and dropped a ball in front of the lake as I could still make a "3" if I holed it out. In a lame effort, I chipped the next shot in the water as well, bringing more loud laughter from the boys.

All these years later, I still sometimes wake up in the middle of the night and hear those guys laughing. It's a nightmare – and a choke – that I'll never forget.

Climbing the Ladder

I was grateful that I met Chip in 1977. We were good friends for the next 30 years. He was the idol of just about every poker player, including me. He had it all: intelligence, money, and respect.

Chip helped me out a number of times in my life when I needed money, usually for $5k or $10k. Every time, he would say something like, "I know you're going to make it, just keep fighting." Once, however, he said, "Mike, don't be discouraged. Let me tell you something: climbing the ladder to the top is more fun than when you get there."

Well, I never believed that then, when I was climbing the ladder, or when I got to the top! Chip was right about almost everything, but I believe he got this one wrong. I'm guessing that Lyle Berman would agree with me, and not Chip, on this. When I saw Lyle after I sold my partypoker shares, the first thing he said to me was, "Isn't it nice to have 'fuck you' money?" Trust me, climbing the ladder was a lot of fun, but it's better at the top.

Once, however, I was in a jackpot where I needed more money, a lot more. I needed $60k. It killed me to have to ask Chip for that kind of money, but I had nowhere else to go. Even though I'd always paid him back, at that time of my life, I didn't have a job, didn't play in the highest stakes poker games, had no outside investment money coming in, and Chip knew I was a reprehensible sports bettor. Friends or not, I knew in my heart that Chip wouldn't go for $60k – nor should he. But, I had to try.

I called him, said I needed to talk to him, and he told me to come over in the morning. That afternoon, I went to my life insurance agent and switched a $100k policy over to Chip's name and made him the beneficiary. I then wrote out 15 checks for the next 15 months for $5k each (so he would eventually get back $75k for his $60k loan).

I took all that over to Chip's house the next morning.

Naturally, he didn't want to loan me that much money. But, he was so impressed that I'd made him the beneficiary of a life insurance policy in case something happened to me and wrote out all the payments in advance, that he gave it to me. And to show you what kind of guy he was, after he cashed the 12th check, he gave me back my last three checks and said, "I appreciate your offer to pay interest, Mike, but I don't want any. I'm just happy you're back on your feet." How blessed can one be to have had a friend like that? Chip was the greatest of all time, on and off the felt.

16 Doyle "Texas Dolly" Brunson

*You judge a hunter by the
number of furs he brings home.*

Doyle Brunson

Doyle Brunson is the Godfather of Poker. He is one of the greatest and most respected poker players of all time. He's a living legend in the poker world – a two-time world champion, a 10-time bracelet winner at the WSOP, a WPT title holder, the ultimate high-stakes cash game player, and he wrote what many consider to be the Bible of poker, *Super System*.

As you learned earlier in the book, I first met Doyle on the golf course at Las Vegas Country Club on my first day in Las Vegas in 1977. I had just flown in from NC the night before and immediately I bet on my friend Danny Robison in a golf game against Doyle. I lost 80% of my bankroll. I was wowed at how good Doyle had played, especially because of his size (which was huge). But even though I lost and hated him for beating me out of my money as we went around the course that day, I couldn't help but admire him.

I later learned that Doyle was a terrific athlete. In high school, he was all-state in basketball and track, and all district in baseball. He went on to become a track and basketball star at Hardin-Simmons College and was even offered a contract with the Minneapolis Lakers. Unfortunately for him, he had an accident one summer while working at a sheet metal plant and injured his knee, thus killing any hopes of playing pro basketball.

When I met Doyle, I didn't know about any of that, but I could see he was a really good golfer. I did know he was the reigning world champion of poker when I met him, but poker results meant nothing on the golf course. No one ever mentioned or discussed them at the golf course.

They were playing for a lot of money, I was pulling for Danny, and Doyle had just met me, but he was quite friendly with me during the round. I told him I lived in North Carolina, and once I brought up basketball, specifically Atlantic Coast Conference (ACC) basketball and how good the North Carolina Tar Heels were, he didn't stop talking, mostly about how good the University of Nevada Las Vegas (UNLV) Runnin' Rebels were. I'm a big Buckeye fan, but when I moved to NC, I learned to appreciate and love ACC basketball. It was by far the best conference in basketball in those days.

I told Doyle that UNLV might be good, but that they could never beat North Carolina. I said the Tar Heels had the best player in the country in Phil Ford, plus Walter Davis and Mike O'Koren, to say nothing about having coach Dean Smith. Doyle said, "Well, you can't believe how good the Runnin' Rebels are. They've got Eddie Owens, Reggie Theus, Glen Gondrezick, and Sam Smith, and those guys fly up and down the court." He was right about that — UNLV averaged 107 points per game that season.

I said, "Doyle, you just can't believe how good the teams in the ACC are and, by playing that good competition, I can't see anybody beating the Tar Heels." He said, "I know they're good, but I just wish you could see the Runnin' Rebels play and then let me know your opinion." Looking back on it, I chuckle because I was so emphatic that day about my basketball knowledge. I had no idea Doyle was ever a basketball player, let alone drafted by the pros.

Back in the mid to late '70s, getting a ticket to the Runnin' Rebel games was tougher than getting one for any show on the strip. At the end of the round, Doyle asked me, "How long are you in town for? Maybe I'll take you to a game so you can see for yourself." (I didn't hate him any more.)

To my surprise, a few days later, Doyle invited me to go to a UNLV game with him. Wow! To not even know me and to invite me to a UNLV game was pretty impressive. I was thrilled to go. He was right about one thing: that Runnin' Rebels team was incredible. They were really fun to watch and unbelievably strong at home, going 19-0 at home that season.

It turned out that both UNLV and North Carolina made it to the Final Four that year. What was a little disappointing to most was that they were the two best teams, but met in the semifinal game. But what a game! North Carolina beat UNLV 84-83. Then, to everyone's shock and amazement, Marquette upset the Tar Heels in the championship game. It was Al McGuire's last game as a college coach.

If you're too young to know who Al McGuire was, you missed out on knowing an original. After coaching basketball for over 20 years (and at Marquette from 1964 to 1977), he became a basketball announcer for another 20 years. He was the first to use slogans like "white knuckler" for a close game and "aircraft carrier" for a big man in the middle. He was great and everybody loved him.

McGuire was a street-smart guy from New York. He would say, "I'm an Einstein of the streets and an Oxford scholar of common sense. I grew up in New York, and if you fall down there, you get picked up by the wallet." He had a rule about recruiting: "I didn't recruit a kid if he had grass in front of his house. That's not my world. My world is a cracked sidewalk."

McGuire would say, "Winning is overrated. The only time it's really important is in war and surgery." Another saying of his was regarding the only mystery in life: "Why did kamikaze pilots wear helmets?"

To keep players eligible, he said, "Our guys took shop and advanced shop. Shop is when they build a chair. Advanced shop is when they paint it." And one of his most famous lines (which is hard to argue with), "Everyone should go to college and get a degree. The following year, they should drive a cab for six months and then tend bar for six months. After that, they'll really be educated."

Beware of Betting the Chalk

Prior to the turn of the century and televised poker, limit poker was all anyone played, at least in the Vegas casinos. I was primarily a $30/60 and $50/100 player back then and those were decent stakes, but weren't near the biggest stakes in the room. Even though I didn't play with the big boys, I felt fortunate because I became good friends with virtually all of the high-stakes players. They just sort of accepted me because of my friendship with Chip and Danny.

When you hang around high rollers in Vegas, there are perks and good things happen. I remember being in Las Vegas for the Muhammad Ali and Leon Spinks heavyweight championship fight on Feb 15, 1978. It was at the Las Vegas Hilton and a lot of the high-stakes poker players were going: Chip, Danny, Doyle, Billy Baxter, Tommy Fisher, and Joey Hawthorne (who wrote the lowball chapter in Doyle's book *Super System*). Lucky for me, Chip and Danny got me a ticket to join them and, needless to say, they were ringside seats. It was the first world championship boxing match I had ever seen and I was really excited about it!

Leon Spinks was in the Marine Corps (1973–76) and was the 1976 Olympic light heavyweight champion. (His brother Michael won the gold medal in the middleweight division that same Olympics.) It was only the eighth pro fight for Spinks, which was the shortest time in history for a guy to possibly win the title. Most thought he was too young, too inexperienced, and too small to be in a heavyweight championship fight.

Ali was "the greatest of all time" and a 10–1 favorite. Most everyone, including me, thought he was a lock. Everyone, that is, except most of the guys I went with. Chip, Danny, Billy, and Tommy all took Spinks getting 10–1.

Long before the main event started, Joey Hawthorne proclaimed with authority, "Ali is the nuts! He won't get knocked out and he will never lose a decision. He's too big a star and it means too much money for boxing for him to lose." I agreed entirely with that logic. Doyle was convinced by Hawthorne to take Ali, so he did. "It's like stealing", Hawthorne kept saying.

My problem was that I had been in town a week, had gotten broke, was leaving town to go back to NC the next day, and had no money to bet, especially to lay 10–1 odds. Chip and Danny knew that I liked Ali and said I could bet them and owe if I lost. How could I pass on that? I bet Ali and laid them $10k to $1k. Doyle and Hawthorne had Ali for much bigger money. I can clearly remember how electric it was in the arena that night. I was there with the big boys, gambling legends in Vegas, and, more importantly, I was back in action!

Ding! Here we go! I had serious concerns at the end of Round 1 as Spinks came out fast and looked good. Ding! It was the same story for Round 2. Spinks had clearly won the first two rounds. It didn't look good at all for the Ali bettors. Doyle was screaming at Hawthorne, "I can't believe you got me in this trap. I just can't fuckin' believe it!"

Hawthorne remained confident. At the end of Round 2, after being cussed out by Doyle, he said to Doyle and everyone sitting around us, "I will take Ali and lay 8−1 and take all the action you like!" Incredibly, no one bet him any more money. I wanted to bet him so bad. But, breaking even or losing $2k didn't seem like the smart thing to do, so I said *fuck it*, and kept my bet. Ding. Ding. Ding. The fight went to a decision. After every round, my head felt like the guy hitting the bell with the hammer was pounding my head. Spinks dominated the fight. It looked like Spinks won at least 11 rounds out of 15. It was a rocking chair. I was sick and I could see Doyle felt worse than I did.

The ring announcer then shouted, "Ladies and gentleman, we have a split decision." WTF? Was it possible? I was sitting right next to Chip and as soon as he heard those words, he said, "If Ali wins this fight, the whole world's on the take." The next words I remember hearing, "And the *new*..."

Chip, Danny, Billy, and Tommy were celebrating and high-fiving. I could have been celebrating with them − and be $10k richer. I was cussing myself out for not betting the same side as Chip and Danny. I stayed at their house all week and could have been rooting with them. Instead, I left town broke and owed them $10k.

Doyle was speechless. I almost felt worse for him than I did myself as I know he lost a fortune. Hawthorne just kept mumbling, "I can't believe it. I can't believe it." Another lock bites the dust.

Leon Spinks was the only man ever to take the title from Ali in the ring. His other losses were non-title contests or bouts where Ali was the challenger. Spinks was stripped of his World Boxing Council title when he opted for a return match with Ali instead of fighting the number-one contender, Ken Norton. In the rematch (for the World Boxing Association title), it was a unanimous 15 round decision for Ali, making him the first three-time heavyweight champion in history ('64, '74, and '78). Guess whom I bet there?

You've Got to Give Action to Get Action

Doyle has always believed, "You've got to give action to get action." In poker, if you don't play a pot for two hours, you're most likely not going to get any action when you finally do play one – nor should you. Smart players are good about accommodating tourists in games. For example, if a tourist was losing in a game and then wanted to flip a coin or make prop bets on the color of the flop (neither of which give you an edge), to keep him happy and maybe keep him in the game, you should give him action, especially if you're winning. Doyle is good at that.

In my life, I've never seen anybody create more action, especially on the golf course, than Doyle. He actually gave a fair game most of the time, but his edge was that he forced his opponents to bet higher than they normally like to play for, to get them out of their comfort zone, and because of that, they choked. Doyle, and his long-time high-stakes golf partner Dewey Tomko, as well as Puggy Pearson, are about the only three guys I've ever known that the more they bet, the better they play. For most of us, it's just the opposite.

When you're around Doyle, just expect to gamble higher – and I don't care what you're doing, whether it's poker, gin, playing golf, making prop bets, or wagering on sports. Somehow, he has that knack to make everyone gamble it up and play higher. You'll read about some of his high-stakes golf matches (one in particular where he and I were partners) in Chapter 20 – Big Action! The guy is remarkable, a true gambling legend.

Doyle is as old school as it gets. He cut his teeth playing poker on the treacherous Exchange Avenue in Fort Worth, TX. Doyle, T.J. Cloutier, and other gamblers from Texas told me what a really tough area it was there in Fort Worth. For quite a while, Doyle traveled the white line in Texas playing in games from one town to the next. For many years, he was partners and traveled the road with Sailor Roberts and Amarillo Slim. All three later became WSOP world champions!

I used to love to talk about the old days, and what it was like traveling the road, with Johnny Moss, poker legend and the first man inducted into the Poker Hall of Fame (1979). He said, "Beating the games was the easy part. Getting out of town with the money was what was tough." He told me about the cheats you had to fade, the law, the hijackers, etc. He also said, "Always keep your money in a rubber band. It saved me $5k once when I was getting robbed after I left a poker game. I reached in my pockets and as I put my hands up, I threw the money in a bush – and they didn't get it." I've put my money in a rubber band ever since Moss told me that story.

I don't think players today appreciate what the old school guys went through – what it was like as a poker player years ago and/ or what it took to survive. I'm also not sure they appreciate what they've got today.

They play in luxurious casinos, can play and quit whenever they like, don't have to worry about getting paid, don't get robbed (at least in the casino), and don't have to worry about getting busted and spending the night in jail. Yes, there are many more great players today, meaning it's not easy to win, but playing against good competition seems a much better proposition than looking down the barrel of a shotgun during or after a game.

Who are the Best Players?

According to Doyle (the title of a column he used to write) the old school guys from Texas were as good as – in fact, even better than – today's young guns. He also believes that the high-stakes cash game players, not the tournament players, are the best players in the world. I'm not sure about his old Texas buddies beating today's whiz kids, but I do agree with him that the best players in the world are the winning high-stakes cash game players.

Years ago at the WSOP, the newspaper *Poker Player* was doing a survey among players to try and rate the best all-round players in the world, as well as the best player in each particular game. A reporter asked Doyle, "Who do you think are the best players in the world?" And Doyle's answer was simple. He said, "You judge a hunter by the number of furs he brings home."

Once, a reporter was doing an article on Eric Drache, the WSOP tournament director at the time. I was standing next to Doyle when the guy said, "Doyle, I hear that Eric Drache is quite a Seven Card Stud player. Just how good is he?" Doyle said, "You're right. Eric is a helluva Seven Card Stud player. In fact, he might be the seventh best Seven Card Stud player in the world." The reporter said, "Wow." Then Doyle continued, "But his problem is that he plays with the top six every day."

We all know that you don't have to be anywhere near the best player in the world to win money playing poker. You don't even have to be the best, or second best, third best, or fourth best player in your game to win. You do have to be better than some, though, if you expect to beat the game. (You would need some real producers in the game to win consistently if you're not in the top half of skilled players in your game.) That story about Eric is one that you should keep in your pocket.

Doyle has been playing high-stakes poker all his life. He was the only person in the world to play the main event of the WSOP every year for the first 30 years. He only stopped in '99 because his best friend Jack Binion had a squabble with his sister Becky Behnen over him building additional casinos in the south, where she wasn't included; as a result of their squabble, Jack sold his remaining interests in Binion's Horseshoe in Las Vegas to Becky, acquired the rights to the name of Horseshoe Casino outside Nevada, and moved to Mississippi. It turned out to be a brilliant move for Jack (a total workaholic) as he later sold his properties for $2 billion!

Out of loyalty to Jack, Doyle and Chip didn't go to the WSOP for three years (until Jack told them to go back and play). Doyle is still the oldest player ever to win a WPT title (at 71). Even today, as of this writing, in his 80s, you can find Doyle at Bobby's room in Bellagio playing mega-stakes mixed games. And he always invites the young guns, and anyone else, to join him.

Doyle's Advice

Doyle's advice to players: if you are having problems, personal or business, solve them before playing poker. He said his biggest losing streaks followed something bad that happened and that severely impacted his focus and concentration. He also said you should calculate your wins and losses by the year, not the month or the day. And finally, according to Doyle, if you can't handle losses, you're in the wrong game.

17 Walter Clyde "Puggy" Pearson

Don't ever worry about money you owe someone else. Let them worry about it.

Puggy Pearson

Walter Clyde, otherwise known as "Puggy", Pearson (1929–2006), was one of the true characters of the poker world. He was from the hills of Tennessee, had nine brothers and sisters, and dropped out of school after the fourth grade to help make money for the family. He joined the Navy on his 17th birthday, became a Navy frogman, now the Navy Seals, and did three hitches in the Navy.

He recognized his talents as a gambler when he was in the Navy.

He was a shark in a world of minnows whether he was playing cards, shooting pool, or loan-sharking. When he got out of the Navy, he had a decent bankroll, and he knew then that gambling, scuffling, and hustling would be his career.

About growing up, he said, "We were so poor that we had to move every time the rent came due." He then added, "I didn't know what shoes were until I left home." His education was the "school of hard knocks", but don't confuse his lack of formal education with not being intelligent. Puggy was a brilliant guy.

Puggy moved to Las Vegas in 1963. He played in the highest stakes cash games in Las Vegas for over 25 years. He played very few tournaments because it went against his grain to "win all the money and then give most of it back". (He used to say he would play every tournament if it were a winner-take-all.) He won the world championship in 1973, along with two other bracelets that year, has four WSOP bracelets to his credit, and was the second living person to be inducted into the Poker Hall of Fame in 1987 (behind Johnny Moss).

Puggy was the only ultra-high-stakes poker player I've ever known who didn't bet on sports or play in the pit. He would say, "Why would I want to bet my money on some goofballs trying to score a touchdown or make a basket? I want to bet my money on *me*." And he didn't hesitate to bet big money on himself – doing anything. He liked to think of himself as the world's greatest rounder.

The Rovin' Gambler

Puggy called himself a roving gambler and owned a bus that he named the "Rovin' Gambler". On the side of the bus in large letters was his name and the quote, "I'll play any man from any land, any game that he can name, for any amount that he can count", and then in very fine print in the corner of the bus, it said, "Provided I like it." That summed up Puggy pretty well. He used to park it outside the Horseshoe during the WSOP and it was quite an attraction.

He grew up tough and came from a background with people

who "did whatever they were big enough to do". He said that, in the old days, when a dispute came up among the gamblers, nobody went to the cops. They solved everything between themselves.

Puggy's skill as a golfer and a pool player, and talent as a poker player, was remarkable. However, he also had a somewhat notorious reputation. You had to keep your eye on him at the poker table as well as the golf course. He took shots in a poker game by shorting the pot, acting like he would bet and then pull his money back if was being called, etc. And as mentioned earlier in the book, he nudged his ball to a better lie on the golf course whenever he got the opportunity. To him, getting the money was the important thing, not how you got it.

Underwater Prop Bet

In the late 1980s, I had some poker players over to my house once for a barbecue. I had a decent size pool in the backyard (20 yards long) and a prop bet came up between Puggy and Tommy Fisher. Tommy wanted to bet he could swim two lengths under water. Someone said they would bet him if he made it three laps. While Tommy was pondering taking the bet, Puggy, who was in his late 50s at the time, said, "I'll tell you boys what I'll do. I'll bet I will go twice as far under water as Tommy does."

That got everybody's attention and Tommy spoke right up, "I'll take that bet for $2k." Well, because Tommy bet on it, so did the rest of us. We bet $1k each, so Puggy was now betting $6k and he took all the action. It was agreed that they couldn't dive in to start. They had to get in the water, push off, and go.

They stripped down to their underwear and Tommy went first. He did just over three laps under water. We were all patting him on the back thinking we had the nuts. Puggy then got in and, as soon as he finished the first lap, I had a feeling we were in trouble. He swam as smooth as any shark in the ocean. Back and forth he went. Knowing he had won the bet, he stopped after seven laps. My respect for Puggy and Navy frogmen skyrocketed after I witnessed that.

Golf is Where it's at

Puggy discovered that there was big action in golf, and he loved big action, so he learned how to play. He got beaten early on, but said to himself: *They put their britches on the same way I do. They won't beat me next time.* He was determined to get better. And boy, did he! He practiced faithfully, hit balls for hours each day, and in just a couple of years he became a scratch player.

Golf is a hustler's dream, and Puggy took advantage of that. A reporter heard that Puggy was a good golfer, and once asked him, "Puggy, I understand you're good at golf. Just how well do you play?" Puggy grinned, wiggled that cigar, and said, "I shoot whatever it takes to get the money." And he could.

Old School Vegas Poker

Puggy wasn't exactly known for being a gentleman with the dealers. (Many old school players fell in that category.) He did give them a big tip, though, if his opponent might have overlooked his hand and the dealer dummied up and didn't point out to that player that they had the winning hand, and then pushed the pot to Puggy. He'd put a green chip ($25) out there for the dealer, wink, and say "thank you".

In those days, fights broke out sometimes when people not in the pot said anything. The unwritten rule was, *if you're not in the pot, dummy up.* Even a number of dealers adhered to it. The logic was that if a player didn't know what he had, he didn't deserve to win the pot.

It was a different time. You may or may not know, but the casinos didn't run the poker rooms in the old days, they were leased out to individuals. They more or less ignored what went on in poker rooms – and let's just say that it wasn't safe to play in *all* poker rooms!

When I first came to Vegas, Johnny Moss ran the Dunes poker room. That's where the big games were held. A number of casino owners played there regularly. This was where and when many of the old school pros like Puggy, Doyle, and Chip built their bank-rolls. Moss was notorious for his bad behavior at the table and totally abused dealers. Following his example, many others did the same. If you didn't have thick skin, and I mean really thick skin, dealing poker in Vegas, especially at the Dunes, would not be a good career move for you. Moss would cuss them out brutally when he lost a pot. He would also chastise them or even fire them if they didn't snatch far more than what would be considered a fair rake. Dealers put up with his antics as he did toke redbirds ($5 chips) when he was winning.

What many didn't see or know about Puggy, though, is that he had a heart of gold, especially for helping out fellow gamblers down on their luck. Amarillo Slim once said that Puggy "was softer than butter on a hot stove". I don't remember Puggy ever missing a funeral of a fellow gambler or not helping out a poker dealer or a family member of theirs that was sick or had died. He would always pass the hat around the poker room and collect money for the family.

Don't Worry About it

Puggy was always good to me. At times, I didn't like the way he behaved at the table, but I admired that he helped so many people. I was "between bankrolls" a number of times in my career, and usually I would go to Puggy to get staked or borrow money. He made money staking me and charged me juice when he loaned me money, so he never minded helping me out. He used to say I was a little oil well for him.

Once, I went to him and said, "Puggy, I need to borrow $5,000." He said, "What for?" I told him that I owed a bookmaker money and needed to pay him. He said, "Let me get this straight. You're coming over to my house, to borrow money from me, to pay him, and then you'll owe me instead of him." I said, "Yes." He said, "Son, let me tell you something. Don't *ever* worry about money you owe someone else, let them worry about it."

I told him I really needed it and that I'd pay him 20% juice and get the money back to him within 30 days. Thus, he would get $6k back for the $5k he loaned me. He inquired, "20% juice, right?" I said, "Yes." And as he was counting out the money, he paused and said, "Son, you've got to give up those sports." I always got the lecture, but I always got the money – with juice.

Backgammon Anyone?

I'd played some poker with Puggy in the early days, but not that much as he was usually playing in the highest stakes games that I couldn't afford. He was only in my games when he was building his bankroll back up. One day in the early '80s, I ran into Puggy as I was going in the Dunes and he was leaving. He said, "Do you want to play some backgammon tonight for $50 a point?"

I had never played Puggy anything heads-up before and had only played a little backgammon in my life. But I knew he was just learning the game himself, like me. I was broke and thought it might be a way for me to get some money. Hey, he didn't say I had to pay that night. So, I said, "Sure. What time and where?" He told me to meet him at Dirty Sally's on Las Vegas Blvd at 8 pm.

I called my brother Tom and told him that I was going to play Puggy in backgammon. I wanted him to go with me in case I lost, as I might need him if trouble broke out. He knew that I didn't play much backgammon but said he would go with me. We met Puggy at Dirty Sally's and we started playing. He was better than me, and I started to lose. The tab ran up to $600 and, apparently, I had a weak poker face. Puggy could sense my nervousness and read me like a book. He said, "You know, we should probably settle up every $500."

I did my best to bluff him and said, "Puggy. Don't worry about it. You know I'm good for the money. Let's play." He said, "I know you are, but it's always better to settle up as we go." I had to fess up and said, "Puggy, I didn't know I would have to settle up tonight. I don't have any money on me, but you know I'm good for it."

He stared at me for what seemed like an eternity and then he started laughing. I said, "What's so funny?" He said, "Hell, I don't have any money either. I was shootin' an air bullet myself." He continued, "Son, I'd love to keep playing you but I've got to go find someone with money. You owe me $600. I'll see you later." For some reason, after that night, Puggy took a real liking to me.

Puggy said he was broke so many times in his life that he couldn't count that high. But he had heart and a lot of talent, and would always bounce back. Finally, when he got older, he got on a rush, won some good money, and decided to build a small shopping center. He leased out the space to a carry-out store and a dry cleaner. Whenever someone spoke to him about it, he smiled and said, "It took me 40 years to learn how to make a mule out of my money."

King of the Gambling World

Thanks to Puggy, I got back in action on a number of occasions. For his birthday one year, I wrote a song about Puggy and had it recorded. It's called, "Puggy Pearson, King of the Gambling World" and is sung to the Davy Crockett theme song. Davy Crockett was a folk hero, frontiersman, soldier, and politician. He was known as the King of the Wild Frontier.

Like Crockett, Puggy was a legend from Tennessee. The first time Puggy heard the song, he grinned from ear to ear. He was truly touched. He said it was his life story. He loved it and played it for everyone. When Mike Eaken first heard the song, he said to me, "That's the smartest thing you've ever done. You'll never be broke again because, after writing that song, Puggy will *always* put you in action. Always!"

Here's the song "Puggy Pearson, King of the Gambling World". The chorus, "Pug-gy, Pug-gy Pearson, King of the Gambling World", is sung between each verse.

Born in a shack in the hills of Tennessee,
he was one out of 10 in a big family.

Dropped out of school while in the fifth grade,
and joined the Navy to see how the world was made.

Pug-gy, Pug-gy Pearson, King of the Gambling World

He learned real fast this was his cup of tea,
all those suckers in the US Navy.
He loan sharked, booked craps, and shot lots of pool,
and the way he played poker, well this was no fool.

Pug-gy, Pug-gy Pearson, King of the Gambling World

He left the Navy as a very rich man,
and he wanted to gamble with the best in the land.
So he packed his bags and headed out West,
to prove to the world, that he was the best.

Pug-gy, Pug-gy Pearson, King of the Gambling World

He always played in the highest games in town,
got broke many times, but you couldn't keep him down.
From gin rummy, backgammon, to all the games you know,
he's just a big shark in a world of minnows.

Pug-gy, Pug-gy Pearson, King of the Gambling World

He became world champ of the poker world,
and to all the scufflers, he had a heart of gold.
He loans out his money and stakes railbirds too,
he's the greatest friend a gambler ever knew.

Pug-gy, Pug-gy Pearson, King of the Gambling World

He learned to play golf, it's a hustler's dream,
and in no time at all became a golfing machine.
A reporter once asked him "How good do you play?"
"I shoot whatever it takes to get the money that day."

Pug-gy, Pug-gy Pearson, King of the Gambling World

He's the gamblin'est man you ever did see,
this backwoods boy from the hills of Tennessee.
He'll play any man any game he can name,
and he landed himself in the Hall of Fame.

Pug-gy, Pug-gy Pearson, King of the Gambling World
[slowing down at the end].

Poker Pioneers

Doyle said Puggy was the kingpin of poker in Vegas for 30 years, from the 1960s thru the '80s. According to Doyle, he was an assassin, a cold-blooded killer at the table. He was fearless and aggressive, and he was phenomenal at all games. He also said Puggy was the greatest pressure putter he ever saw. In golf, he just didn't choke. The more he bet, the better he played.

Puggy Pearson was not only a one-of-a-kind original character: he was a poker pioneer. He came from nothing and rose to the top of the poker world. He also played a key role in helping start the WSOP. I consider the guys who put up $10k to play in those early WSOP tournaments to be poker pioneers. They paved the way for all of us. They deserve our thanks and a tip of the hat. Guys like Doyle Brunson, Amarillo Slim, and Puggy Pearson are a *big* reason for the success of poker today.

18 Stu Ungar

All you can do with two Aces are win
a small pot or lose a big one.

Stu Ungar

When talking about historical legends in the poker world, Stu Ungar has to be at the top, or certainly near the top, of that list. To me, Stuey was the Bobby Fischer of cards. He was a savant. He had a genius IQ, a photographic memory, and, simply, an uncanny knack for card games. Stuey had the quickest mind of anyone I've ever known and was a true high roller.

His natural abilities and raw talent at cards could well be the best of all time. However, he had serious issues that plagued him all his life. He was a degenerate gambler and had a serious drug problem for over 20 years. He went from broke to millionaire and back to broke more times than perhaps anyone in the gambling world.

Halls of Fame

Stu Ungar was inducted into the Poker Hall of Fame in 2001. He was an iconic figure at poker and gin rummy, but in the gambling world he was also a legend at golf, sports betting, betting on the horses, playing in the pit, and craving action 24/7.

If there were Halls of Fame for the following categories, Stu Ungar would be a cinch to be a first ballot inductee in each of them:

- ♠ Gin Rummy Hall of Fame
- ♠ Golf Suckers Hall of Fame
- ♠ Bookmakers' Dream Players Hall of Fame
- ♠ Horse Punters Hall of Fame
- ♠ Drug Dealer Clients Hall of Fame
- ♠ Cocaine Abusers Hall of Fame
- ♠ Quickest Minds Hall of Fame
- ♠ Biggest Tippers Hall of Fame
- ♠ Poker Dealer Abusers Hall of Fame
- ♠ Lack of Appreciation for Money Hall of Fame
- ♠ Youngest Earner for the Mafia Hall of Fame
- ♠ Fastest Eater Hall of Fame (Stuey never stayed through dinner)
- ♠ Degenerate Gamblers Hall of Fame.

Gin Rummy

Stuey was great at all games, but without question he was the best gin rummy player of all time. I have yet to ever hear of anyone who felt otherwise. As was mentioned in Chapter 13, Ungar came to Vegas in the late '70s to play high-stakes gin rummy. All the top poker players of that era were also excellent gin rummy players. They included Doyle Brunson, Puggy Pearson, Chip Reese, Danny Robison,

Sarge Ferris, Tommy Fisher, Bobby Baldwin, Nicky "V", and Amarillo Slim. Stuey played them all and mowed them down like grass.

After crushing them all, he then started spotting them – giving them points, putting them on in all games (they played Hollywood gin, meaning three games at a time), letting them peek at the bottom card on the deck, even peek at the bottom two cards, and it made no difference. Eventually, they all waved the white flag. Stuey once said to me, "Sexton, I suppose it's possible that some day, someone might become a better No Limit Hold 'Em player than me. I doubt it, but it's possible. But I swear to you, I don't see how anyone could ever play gin better than me." Neither do I.

When playing gin rummy, he never sorted his cards into melds after picking them up like nearly everyone else in the world does. He just played them from where they were – and played them fast. And he knew after the third or fourth discard, exactly what the opponent held. It was spooky to watch him play.

I was at the Dunes once watching Stuey play in a $500/$1,000 2-7 draw game. Chip was playing Tommy Fisher $500/1,000 flop gin on the next table. Flop gin means if you knock with 10 or fewer points you get "x" amount, and if you gin or undercut your opponent when he knocks, you get twice that amount. In this case, it would be $500 or $1,000.

We were sitting in a position where we could see Chip's hand. After a few plucks, Chip had only one spread, three queens, and all of a sudden he started discarding them! They played the hand all the way to the end and Chip then had a choice of whether to knock (he had three points in his hand) or throw the hand in and play the next hand. He opted to throw it in for fear he might get undercut if he knocked.

Stuey had only glanced over at Chip's hand once or twice. As soon as Chip threw the hand in, he said, "Chip, you played that hand perfect, but why didn't you knock? You know Tommy's got two black deuces that he can't play on you." Tommy's eyes got wide as he turned up his hand with exactly two black deuces he couldn't play anywhere and said, "I don't believe that."

Chip was just excited that Stuey said he played the hand perfectly. He hollered over to his partner Danny, who was playing stud at the next table, "Danny, did you hear that? Stuey said I played that hand perfectly." And Stuey then quickly yelled out, "Yeah, but he forgot to get the money!"

No Limit Hold 'Em

Many, and put me on that list, consider Stu Ungar to be the greatest No Limit Hold 'Em player of all time. He was scary to watch in terms of instincts and how he just seemed to know when and how to take pots away from opponents. Stuey also hated to lose. He said, "You show me a good loser, and I'll show you a loser."

The guy was incredible. But don't just take my word for it, look at his record. As Doyle said, "You judge a hunter by the number of furs he brings home." Well, nobody in poker history has brought home more fur in big-time No Limit Hold 'Em tournaments than Stu Ungar. He might have played in 35 championship No Limit tournaments in his life, meaning $5k–10k buy-in tournaments. (There were no bigger buy-ins back then.) He won 10 of them! That included three WSOP main event titles and three Super Bowl of Poker titles. To give you an idea of that achievement, other than Moss, if you count his three titles, one of which was a vote between six players, no one else in the world won more than two of those events.

During big events, Stuey thrived on attention from the media and the adoration of the public. He would have lit up like a Christmas tree at WPT events and the WSOP with ESPN coverage. Television and Stuey would have been a match made in heaven.

I know the fields were smaller before televised poker. The players are much better today, and they play as aggressive as, or even more aggressive than, Stuey. I just wish he could have been around in the TV era. I believe he would have not only been the biggest star in the poker world, but whoever was in second place would have been a distant second.

What makes his record even more compelling was that he had a *huge* drug problem for 20 years. It's well known that he was high many times on Day 1 as big tournaments were taking place, including the last tournament he ever played, the '97 main event at the WSOP – which he won. You have to wonder what he might have accomplished in his career without his personal issues.

I can remember meeting Stuey in 1978 when the high-stakes action was at the Dunes. Once, my friend Danny Robison and Stuey were playing together in a Seven Card Stud game. Stuey quit the game. I had been sweating Danny and he asked me if would go with Stuey to his room and bring him back something. I said, "Sure, be glad to."

Stuey and I went up to his room. We entered the room and as I looked over and saw his desk, which had a glass top on it, I thought someone had spilled a pile of sugar on it. It was cocaine! (I was quite naive when it came to drugs.) I couldn't believe it. There was so much of it. And there wasn't even a "Do Not Disturb" sign on his door. All I could think was *if security comes in now, I'm going to jail*. I said, "Stuey, give me whatever you've got for Danny. I want to get out of here." He handed me a brown paper bag and I took it back down to Danny and said, "Don't ever ask me to go to Stuey's room again."

A Railbird's Dream

I remember the first time Amarillo Slim held his Super Bowl of Poker. It was at the Las Vegas Hilton in 1979. I was in Vegas then, so I went over to the Hilton. I was between bankrolls and was standing on the rail watching Stuey playing $100/200 Seven Card Stud. He was killing time while waiting to get in a bigger game. He was on fire, playing every hand, seemingly betting or raising on every street, and winning nearly every pot. Stuey would always say, "Rush, rush, play the rush." And he did.

There was a big crowd on the rail watching this game. Stuey was putting on quite a show. Finally, Stuey had to go to the restroom. He could not stand the thought of missing a hand, so he turned around, saw me, and said, "Sexton, come pick up a hand for me." I looked like Edwin Moses hopping the rail. (Moses won 107 consecutive 400m hurdle events between 1977 and 1987, and two Olympic gold medals. He was also from my hometown, Dayton, OH.)

Stuey took off to go to the restroom and, on the first hand, I picked up 9-10-J with two diamonds. The bring-in was the deuce of clubs and the first guy raised with a 6-up and I called. The guy behind me raised, an ace capped it, and everyone called. On the turn, I caught the 8 of diamonds for an open-end straight and a three flush. Again, the pot was capped and no one got out. On fifth street, I caught a queen for a straight in five. Nobody had a pair on the board nor was there a possible flush draw. At the moment, I had the nuts.

The ace led out and the guy who started with the six raised him. About this time, I see Ungar racing back to the table. My heart was pounding. I knew if I could win this pot that something good might happen for me. Just as Stuey was near the table, I announced, "I raise." Stuey saw the size of the pot and my three-bet, and even though he didn't know what I had, he hollered out, "Yessss!" The fourth player got out but the other two called.

On sixth street, nobody helped but the ace led out again, the other guy called, and I raised again. They both called. On the river, they checked, I bet and held my breath. They both called. One guy had aces up and the other was rolled up with three 6s. I won the pot with a straight. Yes! I felt sooo good. I got up and let Stuey sit down.

I can still hear Stuey laughing. As he was raking in the pot, he roared, "I can beat you guys even when I'm in the shithouse!" Stuey then looked over at the next table and said, "What are they playing over there?" I said it was a $50/100 Stud 8 or Better game. He counted out $1,500, handed it to me, and said, "Here. Get in that game and play for us."

I got in the game and beat it for $2,300. Stuey gave me $1,200. Not only did I have a small bankroll again, but from that day forward Stuey and I bonded. I'll never forget that day. It pays to be in the right place at the right time.

A Night to Remember

Stuey loved action. It didn't matter how much he won at poker, gin, or anything else, he was always back in action as soon as possible. Once, however, he had a great day betting horses. He hit the pick six for $772,000 (two tickets for $386k each). To celebrate, he invited me, Uncle Philly (his mob associate, good friend, protector, and tough motherfucker), and his horse picker, to go with him to the Olympic Garden strip club.

As we drove up in a Mirage limo, the owner was out front to greet us. He welcomed Stuey with open arms. He was excited we were there and said that we were going to be the first-ever to be in the new VIP room. Stuey started handing everybody he saw $100 bills – the valet guy, the doorman, the cashier, the gift store lady, and a waitress. And we hadn't even got inside the club yet!

The owner led us back to the new VIP room and Stuey said to him, "Send your best-looking girls back here for my friends and get us a few bottles of Cristal champagne." Soon thereafter, in came six beautiful women and the champagne. Stuey said to the girls, "Do a dance for my friends", and he tucked a $100 bill in each of their G-strings. They immediately knew they were at the right party.

Word got out about the high rollers in the back and other girls wanted to join the party. They started sneaking in and drinking the Cristal champagne. Things were going great until the club ran out of Cristal. Stuey went ballistic. He screamed at the manager, "How can you embarrass me in front of my friends by running out of Cristal?" The manager said, "Mr. Ungar, I'm so sorry. But, we have plenty of Dom Pérignon."

That didn't soothe Stuey and he continued his rant. I went over to him and said, "Stuey, calm down. It's OK. I like Dom Pérignon better than Cristal anyway." He said, "You do? Well, OK then." He changed his attitude completely, turned to the manager, and said, "Bring us the Dom Pérignon." The party continued – and what a night it was. Stuey took care of everything (probably $15k–20k). Every once in a while, you have one of those nights you put in a frame and hang on the wall. That was one of those nights.

Fire Three Shells

If you ask the top poker players what is the number-one characteristic it takes to be a great player, the majority would answer, "You've got to have heart." That means you have to be willing to fight for pots, even when you don't have the best hand. You take the pot away from your opponent by betting. You have to not be afraid and be able to bluff. I'm not sure anybody in poker history has shown more heart at the table than Stuey.

The best big bet (pot limit and no limit) poker players that I've seen are those that have no value for money. And put Stuey at the top of that list. He started playing gin rummy for the Mafia at 16 and never had a job in his life. Money always came easy for him so he didn't value it.

I had a good friend from Fayetteville, NC, named Harold Simmons. He worked hard all his life. He started working for the power company at 18, saved his money, and later owned pawn shops in Fayetteville and carry-out stores in Myrtle Beach. He loved to play poker, but played conservatively. He was standing next to me while we were watching a PLO cash game at the Stardust years ago during a big tournament. They were gamblin' it up, and finally, after watching several players get caught bluffing, Harold turned to me and said, "Them boys didn't climb light poles for a living like I did, or they wouldn't be bettin' like that."

I was at Bob Stupak's Vegas World one year for the America's Cup of Poker. It was a big event with lots of cash games going on. As I walked by a table where Stuey was playing, he stopped me and said, "Sexton, sweat me for a little while." That was always fun, so I took a seat.

It was a $100/200 blind No Limit Hold 'Em game. Stuey had about $25k in front of him. Right after I sat down, Stuey was under the gun, looked down at the 6-4 of diamonds, and raised the pot to $600. One guy behind him, who had about $20k in front of him, called. The flop came J-10-2 rainbow. Stuey led out for $1,000 and his opponent called. A 7 came on the turn and this time Stuey bet

$2,500. Again, his opponent called.

On the river, the board paired deuces. Stuey now bet $7,000. His opponent thought for a while, shrugged his shoulders, turned the A-10 of hearts face up, and then folded. As Stuey was raking in the chips, he turned to me and whispered, "A lot of guys will bluff at pot, and some will fire two shells, but there are not many who will fire three."

Stuey and I were talking once during the WSOP, and he could see Al J. Ethier walking toward us. (I couldn't see him coming.) Ethier was an old school player who, if he fired three shells, would have the nuts. All of a sudden, Stuey said, "Sexton, I had the worst dream of my life last night. I'm not kidding you. It was the absolute worst!" I bit and said, "Really? What was it about?" And just as Al J. reached us, he said, "I dreamed I was playing Al J. a heads-up freeze-out, with no blinds and no antes."

A Call at 3am

When he was pumped up, for years, Stuey loaned me money or staked me in golf matches. But in the '90s, he was lost in his drug world, down and out most of the time, and I loaned him money. Once, he owed me $7k and I was hurting and needed money. As I was walking toward him, he could read my mind. He put his hands up and said, "Sexton, right now you're at the top of the list, but if you say anything, you're going to the bottom." Knowing he owed a lot of people, I naturally said, "No. No. I won't say anything. Leave me at the top of the list."

Stuey knew I wasn't into drugs. He didn't do any around me, nor would he ever want me around that world. I always appreciated that about him. He would go on three- or four-day binges at times. He called me once at 3 am. My girlfriend said, "Who in the hell is calling at this hour?" I told her it was Stuey, that he was in trouble, and that I had to go get him.

She said, "No. Don't go down there! Please don't go." But I had to go. He had no one else to help him and I just couldn't leave him on the street. I drove downtown to about three blocks from the El Cortez, which is a scary area, especially at 3 am. Then I saw Stuey. He looked awful. He was scraggly, unshaven, and unbathed, with soot all over his fingers. He said he needed to hide as he owed some drug dealers some money. I took him to a motel on Boulder Highway, told him not to call anyone or to leave there for a couple days, and that I would bring him food each day.

The next night, he called me and said he had to move as a drug dealer found out where he was. (He had called a drug dealer to bring him drugs.) I moved him to the Gold Coast, where he stayed for several months. I had put up a Diners Club card to pay for the room. I was shocked when I went to pay the tab at the end of his first month there.

There was $1,400 in pay-for-view movie rental charges! How was that even possible? (Porno movies, that's how.) I was so angry. I was helping him out, didn't have much money myself, and he abused me like that. He was very embarrassed and apologetic about it. I told him if he watched over two pay-for-view movies a week this next month, I was done with him. The next month, there were eight pay-for-view movies on the tab.

He needed to get his life together. I set up a meeting for Stuey to meet with Nolan Dalla, who wanted to write a book about his life. I convinced Stuey to do the book and told him they would make a movie out of it. Then, he could walk the red carpet at the premiere, and he would be a big star. He inquired, "Who's good-looking enough and smart enough to play me?"

Stuey was still at the Gold Coast as the new school year was about to start. He wanted money to buy his daughter Stefanie school clothes. I would no longer give him any cash, but I told him I would give him my J.C. Penney card to buy her $300 worth of school clothes. After they went shopping, he gave me my card back with tears in his eyes. He said, "I can't believe that after all the millions I've made, I don't even have money to buy my daughter school clothes." To hear that from him and to see him so emotional was a powerful moment. He then said, "I will never forget you did that for me. Thank you."

Stuey was given many opportunities to straighten himself out. Chip, Doyle, and Billy Baxter offered to put him in drug rehab a number of times. They also agreed to stake him once he got out. But by then drugs had left him powerless to make rational decisions. Until somebody wants to get help, they're just not helpable. Stuey remained unwilling to get help.

I once asked Chip, "Do you think Stuey was the greatest No Limit Hold 'Em player ever?" He said, "He might have been, but it doesn't matter. He never understood the object of the game." To Chip, the object of the game was to continually grow your wealth, improve your lifestyle, and take care of your family. Chip was right. All Stuey wanted to do was gamble every day as high as he could and go on drug binges.

Stu Ungar was definitely One of a Kind, the name of the book about Stuey's life written by Nolan Dalla and Peter Alson. He had extraordinary talent, but his demons did him in. He was found dead on November 22, 1998, in a cheap motel on Las Vegas Blvd. He was 45.

I was one of three speakers at his funeral. Bob Stupak and Lem Banker were the other two. My last line was, "Let's forgive Stuey for his personal problems and errant ways and remember him for what he was – the greatest player to ever grace the green felt."

19 Billy Baxter

*Poker is like pool. Some days you make every
shot and other days you hit nothing but the rail.*

Billy Baxter

Billy Baxter (born in 1940) has been known as the "Man About Town"
in Las Vegas for a lot of years. His likeability and success are legendary there. The respect he gets in the poker world, sports betting
world, and gambling world is second to none – and deservedly so.

Baxter has been a long-time high-stakes poker player – and I
do mean *high stakes!* He has seven WSOP bracelets, all of which he
won in non Hold 'Em events. (Only Phil Ivey, with 10, has won more
bracelets in non Hold 'Em events.) And Billy, like other top players
back in the '70s, never chased bracelets, as they could make more

money in cash games in the old days. Billy Baxter was inducted into the Poker Hall of Fame in 2006. As successful as he's been on the green felt, his biggest contribution to the poker world came away from the table.

Between 1978 and 1981, Billy filed taxes on $1.25m in poker earnings. He was in the upper tax bracket, meaning he paid 50% of his income in taxes. The IRS contended that poker winnings should not be treated as "earned income" as they claimed it wasn't a business or a trade. They said it was "unearned income", meaning Billy had to pay 70% in taxes on his poker winnings. His accountant advised him to pay the difference to avoid interest and penalties and then sue to get it back. Billy did that.

He filed suit against the US Government to get his money back. The case: "William E. Baxter Jr. vs. the US Government". Billy felt strongly, and rightfully so, that his earnings at a poker table were no different from those of professional golfers, who earned their money on the golf course. Both are games of skill. He simply earned his money at a poker table instead of a golf course.

The district judge from Reno, NV, Bruce R. Thompson, ruled in favor of Baxter's claim for tax refunds. He actually said, "I find the government's case to be ludicrous. Mr. Baxter has extraordinary poker skills. I just wish you (the government lawyers) had some money and would sit down with Mr. Baxter and play some poker."

The government appealed to the Ninth Circuit Court of Appeals, but the court again ruled in Baxter's favor. The government then threatened to take the case to the Supreme Court and tried to make a deal with Baxter, but he held firm and said no deal. The government then backed down and dropped the case.

This case helped all players as they could now enjoy the same tax advantages as skilled athletes. It legitimized poker as a profession. And in 1986 Billy was refunded his $178k with interest. That didn't cover legal expenses, but Baxter didn't care – it was justice for him and a victory for all poker players.

Baxter started his gambling career by hustling pool as a kid in

Augusta, GA. By the age of 16, he had $5k from his pool winnings, an amount unheard of back then. He discovered there were poker and gin games in the back of the pool hall, and put his pool winnings to work. He got married in Hawaii in '75 and on the way back stopped in Las Vegas. He started playing poker and lived in Dunes Hotel for the next nine months (in the Cary Grant Suite).

Those poker games in the '70s were *huge!* The games were great because casino owners Major Riddle and Sid Wyman, with *very* deep pockets, loved to play and were not good players. In addition, Jimmy Chagra, one of the biggest drug dealers in the world, would play in those games to launder money. Every day, you could win hundreds of thousands of dollars, and guys like Billy, Doyle Brunson, Chip Reese, and Sarge Ferris did so. Billy said it was the biggest candy store in the world. He also said there have never been games like that in Las Vegas before or since.

In addition to his tremendous success at poker, Billy became a top-notch sports handicapper, and his strength was betting halftimes. He also got into boxing, and became the boxing manager for several world champions. He managed Roger Mayweather (Floyd Mayweather's uncle and trainer) for most of his 18-year career, as well as Vernon Forrest, who beat Shane Moseley twice.

After he got out of prison, Floyd's dad called Billy and asked him if he would be interested in managing Floyd, who was young and just starting out. Billy passed as he said he was getting out of the boxing business. Billy does point out that neither he nor anyone else has ever lost a bet on Floyd.

I don't think there's anyone in the world who has better gambling stories than Billy Baxter. No one. And with his southern drawl, nobody tells them better, either. Allow me to share a few with you.

Back in the day, Billy could see that a lot of guys with a lot of money were betting on football. So, he went to Doyle to be his partner in a bookmaking operation. They opened a "little store" where players could bet up to $40k a game. Business was good as their customer base included the casino owners, Tony "the Ant" Spilotro (the character Joe Pesci played in the movie *Casino*), drug dealer Jimmy Chagra, poker players, and other big-time gamblers around town.

About a month or so after starting this little venture, Billy got a call at 2 am one night. It was Spilotro. He said, "I need to see you right now. Meet me at the donut shop on Tropicana in 10 minutes." Well, of course his wife didn't want him to go, but Billy knew you didn't want to get on the bad side of Spilotro, so he went. He called Doyle before he went over to tell him he was meeting with Spilotro. Doyle insisted he call him back as soon as the meeting was over.

When he got there, he joined Spilotro in the booth. "The Ant" said, "Starting tomorrow, you have a 25% partner in your little booking operation – me." Billy said, "Well, I'll have to check with my partner Doyle about that." Spilotro pulled out an ice pick and said, "You tell that fat fuck that if he doesn't want me as a partner, that I'm going to take this ice pick and stab him in his big fat fuckin' belly 12 times. And tell him those exact words!" The meeting was over.

Billy called Doyle when he got back to his house. He didn't see any point in ruining Doyle's night and, more importantly, he didn't want to talk about this on the phone. He told Doyle to meet him at 9:30 in the morning for breakfast. Back then, Doyle never got up before noon, but he was at breakfast that day at 9:30. Billy told him the story that they had a new partner. He then gave him the exact quote from Spilotro, that "if Doyle didn't go along with the partnership, that Spilotro would stab him in his big fat fuckin' stomach 12 times with an ice pick." Doyle listened to it all, looked at his belly, and then at Billy's, and said, "Why is he going to stab me? Your belly is bigger than mine!"

Doyle then told Billy that they needed to talk to Benny Binion about this. Benny agreed to set up a meeting with Spilotro. Billy called Spilotro and said, "Benny Binion wants us all to come down to the Horseshoe for a meeting." Spilotro said, "You just had to get that old fuck involved, huh? OK. I'll meet with the old fuck."

A meeting was set up. At the meeting, Benny looked at Spilotro and simply said in a relaxed voice, "These boys are just trying to make a little money. Can you give 'em a pass on this one?" Spilotro was smart enough to know that the one person in Las Vegas that he didn't want to have any trouble with was Benny Binion. He was silent for a minute or so and then said, "OK, Benny. I'll give them a pass on this one."

The business was going fine but, even though they were partners, Billy and Doyle were always betting against each other at everything, including football, as Doyle usually wanted more action. After a round of golf, Doyle would say, "Let's see how they're running today." That meant he wanted to play some gin rummy. Chip Reese, who was pretty new to Vegas at that time, was at the Las Vegas CC with them one day and he and Billy teamed up and alternated playing Doyle gin rummy. They started playing flop gin at $2k/4k a hand, and kicked it up to $4k/8k. Two hours later, Doyle was stuck $200k!

Doyle couldn't believe it. He thought he was getting fucked some way. He said, "I know you're doing something to me. There's no way you two can beat me." He said he wasn't paying unless he could search them and strip them down. He also said he'd be taking the decks home to make sure they hadn't been marked. They were laughing about all this as they undressed and he patted them down. He couldn't find anything, but still said, "I don't know what you're doing to me, maybe putting something in my drinks, but I know there's no way you guys can beat me."

Temporarily satisfied the game was on the square, they started playing again – and continue to raise the stakes. At night's end, Doyle was stuck $900k! After that session, right there on the spot, he told Billy that he was done with him as a business partner. He then grabbed the football schedule and bet Billy $50k a game on nearly every game on the sheet. He went 11-2-1 to get half his money back from the gin session, but their partnership was dissolved permanently. And with Chagra and Spilotro around town, there was beginning to be too much heat in Vegas to operate as a bookmaker. With that, Billy abandoned his enterprise and moved back to Georgia. He returned to Vegas for good in 1986.

Baxter recognized Stu Ungar's talents at gin rummy right away and has always said he was the best-ever at that game. He knew about his uncanny poker ability as well, but he didn't like to get involved with Stuey because he knew that, due to his drug problems, he was a time bomb and could implode at any time. When he did get involved with Stuey, he had some good success with him, but there were also many nightmare experiences.

As you know, Billy staked Stu Ungar in the '97 WSOP main event. The night before the final table, Stuey, with great confidence (and the chip lead), said to Billy, "Billy, this tournament is over. They're all playing for second place." Billy loved hearing that. He called me and told me to bet everything I could bet on Stuey and lay up to -140 on him against the field. I did, but I couldn't get much down as everyone thought Stuey was going to win – which he did. The morning of the final table, I told Stuey that Billy told me to bet all I could on him and lay -140. Stuey loved the fact that Billy wasn't happy "just" winning $1m. It pumped him up and he was determined to win the tournament even more.

Right after his win, Stuey and Billy went to cash out their million, but Stuey had no ID, so they wouldn't cash Stuey out until he got some. He then turned to Billy and said, "Billy, I need some walking around money." Billy said, "Sure." He reached in his pocket and gave Stuey $5k. Stuey barked, "Billy, what is that? I need some fuckin' walking around money, at least $50k." Billy thought, *who needs $50k to walk around*, but he gave him the money.

Years before that win, Billy had staked Stuey several times, but the results were quite different. Once, Stuey was the chip leader of the WSOP main event at the end of Day 1, and was a no-show for Day 2! The next day, when Stuey didn't show up to play, Billy was frantically searching for him. He had security at the Golden Nugget go to his room to see if he was alright. Stuey had apparently done drugs all night and was out of it. They took him to the hospital. Billy raced to the hospital in an attempt to get his horse back in the race, but they told him, "Stuey won't be playing any more poker for at least several days." It was a tough day in the stake horse department. They blinded Stuey off (and he still almost made it to the money).

Another time, Billy was staking Stuey in a No Limit Hold 'Em cash game during Bob Stupak's America's Cup tournament. Billy was sweating him, and Stuey, who was most likely high on drugs, was losing. He was raising and bluffing every pot, thus getting called every time. Billy couldn't take it any more. He stood up and said, "OK, Stuey. Rack 'em up. We're done." Stuey started protesting, saying he was OK, that the game was good, and that he would win for sure. Billy didn't buy it and said, "Stuey, poker is like pool. Some days you make every ball and, other days, you hit nothing but the rail. Today, you're hitting nothing but the rail. Now, rack 'em up."

Baxter is as old school as old school gets. He is the ultimate pro who came from nothing and went all the way to the top. His amicable personality, the way he conducts himself at the table, and the success that he's had in his career sets a standard we all should try to emulate.

In my book, Billy Baxter has always been and will always be "The Man About Town" in Las Vegas. And, oh yeah, if you want to hear the best gambling stories told by the best storyteller, talk to Billy.

20 Big Action!

*When you've got a lot of money,
it's easy to do the right thing.*

Benny Binion

Over the years, poker players have always gambled high on the golf course. In the old days, when I first came on the scene, it was Doyle Brunson, Puggy Pearson, Chip Reese, Danny Robison, Tommy Fischer, Amarillo Slim, Gene Fisher, Dewey Tomko, Hilbert Shirey, David Baxter, Bobby Baldwin, Billy Baxter, Billy Walters, Stu Ungar, Jack Straus, Gabe Kaplan, Big Al, casino owners, drug dealers, and many more.

Since the mid to late '90s until now, there's a new breed of high-stakes poker players who bet big on golf and they include: Huck Seed, Howard Lederer, David Grey, Yosh Nakano, Ralph Rudd, Layne

Flack, Russ Hamilton, Phil Ivey, Daniel Negreanu, David Benyamine, David Oppenheim, Patrik Antonious, Jeff Freedman, Josh Arieh, and Erick Lindgren, among others.

The point is, where there's golf, there's action (or vice versa) – and plenty of it. Most high-stakes poker players love it. And put me on that list!

My Favorite All-time Golf Story

My favorite golf story is the time Doyle Brunson and I played a huge golf match in the late '90s against Howard Lederer and Huck Seed. The bet came about as Doyle was playing in a WSOP tournament, sitting at a poker table with Howard and Huck. At that time, Howard and Huck were playing a lot of golf. Because he had a bad leg, Doyle had played hardly any golf in a year or two, but obviously that didn't stop him from making a bet – and certainly if he thought he had the best of it.

On one of the tournament breaks, I was in the restroom and heard somebody yell, "Your man's got you in a golf match." I didn't know whom he was talking to. I couldn't imagine he was talking to me because I hadn't played much golf in a year. Well, it was Huck, and he was talking to me.

Doyle made them a bet where he and I would scramble our ball from the red tees, the ladies tees, and Huck and Howard would scramble their ball from the blue tees at TPC Summerlin in Las Vegas. The bet was for a $20k Nassau with one two-down automatic press a side, meaning we could win or lose $100k in this 18-hole match. The match was set to take place three weeks after the WSOP ended. (I was broke at the time, but Doyle was staking me.)

The next day at a cash game, Howard was needling Doyle about making the bet, because he knew that Doyle and I hadn't played golf in a long time. He started laughing, so Doyle, becoming slightly embarrassed, threw his chest out, and said, "Well, if you think you've got the nuts, you can double the bet!" Howard, whose laughter then subsided, said, "OK. We'll double it to a $40k Nassau."

After doubling the bet, Doyle came over to me and said, "I just doubled the bet with Howard. We haven't played, so maybe we better go out and see what we can shoot scrambling from the red tees." I agreed. The next day, Doyle and I went out to TPC Summerlin and scrambled our ball from the ladies tee. We hacked the ball all over the place and shot 76, a lousy score in a scramble, especially from the ladies tees! Simply put, we were horrible.

Doyle, who used a crutch and had to put it down when he hit a shot, was hobbling about and moaning the blues all the way around the course, "We're gonna get killed. We're terrible!" In an effort to calm him down, I said, "Doyle, this is the first time I've played in over six months." He said, "I know and I don't care. We're dead. These guys are going to shoot under par as easy as pie. We have no chance. We've got to get out of this bet."

Doyle goes back in the poker room the next day and said to Howard, "I hit some balls yesterday. My knee is hurting and I don't want to throw my leg out of whack again and injure myself worse. You know this will be a tight match. What do you guys want to do with this bet?" Howard said, "What are you talking about? We've got a bet. We want to play. You made a bet and we're going to play it."

Hearing that, Doyle now bluffed at him. He blurted out, "Well, I'll tell you what you can do. You can either double the bet or you can cancel it!" Howard looked at him, shrugged his shoulders, and said, "OK. We'll double!" He called Doyle's bluff. The bet was now an $80k Nassau – meaning we could lose $400k! Doyle got his bluff picked off and he was sick.

Doyle came over to where I was sitting and said, "We're dead. I didn't think they would, but they doubled the bet again." I got up from my chair, walked over to the corner of the room with Doyle, and said, "Doyle, we can play a lot better than we did – a whole lot better. For sure, I can play much better. Here's an idea: The US Open Golf Tournament is in two weeks. You know Harold Henning. He plays on the Senior Tour and is one of my best friends. He'll be off that week. I'll fly down to Florida and I'll train with him for a week. When I come back, I'll be able to shoot par or better by myself from the ladies tees."

Doyle thought about it a minute and said, "That's a pretty good idea." And now, I'm hemming and hawing around because I couldn't really afford to fly to Florida and be gone a week. I said, "Doyle, I'm broke. I barely have enough money to even get down there. I might need a little training money." Doyle reached into his pocket and pulled out two flags ($5k chips). He flipped them to me, and said, "Go train." Doyle knows how to take care of his men.

I called Harold and told him I was coming. He loved hearing about the bet and wanted me to come down and train. He said he would get my game in shape. We played golf every day and by the end of the week I was hitting it good and was playing as good as I was capable of playing.

I came back to Vegas feeling good. Even with all the money he bet, Doyle still hadn't played. He said he had hit balls twice. Go figure. Anyway, he sent me out to TPC Summerlin with a guy to watch me play 18 holes. This guy was a good friend of Doyle's and a really good player, a 1 handicap. But, he wasn't there to play. He was just there to watch me play and give his assessment of my game to Doyle. He also knew how Howard and Huck played, so he would get a pretty good idea of how we would fare in our match with them.

I hit the ball great (for me) all the way around. On every hole, this guy was shaking his head looking at where my tee shot was and where he thought they would hit it. He felt we would be 30–40 yards in front of them on nearly every hole. And he knew we had a big advantage on the par 3s. He kept saying, "Nice shot. How are they going to win? How can they beat this?" I shot even par from the ladies tees. Doyle figured to help me a number of times, so he thought we would be really tough to beat.

Doyle had orders for us to come right over to his house immediately after we were done. We get there and Doyle said, "How did he do?" And the guy said, "I'll tell you how he did. He played great! You two have got the nuts." Doyle looked at the guy and growled, "We've got the nuts? We've got the nuts, do we? Well, if we've got the nuts, how much are you betting on us?" He looked at Doyle and said, "I want to bet $5,000 Nassau on you."

Doyle popped up in his seat like a Jack-in-the-box. He couldn't believe his ears. (Doyle later told me this guy had never bet over $500 on anything in his life.) He said, "You want to bet $5k Nassau on us?" And the guy said, "I sure do." Doyle, grinning from ear to ear, said, "That's good enough for me."

The next day, Doyle goes back to the poker room and gets in a cash game with Howard. And he goes through his whole routine again. He said, "I hit some balls yesterday and I could feel a twinge in my knee. If I play golf, I'm afraid I might really mess it up. I don't want to injure myself. What do you guys want to do with our bet?" Howard said, "Doyle, you made a bet and we're playing it next week."

Doyle then threw out his chest again and bellowed out, "Well, I'll tell you what you can do. You can double the bet or you can cancel it!" Howard thought for a little while and said, "OK. We'll double again." And Doyle screamed out, "Yessssssss!" The bet was now for $160k Nassau, meaning we could win/lose $800k in one round of golf.

Needless to say, all the poker players and gamblers in Las Vegas knew about this golf match. The day of the match was one of the hottest days of the summer, but that didn't stop anyone from coming out to sweat the match. It looked like a PGA tour event. There must have been 50 carts that followed us around, and everybody was betting big money one way or the other. I was excited because Doyle was giving me a $15k freeroll on every bet – meaning I could win $75k if we scooped!

As we reached the first tee, I was suddenly feeling pretty nervous. It wasn't the crowd that bothered me, it was my fear of letting Doyle down. He was putting all his faith – and money – on me. He was giving me a huge opportunity and I knew, for us to win, I had to play well.

My heart was pounding as I stepped up to hit that first tee shot. I said to myself, *just stay calm and hit the ball*. Fortunately, I hit a decent shot, which automatically took away some of my nervousness. I hit a pretty good second shot as well and we were 15 feet away for birdie. They were 35 feet away. They missed their putt. I lipped my putt out on one side of the hole and Doyle lipped his out on the other side. It was an opportunity missed. Damn.

We birdied number 2 and we birdied number 3 (an easy par 5), but they parred them both. We were two up after three holes! Doyle started laughing and shouted out for all to hear, "I've forgotten more about golf than these two guys will ever know!" He could have been right about that.

On the fourth hole, I hit two good shots to about 12 feet from the hole. They were a good 45 feet away. Howard putted first and didn't come within 10 feet of the hole. Huck then stepped up and knocked it in the hole. Wow! And then sadly, just like on number 1, I lipped out on one side of the hole and Doyle lipped out on the other side. What a turnaround. It looked like we were going to go up 3 and 1 in this match, but now we were back to 1 and 1. We were a little shell-shocked.

We tied 5-6-7 and 8, so we were 1–1 going into number 9 (a reachable par 5). Huck crushed a drive and luckily, with all the pressure on, so did I. He then flew his second shot to the back of the green – a great shot – and things did not look good for us. They were a cinch to make a birdie from there.

My second shot was probably the best shot I hit all day. I hit a perfect 3-wood down the left side and it rolled up between the traps to the front part of the green. Both teams two-putted, so we finished 1–1 on the front nine.

It was a heck of a match. They birdied 10, we birdied 11, and we were even on the back nine going into number 15, the shortest and easiest par-4 on the golf course. The good players can drive that hole. I could come close to driving it myself on occasion from the red tees. They didn't hit a good tee shot for them, but still had an easy wedge into the green. I hit a great tee shot and we were exactly flag high between two bunkers, no more than 20–25 feet from the hole. Their second shot wasn't that good – about 20 feet away. This was an opportunity for us. It was our chance to birdie and perhaps go 1-up on the back nine.

The green is elevated, so we were debating whether to chip the ball up the hill or putt it, which we could easily do as the fairway grass was very short. The flag was on our side of the green so it would be tough to stop it close if you tried to chip it. Doyle said, "I think we should putt it up the hill." I agreed. I putted first and my ball got to the top of the hill and then came rolling back down. Shit. Doyle got up there and did the same thing! The ball came right back down to us. It was pathetic we didn't get a ball on the green. We were in exactly the spot we were before we hit the previous shot.

We got the next one on the green but not that close. They missed their putt, but so did we. We made our only bogey of the day on the easiest hole on the golf course and we were only 20 feet from the flag after our tee shot! You could see the steam coming off of Doyle's head. He couldn't believe we bogeyed that hole – and neither could I. We were now one down on the back nine and even on the Nassau.

Sixteen is a par-5 hole that's reachable for long hitters. Huck, pumped up after watching us bogey the last hole, flushed his drive. The red tees are *way* up on this hole and I crushed my drive – as good as I could possibly hit it. The second shot is all carry across water. They were 240 yards out and we were 160 yards away. The large gallery went up ahead and gathered on the hill behind the green. Seeing the crowd on the hill made it feel like we were playing in the Masters.

The flag was tucked in the front left corner of the green. Howard laid up and Huck hit it on the screws. It looked like he hit it stiff. He must have been too pumped up, though, as it flew directly over the flag and went over the green into the back bunker. Doyle wanted me to hit first. He couldn't fly it anywhere near that far but could lay it up if I didn't get across the water. I hit a seven wood and hit it perfect.

It looked like my ball was coming right down the flagstick. My ball hit about 10 feet from the hole, right at the top of the bank, and then rolled back in the water. Heartbreak. You could hear the crowd groan. Doyle, dismayed my ball went in the water, dubbed his shot over in the left rough. Now we've got a 110-yard shot out of the rough, over the water, and the pin is on the front left, meaning there wasn't much of a chance for us to get it close.

I hit it on the green, but long, and we were a good 45–50 feet from the hole. It was a downhill putt that broke 10–12 feet to the left. We were sick about how we had fucked up these past two holes. We got even sicker as Huck blasted the ball to about 6 feet from the hole. What a shot! (Huck played like a touring pro on this day. He really was amazing.) It looked for sure like we were going two down on the back nine and one down on the Nassau.

I putted first and the ball didn't come close to the hole. Things looked bleak. Doyle stood over his ball and then stroked it. Before the ball got halfway to the hole (and remember, it was about a 45-foot putt that broke 12 feet to the left), Doyle started screaming, "It's in! It's in! It's in!" Incredibly, the ball went dead center in the hole! The crowd erupted in a roar. Doyle and I were high-fiving. It was the most electric moment in golf history, at least to me. What an amazing putt! Sadly, they made their birdie to tie the hole and remain one up on the back nine.

But, that putt of Doyle's broke them down so bad that they hit it way right on number 17 (par 3) and they bogeyed that hole. And to top it off, we won number 18 as well. We ended up winning two bets for the day – good for $320k. I was elated. I played well, we won, and I got $30k! Thank you, Doyle!

In hindsight, it was a much tougher match than we thought it would be. It was lucky for us that Howard played so badly. He choked nearly all the way around, but Huck played lights out. It really was one of the most exciting matches that you could ever witness. I can assure you that all those that were there will never forget it, especially that putt Doyle made on number 16.

Our group, Doyle's close friends who bet on us, went with us to Ruth Chris steakhouse on Flamingo to celebrate. It was a fun party and a phenomenal day. It was one of those days you put in a frame and hang on the wall – which I've done. That picture of Doyle and myself celebrating is front and center on my office wall.

My Wedding Day

In May 2007, a bunch of us went to Kona, HI, to play in Ralph Rudd's golf tournament. I had been dating Karen (poker room host at Bellagio) for about six months. We decided just a few weeks prior to going to Hawaii to get married while we were there. The problem was, we couldn't tell anybody, because we didn't think it was right to invite golfers to our wedding, but not our friends and families, who wouldn't have had time to make arrangements to attend. Karen made all the arrangements for us to be married at the Four Seasons in Kona. It's as nice a hotel as you will find anywhere in the world.

The day we arrived in Hawaii, we were taken to the golf headquarters hotel, about a mile or two from the Four Seasons. Karen and I slipped out to get our marriage license and go over to the Four Seasons to finalize our wedding plans. Once there, we inquired about staying there as well. Luckily, they had one room left. We were thrilled to get the room.

When Phil Ivey and a few others found out we were staying at the Four Seasons, they were jealous and tried to get a room there as well – even though all our rooms at the other hotel had already been paid. To their dismay, they couldn't get in the Four Seasons for two days.

The golf tournament was set up for four days, but on Day 4, playing was optional (where guys could play golf or take the day off to be with their wives or girlfriends). That was the day Karen and I were going to get married.

Ivey and I arranged for us to play golf together every day. We agreed to play $20k–50k Nassaus. Richie Sklar and I would play Phil and Matt Othick or Phil and Danny Dotson, who was Phil's coach and caddie. We were about even after two days of play, and on Day 3 we played a morning round and again broke even. I had promised Karen I'd spend the afternoon with her, getting massages and going to the beach. They all wanted to play more golf, so I let Richie make a match and play against them.

That night, when we met for dinner, I got the news. Richie had lost, and lost big – $300k! I was sick. All I could think about was *how was I going to get my money back*. The only way was to play the next morning – on my wedding day. But, since he obviously didn't seem to be playing too well, I decided to do it without Richie as a partner.

After dinner, we (just the guys) went to the bar to discuss playing the next day. I gave them an option of playing me a $50k Nassau where I scrambled my ball from the front tees (with Phil on my tee but Matt and/or Danny on the back tees) vs. them scrambling their ball, or they could play a best ball match where I played two separate balls (I was my own partner) vs. Phil with Matt or Phil with Danny as a partner. They chose to play the best ball match and Phil selected Danny as his partner. I told them I had to tee off early and could only play 18 holes. I was getting married at 2 pm, but they didn't know it.

After setting up the match, I now had to figure out how to tell Karen I wanted to play golf on our wedding day. (And, no, she didn't have any idea of how much we were gambling for on the golf course.) Hmmm, I came up with a plan and hoped it would fly.

I told her that while she was getting her hair and nails done in the morning I could play golf and be back in plenty of time for the wedding. She wasn't thrilled about it, but finally said, "You can play, but if you're not back here by 1 pm, there will be no wedding." Life's a gamble, so I opted to play. I guaranteed her I'd be back.

The next day, the morning of our wedding, I played great – honestly, over my head on the front nine. I beat them 5-3-1 to win three bets. They wanted a spot on the back nine but I refused to change the game. Truthfully, I didn't care if they quit as I would be $200k winner. Danny said he was quitting and paying off, but Phil and Matt said they would play the back nine – and not only would they play, they would double the bet to $100k! I said OK.

I continued playing well and won 2-up on the back nine. I'd also won a $20k prop bet along the way to total a $320k win for the day. What a wedding present! I actually got winner from Richie's fiasco the day before. They screamed and hollered when I wouldn't play any more, but I told them I *had* to go. Remember, they didn't know I was getting married. We didn't tell anyone. That round of golf was the most money I've ever won on the golf course.

I made it back to the Four Seasons by 12:30 pm. The wedding, and the whole day for that matter, was beautiful. After the ceremony, we had a fantastic, private champagne dinner on the beach. Life just didn't get any better. As we were walking back to our room, the first person who saw us after getting married was Matt. He said, "I knew it. I knew it had to be something like this for you to not play more golf. Congratulations!"

The marriage lasted 6½ years – perhaps too much golf and, for sure, too much gambling. But we produced the most wonderful son anyone could hope for – Ty Michael Sexton, born 8/21/08 – the happiest day of my life! Even though it didn't work out for Karen and me, I'm blessed because I know that I couldn't have a better mother for my son. She is a great Mom. We get along well and co-parent beautifully. And Ty is the best!

One thing is for sure, *I'll never forget our wedding day!*

"Kick It Up"

We finished our round of golf at Shadow Creek and ordered drinks in the bar. Someone said that Bobby Baldwin just arrived and was on the driving range. After we finished getting a bite to eat, Doyle and I went out to the range to say Hi to Bobby. He had just finished hitting some balls and was headed over to the chipping green.

After hitting a chip or two from about 20 yards away, Bobby asked if we wanted to chip some – just for a little sweat bet. Doyle said he would do it, so I said I would too. We went and got our clubs and Bobby said, "We'll all hit from the same place, and whoever is closest to the hole wins – say $5k from each of the other two." This was a little sweat bet to Bobby – where you win $10k on one chip shot. Doyle said "OK", and as I had recently received a good sum of money for selling my partypoker shares, I went along with it.

Bobby was a much better golfer than me, but I was better than Doyle. I was a pretty good chipper and putter, and Doyle was as well. I didn't think I was a big dog to these guys, so I thought I'd try this for a while. Doyle got out his grooved wedge, meaning he could hit a shot and make it stop on a dime with this club. All of a sudden, after seeing him hit a few warm-up shots, I didn't feel like a better player than Doyle. And I knew I wasn't better than Bobby. What the hell, life's a gamble.

After chipping 10 minutes or so, I was $20k loser. I suggested we move to another spot and Bobby said, "That's a good idea. Let's say whoever wins gets to pick the next location we chip from." Out of courtesy to me since I was losing, Bobby told me to pick the first new location. That new plan didn't work for me, either.

After another 10 minutes, I was now $30k loser, and Bobby said, "Let's kick it up." Doyle agreed, and we went to $10k a chip. I was stuck, so I agreed. After another 15 minutes, I was $60k loser! Bobby was $40k winner and Doyle was $20k winner. And again, Bobby, laughing, said, "Let's kick it up." So we went to $20k a chip, meaning you could win $40k on one chip shot! I was definitely swimming with the sharks – and great whites, at that.

Moving around to different locations didn't seem to help me at all. It wasn't much longer until I was $140k stuck. Bobby was up $80k and Doyle was up $60k. And one more time, Bobby said, "Let's kick it up!" Doyle chuckled and said, "It's OK with me." I said, "Fuck it. Let's do it."

After a few more chip shots, I was $240k loser! I was kicking myself for getting in this trap. *We just went out to say Hi to Bobby*, and here I was, absolutely buried. What was I thinking? Somehow, I fortunately got on a small rush winning a couple chips and we quit shortly after that. I ended up losing $60k for the chip session, but I felt like I won $200k!

Big-time Poker

I had the good fortune to be around the big-time players in Vegas since the '70s. Even though I didn't play in those big games back then, I was good friends with Danny Robison and Chip Reese, so I got to know – and later became good friends with – Doyle, Puggy, Stuey, Amarillo Slim, Billy Baxter, and all the biggest players.

For most of my career, I played medium high-stakes poker ($30/60, $50/100, and $75/150). I didn't really play "big-time" poker until 2004, which is when I came into a substantial sum of money when I sold my partypoker shares.

Most of you would be shocked to know who the biggest winners in poker are. It's not the player of the year on the WPT, WSOP, EPT, or GPI (Global Poker Index). It's not anyone you see on any tournament-ranking list. They're not even close to the biggest winners in poker. It's people you've probably never heard of, as most of the biggest poker games in the world don't take place in casinos, they take place in private home games with rich businessmen.

I had the pleasure of playing in the biggest game in Beverly Hills for several years. We played at a billionaire's house where he brought in the best chefs in Beverly Hills to prepare dinners, and he picked up the tab for dealers, cocktail girls, massage girls, and everything else, including fine wine. It was also rake free. We were his guests and he took care of everything. It was poker heaven. (I've opted not to name him, or other players in that game – other than the pros – in this book out of respect for their privacy, even though they never requested me to do so.)

The players included several billionaires, a number of rich businessmen, Hollywood studio moguls, actors, directors, etc. Everyone settled by check at the end of the game. Some of the biggest celebrities in the world popped in on occasion just to say Hi. On occasion, a top pro (Doyle, Ivey, Durr, etc) was invited to play because the host billionaire enjoyed the challenge of playing against these noted poker superstars. Nobody else did.

Once, Tom Durr – a young, online sensation and high-stakes guru, considered one of the best players in the world by most players back then – was invited to play. I'll never forget the look on his face when he first arrived. He looked around the table and saw nothing but rich, old guys. You could sense he knew he was in paradise.

It was a $50k buy-in No Limit Hold 'Em game, with $300/600 blinds. A straddle, which is an additional blind double the size of the BB, was not mandatory, but was put on by most players, making the game much bigger. Durr sat down and the hostess gave him $50k. He looked around the table and noticed several guys had $200k or more in front of them and the host had $1m in front of him. After two or three hands, he inquired, "Am I allowed to buy more chips?" The host said, "Sure. Buy as many as you like." Durr said, "I'll take another $200k please."

I had played in a couple poker games with Durr prior to this, but they were $10k buy-in PLO or PLO Hi/Lo split games. I'd heard about how good he was in No Limit Hold 'Em, but I had never played in a big buy-in, deep stack, No Limit Hold 'Em game with him before. It didn't take me, or anyone else, very long to realize that Durr was the real deal. He played a lot of pots. He raised continually and was very intimidating. In 45 minutes, he was up $560k! At that point, I know he thought he was going to win $2m–3m that night.

What impressed me as much as his skill was the way he conducted himself. You never know how a young guy is going to react in that environment. He was friendly, cordial, and handled himself beautifully. He also gave tremendous action, which the host loved. Durr was betting or raising all the time. He put constant pressure on you and gave you no air.

Durr was drawn out on in several huge pots but never whined or moaned about it, just politely said, "Nice hand, or nice catch." As a result of those bad beats, he only ended up winning $60k for the night, but he made an impression on me and everyone else who was in that game, I can tell you that. As much as we all liked him, we knew having him in the game wouldn't be in our best interest.

The "One Drop"

Most everyone knows about the "One Drop" tournament at the WSOP. It's a $1m buy-in with $111,111 from each entry going to the One Drop charity. The One Drop charity event was the brainstorm of Guy Laliberte, creator of Cirque de Soleil. The first One Drop took place at the WSOP in 2012. It was capped at 48 players – and sold out!

I was fortunate enough to get to play in that tournament – extremely fortunate. A good friend staked me in the One Drop tournament. It was the billionaire who hosted that Beverly Hills game. How lucky was I to get a 50% freeroll in a $1m buy-in tourney?

It came about one night at his game. When they announced the One Drop tournament, it was naturally the topic of conversation at most poker games, certainly in the high-stakes games. As it was being discussed in our game, the host said, "Mike, you should play in the One Drop." I smiled and said, "I can assure you that I'll be available and would love to play."

He mentioned later that he might stake me in it, that it would be fun to sweat. And he did! A little background on why he would stake me. I helped him with his game when he first started playing poker and then later helped him when he started playing heads-up matches for really big money. And he had pretty good success in those matches, so this was a way to reward me for helping him.

Just as my man was about to wire the $1m One Drop entry fee to my bank account, I said, "Did you know there's a $50k buy-in Players Championship mixed-game tournament a couple days before the One Drop? I'm going to play in it and you can have a piece." He said, "That's a good idea. Let me wire you $1,050,000 and we'll be partners in both events." I was now being staked in the biggest two buy-ins at the WSOP. Life doesn't get much better.

That inaugural One Drop tournament was an historic, thrilling, heart-pounding event to play in. Nine places were paid and first place was over $18m! My man was getting a good sweat, as I was still alive as we reached the final 10 players. We merged to one table and we were about to see who would go out on the biggest bubble in history. The guy who was tenth got *zero* and the ninth place finisher received $1,109,333. I was one of the short stacks at the table, but I was determined (and praying) *not* to be the bubble-boy.

I thought that, with that kind of money at stake, it might take a pretty long time to eliminate someone. I was mentally prepared to last, no matter how long it took. On the very first hand that was dealt playing 10-handed, blinds were 150/300k and Sam Trickett, in second chip position with 32m in chips, made it 800k to go. Everyone folded around to me. I was in the small blind and folded as well. The big blind was a Russian I didn't know. He was one of the three short stacks at the table. He moved all-in over the top of Trickett's raise for just under 5m. In just a few seconds, Sam shrugged his shoulders and called. He then turned up a K-8!

II couldn't believe he made a snap call for $4.2m with just a K-8. To everyone's amazement, the Russian then turned up a Q-10 off-suit. Sam had the best hand! He flopped an 8 and won the pot with two 8s. In one hand, we were "in the money". I looked at Trickett and said, "Sam, you'll always be my hero!" It was sweet. I was in the money for over $1m and my man and I were going to show a profit. It was just a matter of how much.

Nine made the money, but only eight made the TV show the next day. On the very next deal, I was in the BB and it folded all around to Antonio Esfandiari, who was in the SB. He was the chip leader with 34m prior to the previous hand, and he made it 900k to go. That raise was suspicious to me because in the entire tournament Antonio had never tripled the size of the BB. He just didn't raise that much.

I looked down at the J-10 of diamonds. Now what? You could make a case for moving all-in or calling, possibly even folding, especially in an event this big. I contemplated moving all-in but opted to call and look at a flop. The flop came A-J-3 with the ace of diamonds. I was trying to figure out what I would do after Antonio bet but, to my shock and surprise, he checked! What was going on? Antonio never checks.

Was he trapping? Should I bet? If so, do I move all-in or bet like 1m? If I bet 1m and he check-raises me all-in, then what? All of this was whirring through my head. I finally opted to check right behind him. On the turn, the 6 of diamonds came off, giving me a flush draw to go with my jacks. Antonio now led out for 1m. Honestly, I didn't consider folding. It was either call or move in. I knew that whatever he had, I was at least drawing live, so I moved all-in over the top.

He then sat up in his chair and said, "Wow, Mikey. Did you really flop aces and jacks?" I tried not to flinch after that statement. He took a pretty long time to act, murmuring things like, "I don't see how I can fold this hand." He finally said, "I call." He showed me a 6-3 offsuit, giving him two pair, and I said, "You've got the best hand. I've got jacks with a flush draw."

Hearing that, he turned to his rail and raised his hands up in the air. He wanted to let them know he had the best hand. When he turned back around, he said, "Where's my hand?" The dealer didn't realize he called and mucked it! Wow. I then told the dealer, "He absolutely called and showed me a 6 and a 3." Antonio and others agreed.

The dealer went to the muck and brought Antonio's 6-3 back out, giving him two pair. The floorman nodded for the dealer to proceed. I had 16 outs, but blanked on the river, and busted out in ninth place. Everyone was celebrating and high-fiving because play was done for the day. It took two hands to go from 10 to eight players. What was the price on that? It was tapioca pudding for me. I was out and they were all coming back for the TV show the next day.

The brass from Caesars' saw what happened. They called me over right after the hand and thanked me for not making a scene about Antonio's hand being in the muck. I never considered making a scene. Antonio did *nothing* wrong. He said "call" and showed me his hand. To me, that was it. He shouldn't have been penalized for a dealer mistake.

Obviously, looking back on how I might have played the hand differently, I wish I had moved all-in before the flop or bet on the flop, where it was highly likely that I would have won the pot rather than go broke. I should have moved all-in pre-flop because my gut told me Antonio didn't have anything. But, it's easy to play the red board (playing the hand when you know your opponent's hand). In the end, I don't really fault myself too much for the way I played the hand – but I wish I'd moved all-in pre-flop!

The two guys that played key roles in my One Drop finish, Esfandiari and Trickett, finished first and second in the tournament. Antonio got $18.1m and Sam took home $10.1m. It was the largest prize money in poker history. In fact, it was the biggest prize money for any sporting event in history. I was happy for both of them.

My stake horse was pure class. I didn't cash in the $50k Players Championship but cashed for over $1.1m in the One Drop. I told him that, after the two entry fees and dealer toke, we had $55k left to split. He said, "That's OK, Mike. Just send me back the entry fees and you keep the rest." That whole event was an amazing experience. And for sure, I had the best stake horse in the entire world!

The next year (2013), the buy-in for the One Drop was lowered to $111,111 and I played again. If you're looking for a trivia question, "Who were the only two players in the world to cash in the One Drop tournament in each of its first two years?" Answer: it was Antonio and myself. In year two, they paid 24 places and I finished 16th ($209k). Antonio finished in fourth place for $1.4m. I always say about us cashing, "Antonio made the most money possible (almost), and I made the least."

Know your Opponent

In the mid '90s, Puggy's golf game had declined somewhat, but he could still shoot in the low 80s. He was a little better than me. Tommy Fisher said he had a match for Puggy and one for myself. He told us that he had a man who was in his 30s, wasn't a tour player, and who would play us where we would all play from the blue tees at TPC Summerlin. He said the guy would give me a stroke a hole and give Puggy a stroke on all the par 4s and par 5s and a half stroke on all the par 3s. He also said we had to make a minimum bet of a $5k Nassau. He then said our opponent was Jamie Crow, who I'd never heard of.

Puggy said he didn't care who it was, that he would take the bet. I wanted to take the bet as well, but I didn't have enough money to bet $15k, the minimum bet allowed. At that time, Puggy said he didn't have enough to stake me, but told me to call Billy Walters, who was an entrepreneur, golfer, and the best sports bettor of all time. I knew Billy as he used to live right next door to Chip at the Las Vegas Country Club (and he also won Amarillo Slim's Super Bowl of Poker in 1986), but I'd never done business with or borrowed money from him. Puggy said he'd call him and OK the loan for me.

I went to pick up the money from Billy. When I got there, he said, "Mike, I'll loan you the money, but I don't think you should fuck with Jamie Crow on the golf course. He is really good – and I mean *really good!*" Billy owns a number of golf courses in Vegas, is a good golfer himself, and is a gambler extraordinaire, so you have to respect his opinion. But still, a stroke a hole.

He continued, "This guy spots the tour pro who lives next door to Chip at TPC Summerlin one a side." I asked, "If he's that good, why doesn't he play on tour?" Billy said his dad was the founder of Cobra Golf and he didn't need or want to grind it out on the tour. He warned me again about how good this guy was, but gave me the money and wished me luck. Life's a gamble. I was going to take a chance as I was getting *a stroke a hole!*

On the first tee, Tommy introduced us to Jamie Crow. Puggy looked at the guy and said, "Pal, I might not win today, but I like my game. *Nobody* has ever given me strokes on every hole on the golf course." I was hoping to shoot an 86-87 where I thought I would be very tough to beat. Remember, this was not a medal bet, but a match play bet where I got one shot on each and every hole. That's a big spot.

I hit two decent shots on number 1 and was just short of the green. I chipped up to about 6 feet where I was putting for a par. Jamie was putting for birdie from about 18 feet. With my spot, we were playing even from here. Being a pretty good putter, I loved it. If he missed, I'd be on a free roll to win the hole. Obviously, if I could get in this position on most holes, I'd be a huge favorite in the match.

Jamie's putt broke about 2 feet, but he drained it dead center. It was a pure putt. That was not a good sign for me. I lipped my putt out and, just like that, rather than being one up like I thought I might be, I was one down. Losing that hole was a mental disaster for me. I dogged it from there and lost four up on the front nine. I was two down on the back nine after number 17, so I got scooped for $15k. Jamie drove it like Robin Hood and shot the easiest 66 I've ever seen – never threatened a bogey. Puggy played well, but still lost one bet. Billy was right. I shouldn't have fucked with this guy.

Care to Settle?

I've seen two guys in my life that have an aura and mystique about them that turn all heads when they enter a room in a poker environment – Stu Ungar and Phil Ivey. Their poker talent is unquestioned, as is the tremendous amount of gamble in them. They had the balls to bet sky-high on everything – and I mean everything.

You know about Ungar's achievements in tournament poker. Ivey has proven himself in all phases of poker – cash games, tournaments, and online poker. He has 10 WSOP bracelets and a WPT title to his credit and plays in the highest stakes cash games he can find all around the world.

I was in a poker game with Ivey two weeks before the first-ever $50k buy-in HORSE tournament at the WSOP in 2006. He asked me what price he could get on himself to win. I thought there would be about 150 entrants (there were actually 143), of which the vast majority would be *very* good players, so I told him 30-1.

He originally scoffed at that price and asked for 60–1, which I rejected. He then asked for 50–1 and then 40–1, which I also turned down. Finally, he pitched two $5k chips at me from across the table and said, "OK, I'll take 30–1 on myself to win for $10k. I told him he had a bet. He smiled as he loved getting an extra $300k worth of action.

A few minutes later, he threw me two more $5k chips to bet another $10k at 30–1. I pitched them back to him and said, "The line moved to 25–1." He said, "What? Don't be such a nit." He almost took the 25–1, but he didn't. Isn't it amazing when someone isn't satisfied winning $1.8m? Guys like Ivey and Ungar always wanted more.

It was now sweat time for me. If Ivey would win the HORSE tourney, I would lose $300k! There was tremendous fanfare as the tournament started as this was the largest buy-in tournament in WSOP history. I played in the tournament but was distracted watching Ivey and thinking about losing $300k. That's probably one of the reasons I went out on Day 2.

As the tournament progressed each day, I kept checking to see if Ivey was still in. Sadly, he was. Ivey made it all the way to the final table, but was in seventh chip position out of the remaining eight players. But still, I hated my bet. Ivey was an assassin and if he got some serious chips, I knew he would be tough to beat.

I decided to go down to sweat the final table. I got in a PLO game not far from where they were playing the final table of the HORSE tourney. Before the final table started, Ivey walked by with a big grin on his face and said, "Hey, big boy. What do you want to do?" Not wanting to lose $300k, I said, "I'll give you $75k profit to off the bet." It seemed more than fair to me, but he laughed and said, "Just because it's you and you were nice enough to give me a little action, I'll take $100k." I said, "No. $75k is more than fair. Good luck to you."

He walked over to start the final table and Greg Raymer, the 2004 world champion, who was in my PLO game, got his calculator out, started clicking numbers, and said, "It's impossible for him not to take $75k! Impossible! According to his chip count, his equity is just under $30k." Everyone laughed and I said to Raymer, "You don't know Ivey very well. He would never take equal equity. And he probably would like to beat me out of $300k as much as he wants to win the $1.8m first place prize."

As players started busting out of the final table, Ivey wasn't one of them. I was getting more nervous. With three players left, Ivey was still there with Chip Reese and Andy Bloch. They took a break and Ivey strolled over to our table. He was grinning wider than before and said, "How do you like it now? What do you want to do now?"

He was in third chip position and only had about 18% of the chips. I said, "I'll give you $100k." He turned that down but said he would take $125k. I told him I wasn't giving him a dime more than $100k and wished him luck. He made no deal and, as he was walking away, he hollered out, "Let's gamble!"

On the first hand back after the break, Ivey was all-in. My heart was pounding and I was holding my breath. Luckily for me, he lost the hand and busted out in third place. Whew! That was fun, but it was a tough sweat to make $10k when I could have lost $300k. The following year, Ivey pitched me another $10k and said, "I want the same bet as last year, 30–1 to win the HORSE tournament." I said, "You've got a bet." This time, though, it was much more enjoyable as he busted long before they reached the final table. I just can't help myself laying 30–1 in a tough 150-player field – even if it is Phil Ivey.

Isn't this Fun?

We were at La Costa for a golf outing once and after one round, while having lunch, Doyle made a nine-hole match with Bobby Baldwin. He bet on my man, Richie, who was scrambling two balls from the tips, against Bobby, who would scramble three balls from the blues but only got two putts. Doyle bet $100k on the match. I bet $80k on it, Dewey Tomko bet $35k, and Big Al bet $30k. That meant Bobby was betting $245k on one nine-hole match. He loved that kind of action.

They tied the first five holes. Number 6 is a long par 5 that doglegs left and is all uphill, meaning it plays like 600 yards. Both reached the green in three shots. Bobby had a 40-foot downhill putt and Richie had a 25-foot uphill putt. Bobby missed and Richie made it to take a one up lead. They both parred number 7. Number 8 is a long, tough par 3 with water in front of the green. It's especially tough from the tips. Bobby had a big edge on this hole, but both players made par.

Number 9, the final hole of this match, is the toughest par 4 on the course. It's an uphill, dogleg right, with water all along the right hand side. It's about a 280-yard carry across the water. Richie bombed it – hit it perfect and was a wedge away. Bobby had to go left off the tee as he couldn't carry it across the water. He was about 200 yards out, all uphill, meaning it played at least 225 yards. His best shot was about 30 feet short, just right of the green. Richie hit his second shot 20 feet underneath the hole, which was in the center of the green. Bobby had to hole it out and then have Richie miss to break even.

Bobby's caddy walked off the exact distance and he decided to putt it. He came up 15 feet short and 15 feet left on his first putt. Doyle was behind the green talking to Big Al on the phone as he was keeping tabs on the match and his $30k. Just before Bobby hit his second putt, Doyle was chirping on the phone to Big Al and told him, "We've won." Bobby then proceeded to hole out his putt for birdie!

Richie, who fell to his knees and couldn't breathe after watching that, made a better than expected effort to make his putt. He got them both to the hole, something very unusual for Richie. The first putt was close and the second one lipped out. Bobby then went over to Richie, put his arm around him, and said, "Isn't this fun?" Richie replied, "Fun? I can't swallow a bee bee right now."

The Big Take-off

Doyle had set up a three round match at Shadow Creek where Dewey Tomko would play David Benyamine a different match each day for $50k per day. On Day 1, Dewey would spot David one and a half shots per side in a match play bet. On Day 2, Dewey would play David even in a match play bet but lay him 2–1 odds on the money, and on Day 3, they would scramble their ball from the back tees and play even. Most thought, like Doyle, that Dewey was the nuts. Those people must have had New England against the Bears in the '85 Super Bowl. (To give you an idea of that outcome, the Bears were ahead 44-3 at the end of the third quarter in that game.) They didn't realize how good Benyamine had become at golf.

Dewey was a very good player for a long time. He still played well at the time of this match, but wasn't as good as he used to be. David had only taken up golf a little over a year ago, but he had gotten quite good. I've never seen anybody improve as much in one year as Benyamine did. Even though David was on the heavy side physically (playing too much poker and not exercising), he once considered becoming a pro tennis player, so you knew that he was a great athlete at one time. It sure didn't take him that long to get in golf shape.

Dewey lost on Day 1. On Day 2, Benyamine shot a 74 and won again. After that round, Doyle said, "He didn't miss a shot. He looked like a pro. If I didn't see it with my own eyes, I wouldn't have believed it." On Day 3, it was a homicide as Benyamine scrambled to a 64 to win easy. He scooped the pot.

The big take-off Doyle and Dewey were looking for crash landed in their face. As Amarillo Slim liked to say, "Sometimes the lamb slaughters the butcher."

It's One Thing to be a Sucker, it's Another to Remain One

Many of the high-stakes poker players who take up golf are *it* in the early part of their golf career. Their game doesn't match their craving for big action. They bet high but don't play well enough to win. They are the limping gazelles who everybody is trying to fleece. In gambling, it's called "paying your dues".

Stu Ungar had too much gamble in him to win. Even though he had a genius IQ, he didn't apply that intelligence when it came to golf and was a limping gazelle on the golf course all his life. The new breed of high-stakes poker players, however, were much better in the catching on department. They paid their dues early on but became tigers later. That included Phil Ivey, Daniel Negreanu, and – as you learned in the story above – David Benyamine.

After being punished for a few million early on, Ivey latched on to Danny Dotson, a phenomenal golfer at one time, and life-long golf hustler. Ivey's game improved 20 shots within a year. Furthermore, Dotson had to approve all of Ivey's bets before he teed off. Dotson nixed nearly all of his proposed bets, so Ivey fell off everyone's radar.

Negreanu, who also lost quite a bit in his early golf days, got himself a full-time coach and advisor. His coach's name was Christian Sanchez. He was a terrific player who worked with Negreanu all the time. Daniel improved at least 20 shots in a year as well.

Benyamine was helped by Chris Perry. Chris is quite a player himself, and obviously a good teacher as well. To many in our little gambling world, Chris was dubbed Coach of the Year.

It's one thing to be a sucker, it's another to remain one. When it comes to gambling at golf, you can take Ivey, Negreanu, and Benyamine off the sucker list.

'BIG' Gambler

It wouldn't be appropriate to have a chapter on "big action" and not mention one of the world's biggest gamblers of all time. This guy could well be the most incredible gambling story ever in Las Vegas. Forget about Nick "the Greek", the legendary high roller. Meet Archie Karas, a Greek immigrant who was born Anargyros Karabourniotis.

Archie went on a winning streak playing pool, poker, baccarat, and shooting dice from 1992 to 1995, which will be talked about in gambling circles forever. He started with a $50 bankroll and ran it up to $40m! According to Jack Binion, Archie was the highest of all high rollers. He said, "Archie wasn't trying to win money. He was trying to win the casino."

Archie started his incredible run by playing nine-ball with a casino executive for $500. They kept raising the stakes, and two and half months later Archie had a decent size bankroll. He took that bankroll and put the word out that he would play anyone heads-up poker in Razz or Seven Card Stud. And the biggest names in poker lined up to play him for stakes that were unthinkable at that time ($8k/16k up to $20k/40k).

Archie was a fearless gladiator on the green felt and always considered himself to be the best heads-up poker player of all time. It was hard to argue with that as he beat them all. He started with Stu Ungar who was being staked by Lyle Berman, and beat him for $500k, and then took on Chip Reese the same day. He beat him for $700k for a total of $1.2m!

Next on his list of victims were Doyle and Johnny Chan. They discovered that Archie was no easy mark. He was more like Tony the Tiger playing heads-up – very tough to beat. He played Chip about 25 times, and once he beat Chip for $2,022,000 in one session – the most Chip said he ever lost. Without question, Archie was the uncrowned king of heads-up poker. Between his poker winnings and shooting a little dice, his bankroll grew to $17m in six months.

Running out of high-stakes poker action, he turned his sights to the dice table. And he couldn't play high enough. He got Jack Binion to bump his limits up at the Horseshoe from $20k to $100k. Archie kept winning and wanted to play higher. Jack said he could bet $300k on the pass line and come bet line, but couldn't take odds if he bet that much. (It was this tactic that got Jack his money back.)

Playing sky-high in the pit all over town (but mostly at the Horseshoe because that's where he could play the highest), he built his bankroll up to $40m within two years! I was sitting next to Doyle, playing in a WSOP tournament, when Jack came over to the table and showed Doyle and me the new $25k chips the Horseshoe had just acquired. They were larger than the $5k chips and had a picture of a stagecoach on them. Jack said, "Archie made us get these. He has nearly every $5k chip we have in the casino in his boxes, $18m worth, so I had to get these $25k chips for Archie so we could get our $5k chips back."

I vividly remember watching Archie in action, both in poker and in the dice pit. Once, I saw him get two racks of $5k chips ($500k a rack) and he took that $1m to the dice table. He bet $1k on the pass line and took $100k odds. He came out for two more numbers for $1k each, and took the same $100k odds on each number. Seven out. He did the same thing the next roll. Seven out. And he did it a third time, betting the remaining money on all the hard ways. Seven out. In less than 10 minutes, I saw him lose $1m!

Although I lived in town, I had gotten a room at the Horseshoe for the month of the WSOP in 1994. At the end of the series, I was talking to Jack Binion and said, "Jack, I've had a tough month here and want to know what you want me to do." He said, "What do mean, Mike?" I told him I'd gotten broke during the series and didn't have any money to check out. I continued, "You can comp me or I'll just keep the room until I make a score and I'll check out then. It's your choice." I was kidding about not having enough to pay for the room, but not about the bad month.

He stuttered and said, "Mike, we've had a tough month, too. Archie's been killing us and we need all the money we can get." Just as he finished his sentence, I saw Archie walking across the casino. I hollered out, "Archie! Come over here a minute." Archie walked over and I said, "Archie, I've gone busted here and I was hoping Jack could comp my room. He said he couldn't because you're winning too much money. Can you go shoot a little dice and dump off a million or so, so he'll take care of my room?"

Once, I saw a sign in a casino exec's office that read, "If you're broke, let the door hit you where the good Lord split you." I'm pretty sure that's what Jack was thinking about me right then.

Archie said to me, "Mike, I'd like to play, but he won't let me bet enough." Jack then said, "Archie, I've told you a hundred times that your current limits are all we can stand. If you find anywhere else in town that lets you play higher, go play there – and good luck to you." Later that day, after packing up, I went to the front desk to check out and discovered that Jack had taken care of my room. Don't believe what you hear about Jack being cheap.

Archie's luck finally ran out. Even though he went completely broke, it wasn't from playing poker. He did well there. He lost it shooting dice and playing baccarat. He blamed nobody but himself.

Archie said his biggest mistake was keeping too much cash at the Horseshoe. His urge to gamble was too strong. One night, he brought the key to a box that had $2m in it. He lost that, didn't have any of his keys to other boxes, but was steaming and wanted to gamble more. He told them to drill the other boxes. They gladly did. He ended up losing $11m that night. He also blamed himself for not pressing Jack more about giving him odds on his $300k pass line bets. In case you ever get $40m, you can now avoid making these same mistakes Archie made.

In addition to losing back all his money, his life took another bad turn years later. In fact, it was far worse. On Sept 24, 2013, Archie was arrested for allegedly marking cards at a blackjack table by the Barona Gaming Commission. He was found guilty and sentenced to three years of probation. Prior to that, he had been arrested four times in Nevada since 1988 for allegedly cheating at blackjack. (He took plea bargains in each case to reduce the charges from a felony.) As a result of all of that, the Nevada Gaming Commission voted unanimously to put Archie in the "Black Book", officially known as "Nevada's List of Excluded Persons".

Archie became the 33rd person in history to make it on to that undistinguished list. It was a sad fall from grace for the guy who was once the man at high-stakes poker and the biggest gambler that Las Vegas had ever seen.

21 In Conclusion

A gambler never makes the same mistakes twice. It's usually three or more times.

Terrance Murphy, a.k.a. 'VP Pappy'

When I look back on my life, I realize how blessed and fortunate I've been. I have a great family, grew up in a wonderful era, went to a great high school, got a scholarship to college, joined the Army and missed going to Vietnam, and had jobs that I've truly enjoyed my whole life. And the icing on the cake for me was to have had a son at age 60.

Everyone looks back on things and wonders, "What would have happened if...?" Poker players do it after nearly every hand they play. And most people wonder about other things: did they choose the right college, take the right job, pick the right spouse, move to the right city, etc, etc. Life's a gamble. Life is like poker – you just try to make the best decision when it's time to make one. That's all you can do. Sometimes we get it right and sometimes we get it wrong.

If you're a gambler, or especially a tournament poker player, the following quote by Vince Lombardi is one you need to heed: "It does not matter how many times you get knocked down, but how many times you get up." Those who take risks will most likely fail a lot, especially tournament poker players. If you're a gambler, chances are you'll get broke more than you would like to admit. I always liked what Puggy Pearson said, "It's OK to get broke. It's not OK to stay broke."

I've been broke more times than they say "O-H-I-O" during a football season at Ohio State. It was always for the same reason – betting sports. It's been my drug of choice, and my only drug, for 40 years. When I was young, I used to win six days a week playing poker and still didn't have enough to pay the bookies on Monday. That is sick. I'm not proud of it, but it has played a large part in my life, and not a good part. It cost me millions and, most likely, three marriages.

Honestly, for the vast majority of the years of my life, it really never bothered me to go broke as I knew I could get back in action. I could always borrow money and/or get staked. Danny Robison once said to me, "As long as you can ante up tomorrow, what difference does it make?" Sadly, I adhered to that philosophy. If I hadn't had "borrowing power", I might have quit betting sports a long time ago – but maybe not.

An old poker player once said to me, "It's not important to be a millionaire. It's only important to live like one." I've pretty much lived like that whether I had millions or was sitting on empty. I wouldn't recommend everyone adhere to that philosophy, but I pretty much did. A businessman who used to play poker with us once said to me, "It's a lot more impressive to be able to borrow a million than to have a million." That is true for sure.

Money management has never been my strength – at all. I could write a book on what "not to do" with regards to money management. I've made millions as a player and many more millions on the business side of the game. Yet, when I had big money, I just made bigger bets. Everything is relative.

All this stuff about having "x" number of buy-ins to play a certain level of cash game was folly to me. I was only concerned about having enough to buy into the game that day. I was the reverse of the Kelly Criterion. (The Kelly Criterion is about preventing the destruction of your bankroll by requiring smaller and smaller wagering when your funds shrink. It does allow for larger wagering when your bankroll grows.) It sounds good – and I'm sure it is and would recommend it for you – but it was never a consideration for me.

My favorite story when it comes to bankroll management, being in debt, etc, came from my friend and fellow poker player Thor Hansen, another who didn't adhere to the Kelly Criterion. He was one of the chip leaders at the end of Day 1 at one of our WPT events in Season 2. First place was over $1m. A reporter was interviewing him after play finished and said, "Thor, congratulations on being a chip leader. What will you do with all this money if you win this tournament?" Thor said, "I'll pay back a few debts." The reporter then continued, "What about the rest?" And dead serious, Thor said, "They'll have to wait."

I've seen many a player come into serious money and then get broke and/or have serious IRS issues because they didn't have money to pay their taxes when it came time to pay them. In most cases, I'd say it was their ego that crushed their bankroll. Most who win a big tournament suddenly think they are better than they really are. They go and play in bigger cash games than they probably should, or start playing in more and much bigger buy-in tournaments. When they start losing, most don't drop down to a level they can beat. Their pride prevents them from doing so.

I've also seen players seek out a partner (meaning you put up half the money and they put up half the money) to play in a higher game. For example, they might normally play $15/30, $20/40, or $30/60 limit poker and yet they now want a partner so they can play in a $50/100 or $75/150 game. That never made sense to me. Remember this: as a basic rule, *the bigger the game, the better the player*. Even though the player would be more likely to win in the lower limit game (and percentage-wise, win the same amount), the player just wanted to play higher. This syndrome could definitely be ego-related.

The beauty of poker is the freedom it provides you and that you're your own boss. In seminars, I like to say that playing poker is like running a business. You are the company CEO and make all the decisions for the company – when to play and what level of game to play in, you make all the decisions in the game, say when to quit, etc. You also promote yourself whenever you want (play in higher games). If your company is not successful, you have no one to blame but yourself.

Eric Drache, another who never applied the Kelly Criterion to his bankroll, once said this about who's a professional poker player and who isn't: "If you play and win, you're a pro. If you play and lose, you have an addiction." Addictions don't just apply to poker players but to everyone in life. Whether it's drugs, drinking, betting on sports, playing in the pit, betting horses, or spending a lot of time with hookers or in titty bars, to survive, you need to be strong enough to avoid and/or overcome these addictions. It's tough to always stay on the straight and narrow path, especially if you live in Vegas, which is a 24-hour town.

Earlier in this book, you learned about a number of legendary players who ruined their lives by doing cocaine. Because Doyle saw so many destroy their lives and those of their family by doing cocaine, he once said, "If I knew I had 30 days to live, I'd get on the cocaine train. It must be powerful stuff."

On another note, I want to thank "the boys" from those games in North Carolina I used to play in back in the '70s and early '80s. That's where I cut my teeth as a pro. To this day, I've never enjoyed playing poker as much as I did in those games.

I ran a game in my apartment in Fayetteville, NC, two days a week for nearly 10 years with two good friends, Don Gianattassio and Terry Keith. I also drove 100 miles to Nashville, NC, to play twice a week. That game was special. It consisted of a few pros, but mostly businessmen and tobacco farmers. It started at noon on Mondays and Thursdays, and if you weren't there at noon, you couldn't get a seat.

We only played one game there. What was it? Well, it's probably a game you've never played or ever heard of – it was Seven Card Stud Hi/Lo split, *all cards down*, with a forced bet rotation where you had to "bet or get out". There was no checking and the bets increased to $10, $20, $30, and $40 along the way. The last bettor on the river declared first. If you declared both ways, you had to win both ways. You lost if you tied one way or the other. Reading opponents and maneuvering where you bet on the river were great skills in that game.

The eighth wonder of the world is that the game in my apartment was never busted by the law and never robbed in all those years – and everybody in town knew about it. There was always money there, as the bookmakers in town settled up there every week. We played dealer's choice and had a rule, "If you can explain it, you can deal it." Because of that, I became extremely versatile and accustomed to playing all games. That's been an asset throughout my career.

The highlights of my career as a player:

♠ Won my first WSOP bracelet in Stud 8 or Better in 1989. (In '90, as I was walking from the Golden Nugget to the Horseshoe to play in the Stud 8 tourney, I bumped into Stu Ungar. He said, "Sexton, anybody can win a poker tournament. Defending, that's where it's at." I was shocked that he even knew that I won this event the previous year. It really pumped me up to defend, and I almost did. I took a terrible beat with six left, or I might have won it.)

♠ Won the inaugural World Poker Finals $10k buy-in No Limit championship at Foxwoods in 1992.

- ♠ Won the Summer Four Queens No Limit championship event in 1996 and successfully defended that title in '97.
- ♠ Won the Grand Prix de Paris in Paris, France, in 2000 (which at the time was the largest event in the history of Europe).
- ♠ Won the WSOP TOC in 2006 ($1m). I beat Daniel Negreanu in a seven-hour heads-up battle.
- ♠ I cashed in the first two (and the only two I've played) WSOP One Drop tournaments in 2012–13. The buy-ins were $1m and $111,111. (Antonio Esfandiari was the only other player to do so.)

I've had more than my share of success as a player in tournaments and cash games. I was very proud of creating two mega events in poker, the TOC of Poker and the partypoker Million. On the business side, I helped partypoker become the number-one online poker site in the world. You may or may not know, but prior to UIGEA being passed in 2006, partypoker had 58% of the entire online poker market!

I've also had the privilege of working as a commentator with Vince Van Patten since day one of the WPT. I can't say enough good things about the WPT, how it changed the poker world forever, and the professionalism of everyone who works there. WPT President Adam Pliska, who has done a tremendous job of expanding the WPT globally, calls the WPT "a family". It really is – and I'm proud to be a part of it.

But nothing will ever top the highlight of my career – which was being inducted into the Poker Hall of Fame in 2009. That isn't about having a good year or winning a couple of tournaments. It's a career achievement award. It's a tremendous honor to join the icons of the game, forever. (A trivia question: who was the first player ever to be *voted* into the Poker Hall of Fame? Here's a hint: he wrote a book called *Life's A Gamble*.) I was also privileged to receive the Lifetime Achievement Award at the American Poker Awards in February 2016.

I'm sharing my story, both of having had a successful career in the poker world as well as the downside of being a degenerate sports bettor all my life, in hopes that someone may benefit from the mistakes I've made. It's hard for normal people to ever understand how or why high-stakes gamblers bet as much as they do. I recognize that people who get a paycheck will never understand it.

For most of my life, I always bet above my bankroll. It was easy to do. With a bookmaker, you don't have to post up any cash. You settle later. If bettors had to post up like they do in Vegas sports books, the amount bet would probably go down 80%, and the earn of the bookmaker would decrease dramatically. It was easy to bet the sheet when you didn't have to post up. And if you lost on Saturday, you just bet more on Sunday trying to get out. It was a downward spiral, week in and week out.

When I did come into big money, I just increased my wagers. In football, I went from $1k–2k a game to $50k–100k a game. Yes, it's crazy – and, sadly, I paid the price for it. I lost millions. I increased my action on the golf course as well. I used to bet $1k on a round of golf, but then I started betting up to $50k a hole. I loved betting big, but I was out of control.

Having a son at my late age was certainly a wake-up call for me and helped me put my values in order. It's also toned down my sports betting substantially. However, life's a gamble, and I still enjoy taking a risk occasionally.

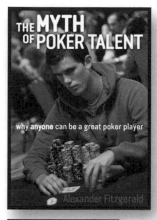

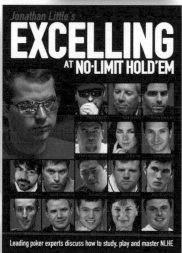

"Life's a Gamble brings back a lot of fond memories for me. I loved it and I'm betting you will too."

Jack Binion (casino owner & Founder of the WSOP)

"If you didn't already realize the role Mike Sexton has played in the growth of the poker industry, you will when you read Life's a Gamble. Mike's life story is the history of the game itself. This book isn't a gamble at all. It's a lock. For any poker player/gambler, this book is a must read."

Nolan Dalla (writer/poker historian)

"In my position as publisher of Card Player magazine, hiring Mike Sexton was one of the best moves I ever made. He has been a great poker ambassador for more than 25 years. Life's a Gamble provides insight into the role he played in creating the 'poker explosion'. It is also the most entertaining read I've had in a long time. I couldn't put it down! I'm sure you will love it, too.

Linda Johnson (First Lady of Poker - member of the Poker Hall Of Fame)

"Mike Sexton was well ahead of everyone else when it came to recognizing the future of poker. He went from poker player to one of the most successful people in the poker industry. He played a key role in the development and growth of online poker (PartyPoker) and televised poker (World Poker Tour). Life's a Gamble gives you an inside look to all that plus many entertaining stories on some of the most infamous figures in poker."

Lyle Berman (entrepreneur & member of the Poker Hall of Fame)

"Mike Sexton has been poker's preeminent ambassador since the 90's, with his creativity and vision always on display. Mike played and continues to play a critical role in the creation and growth of the World Poker Tour. Life's a Gamble tells the fascinating story of Mike's life – how he got into poker, the passion he has for the game ... and how he has worked tirelessly to bring the game of poker to the forefront, making sure it finally got and continues to get the respect it deserves."

Steve Lipscomb (Founder of the WPT)